Educational Leadership in an Age of Accountability

SUNY series, Educational Leadership
Daniel L. Duke, editor

EDUCATIONAL LEADERSHIP IN AN AGE OF ACCOUNTABILITY

The Virginia Experience

Edited by

Daniel L. Duke
Margaret Grogan
Pamela D. Tucker
and
Walter F. Heinecke

State University of New York Press

Published by
State University of New York Press, Albany

For information, address State University of New York Press,
90 State Street, Suite 700, Albany, NY 12207

Production by Judith Block
Marketing by Patrick Durocher

Library of Congress Cataloging-in-Publication Data

Educational leadership in an age of accountability : implementation in Virginia / edited
by Daniel L. Duke . . . [et al.].
     p. cm. — (SUNY series, educational leadership)
   Includes bibliographical references and index.
   ISBN 0-7914-5675-7 (alk. paper) — ISBN 0-7914-5676-5 (pbk. : alk. paper)
    1. Educational leadership—Virginia. 2. Educational accountability—Virginia. 3. School
improvement programs—Virginia. I. Duke, Daniel Linden. II. SUNY series in
educational leadership.

LB2806 .E423 2003
379.1'58'09755—dc21   2002067030

10 9 8 7 6 5 4 3 2 1

CONTENTS

INTRODUCTION

MARGARET GROGAN

Do we need a new prescription for educational leadership? Many would argue that we do—that conditions of schooling have changed so much in recent years that the old prescriptions are not helpful anymore. Few would argue that educators are not facing many different demands now. The current context within which educational leadership is developed and exercised reflects a culmination of years of ferment and public dissatisfaction with the schools in the United States (Murphy, 1999). Scholars and practitioners have offered a variety of predictions regarding leadership trends and recommendations for change (Brunner & Björk, 2001; Duke, 1996, 1998; Elmore, 1999; Ferrandino, 2001; Grogan, 2000; Houston, 2001; Leithwood & Duke, 1999; Murphy, 1999; Tirozzi, 2001). Despite differing opinions on the emerging nature of school leadership, there are agreements that tomorrow's leaders must respond to the shifting economic, social, and political forces that are reshaping public education. To be aware of the past is helpful, but to know the present is vital.

Duke (1996) argues that the facility to prescribe leadership needs depends on being able to "address the conditions perceived to necessitate leadership" (p. 841). The chapters of this book address such conditions in Virginia, conditions created by the implementation of a new statewide educational accountability system. The focal question that has guided the authors' thinking is: In light of the statewide accountability initiative, are educators (1) continuing to rely on conventional notions of educational leadership, (2) resorting to a managerial model, or (3) developing new or hybrid forms of educational leadership?

Researchers have tried to understand leadership by focusing on various aspects of the phenomenon. Recent years have seen increased attention to the interactions between leaders and the contexts in which they lead (Duke, 1998). These contexts are characterized by followers, belief systems, norms, and organizational structures. Another focus of attention has been how leaders identify and solve problems (Leithwood & Steinbach, 1995). Presumably, Virginia's new accountability plan has generated conditions in schools and school systems that

1

might be regarded by educators, and others, as "problems." Dealing with these problems can be expected to require considerable interaction between educational leaders and those they supervise and serve. The contributors to this volume have made an effort to determine the kinds of problems posed by systematic accountability and the nature of the interactions that have resulted from efforts to address these problems.

The story of Virginia's initial responses to a major accountability initiative is a complex one. Although many benefits and costs have been identified, there is one overarching effect of the reforms that stands out clearly—the importance of high-stakes tests. The Foreword to the Standards of Learning (1995) explains that:

> A major objective of Virginia's educational agenda is to give the citizens of the Commonwealth a program of public education that is among the best in the nation and that meets the needs of all young people in the Commonwealth. These Standards of Learning chart the course for achieving that objective.

Consistent with what is happening all over the country as Heinecke, Curry-Corcoran and Moon point out in chapter 1, what the Virginia story reveals is that the present focus is primarily on high-stakes testing though it is only one part of the whole. The state describes the Standards of Learning, school accreditation, and the report card as other equally important initiatives in Virginia's educational agenda (Foreword, 1995). To be sure, it could be that the tests embody the reform in its early years because they represent the most radical departure from earlier methods of assessing student achievement. Or it could be that the tests attract more attention because they are the most flawed part of the reforms in their current form. Whatever the case, the chapters in this volume illustrate the need for a concerted effort to put testing back into perspective so that the goal of improving instruction to facilitate student learning can be at the center of reform.

The Virginia story confirms the need for a new model of educational leadership. Leaders who are proactive and adept at designing and nurturing learning environments are needed at all levels. Educational leaders must keep the big picture in mind. Rather than being consumed by the managerial demands of their work, they should constantly interrogate the conditions under which they are being asked to deliver instruction. Instruction must be at the heart of their work, providing the foundation for helping students to develop into competent, compassionate and connected human beings. Tirozzi (2001) asserts that "preparing teachers for the "age of accountability" requires enlightened leadership" (quotation marks in the original, p. 438). To be enlightened means to strive to achieve the larger goals of the reform movement. It is worth noting that Virginia officials describe the standards as minimum requirements, encouraging schools to go beyond them to enrich the curriculum to meet the needs of all the students (Foreword, 1995).

The new model for educational leadership suggested by the following research entails teamwork and shared responsibility. Even enlightened educational leaders cannot bring about change single-handedly. The Virginia story suggests that educators need to accept the state as part of the "team." If, as Heinecke, Curry-Corcoran, and Moon suggest in the first chapter, "professional influence has been replaced with political control [and] local control replaced by state control" educators must be sensitive to the state's political culture. School and district leaders cannot stay focused only on internal affairs. They must become educational activists. Instead of resenting the erosion of local control that current reforms symbolize, local educational leaders must find ways to have their agendas recognized and incorporated into future iterations of statewide reform. Bridging the divide between those in the field and those in government, is, of course, an enormous challenge, but one that has to be undertaken.

Leadership in an age of accountability, as it is described in the following chapters, is an emerging response to a strong state presence in schools and districts. As the chapters unfold, the impetus to meet the challenge outlined above becomes clear.

The first chapter provides the national context within which Virginia's reforms are nested. Heinecke, Curry-Corcoran, and Moon review the historical development of the notions of accountability that have driven similar reforms in most of the 50 states of the country. They also provide a succinct overview of various state accountability plans, plans that reveal the values and purposes of policy makers who are changing the conditions under which leaders must work. We learn how accountability is defined, and what beliefs undergird it, and we gain insight into the broad challenges posed by the national standards and assessment reforms. The chapter offers a rich backdrop for subsequent discussions of Virginia's experiences with accountability.

The Evolution of Educational Accountability in the Old Dominion, the second chapter, narrows the focus to accountability reform in Virginia. Duke and Reck trace early policy initiatives from the 1970s through the early 1990s, then examine the politics surrounding the adoption and implementation of the revised Standards of Learning and statewide tests. They conclude with some lessons about statewide accountability initiatives that bear consideration by contemporary educational leaders both within and outside the Commonwealth of Virginia.

Chapter 3 reports on the initial efforts of 16 Virginia high schools to respond to the new accountability measures. Speculating that the schools facing the greatest challenges are those with relatively poor student performance on state tests and low levels of financial resources, Duke and Tucker explore the implications of these factors. They note promising developments including an overall increase in test scores across Virginia, heightened levels of cooperation among teachers and administrators, and the emergence of principals as instructional leaders. They also identify several areas for concern, including the fear that course content will be limited to what is tested, the elimination of electives, loss of teacher autonomy, and triaging of students.

In the next chapter, Tucker builds on the study reported in chapter 3. "The Principalship: Renewed Call for Instructional Leadership" focuses on the high school principal's role in instructional activities. Tucker argues that "Virginia's accountability initiative has introduced an external challenge for schools and educators with relatively little instructional guidance" (p. 172). She concludes that principals clearly see their ability to address instructional issues as a key to their effectiveness, but she also questions whether it represents instructional leadership as we know it or a reinvented form.

Grogan and Roland also report on high school principals' responses to Virginia's accountability plan in chapter 5. In addition, their study includes the voices of teachers who were successful in preparing students for the end-of-course tests in seven different high schools in Virginia's Region V. The study was commissioned by the Best Practice Center in that region to discover replicable classroom strategies used by successful teachers and key principal actions that supported teachers' efforts. The authors conclude that district assistance is important, but that its effectiveness depends, ultimately, on the engagement of teachers and principals.

Chapter 6 broadens the leadership lens to include department chairs. "The Impact of Virginia's Accountability Plan on High School English Departments" provides an opportunity to understand the role of department chairs in efforts to achieve educational accountability. Duke, Butin, and Sofka surveyed English department chairs across Virginia to gather their perceptions of how reforms affect teachers and teaching in their departments. The authors offer suggestions for how the role of the chair can be strengthened to facilitate staff development and student success.

The next chapter focuses on student achievement gaps that have been revealed by Virginia's new Standards of Learning tests. Discrepancies in test scores for Black and White students were the focus of interviews with 15 superintendents. Grogan and Sherman found that very little is being done at the moment to eliminate the achievement gap specifically. The authors discuss the context of superintendent responses and issue a call for targeted action to address the problem.

In chapter 8, Tucker and Grogan examine the data from several of the studies reported in the book in order to understand educators' moral concerns related to the accountability plan. They ground their discussion in a review of educators' beliefs and attitudes prior to the reforms, and adopt Starratt's three-part analytical framework involving the ethics of care, justice, and critique in order to come to terms with current misgivings about accountability measures. Tucker and Grogan invite educators to work toward refining and strengthening the reform to ensure that the goals of accountability are consistent with the goals of equity and social justice.

Duke, Grogan, and Tucker conclude the volume by reflecting on educational leadership in an age of educational accountability. They describe the changing context of educational leadership, consider both the benefits and possible costs of accountability in its present form, and discuss the implications of the reforms for preparation, recruitment, selection, and evaluation of educational leaders.

REFERENCES

Brunner, C. & Björk, L. (2001). *The new superintendency: Advances in research and theories of school management and educational policy*. Oxford: Elsevier Press.

Duke, D. (1996). Perception, prescription, and the future of school leadership. In K. Leithwood, J. Chapman, D. Corson, P. Hallinger, & A. Hart (Eds.), *International handbook of educational leadership and administration* (pp. 841–872). Dordrecht: Kluwer Academic Press.

Duke, D. (1998). The normative context of educational leadership. *Educational Administration Quarterly, 34*(2), 165–195.

Elmore, R. (1999, September). Leadership of large-scale improvement in American education. Paper prepared for the Albert Shanker Institute.

Ferrandino, V. (2001). Challenges for 21st century elementary school principals. Phi Delta Kappan, 82(6), 440–442.

Foreword to the Virginia Standards of Learning (1995). Available: http://www.pen.k12.va.us/VDOE/Superintendent/Sols/foreword.pdf.

Grogan, M. (2000). A reconception of the superintendency from feminist/postmodern perspectives. *Educational Administration Quarterly, 36* (1) 117–142.

Houston, P. (2001). Superintendents for the 21st century: It'a not just a job, it's a calling. *Phi Delta Kappan, 82*(6), 428–433.

Leithwood, K., & Steinbach, R. (1995). *Expert problem solving*. Albany NY: SUNY Press.

Leithwood, K., & Duke, D. (1999). A century's quest to understand school leadership. In J. Murphy & K. Seashore Louis (Eds.), *Handbook of research on educational administration,* 2nd ed., 45–72. San Francisco: Jossey-Bass.

Murphy, J. (1999). *The quest for a center: Notes on the state of the profession of educational leadership*. Columbia, MO: The University Council for Educational Administration.

Tirozzi, G. (2001). The artistry of leadership: The evolving role of the secondary school principal. *Phi Delta Kappan, 82*(6), 434–439.

Chapter One

U.S. SCHOOLS AND THE NEW STANDARDS AND ACCOUNTABILITY INITIATIVE

WALTER F. HEINECKE
DANIEL E. CURRY-CORCORAN
AND
TONYA R. MOON

INTRODUCTION

The discourse of American educational policy in the 1990s has been dominated by "accountability," the notion that we must hold schools, parents, and students accountable for attaining high standards. Currently, educational accountability is the major reform initiative affecting all levels of education in the United States. As we conclude this chapter, the U.S. House of Representatives and Senate just approved most of President Bush's education plan to increase accountability for student performance in American schools. The new legislation, reauthorizing the Elementary and Secondary Education Act (ESEA), will tie federal education funding to improvements in student test scores. To receive federal funding, states will be required to test annually all students in grades 3–8. This legislation represents the ongoing effort of a movement for measurement-driven accountability reform which has gained momentum in the 1990s. While there has been considerable variation in the concept of accountability reform as it has spread among the states, common components of state accountability systems include: (1) aligning standards and assessments, (2) rating schools and reporting school or district performance, and (3) creating consequences for schools that fail to perform adequately.

There are two fundamental models of accountability on the policy agenda, a market-oriented approach and a state-regulated approach. In the market version, schools are held accountable for student performance, usually on the basis of standardized test scores. Schools that do not meet performance standards are labeled "failing" and students are given the choice and, under some proposals, the financial vouchers, to switch schools.

In the state-regulated model, students and schools are held accountable for achieving high standards based on standardized test results, schools are rated, and "underperforming" schools are subject to various consequences such as public humiliation, state sanctions, loss of accreditation, state takeover, and the reassignment of personnel. In some models students also may be sanctioned for low performance through retention in grade or denial of graduation privileges. Policy advocates of the market-oriented approach have failed to win widespread support at the national and state levels. Hence this chapter will focus on state-regulated accountability systems. It is important to note, though, that the prospect of a market-oriented model looms in the background as an alternative to the state-regulated model of school reform.

The accountability movement has influenced state education policy in varying ways depending on the political culture of the state. Despite the differences in the political culture and education systems of the states, most of the 50 states are currently working on, or have already developed, accountability reforms with statewide standards and assessments (Goertz & Duffy, 2001; Harrington-Lueker, 1998; Lane, Parke, & Stone, 1998; Ramirez, 1999; U.S. Department of Education, 2001). The central thrust of this reform movement is to promote high standards by holding schools and students accountable for outcomes rather than inputs or regulations. It is the form of these outcomes that continues to be at issue. Behind the technical debate about various reforms centered on standards and accountability lies an ongoing debate over fundamental values and purposes of education. Should our educational policy promote quality and excellence, equity, efficiency, or liberty and choice (Marshall, Mitchell, & Wirt, 1989)?

Virginia, like many other states, is in the throes of a massive accountability reform effort. Virginia has been cited as one of the states in the forefront of the accountability movement (Edusource, 1998; U.S. Department of Education, 2001). The purpose of this book is to explore Virginia's accountability plan and its impact on educational leadership in the Commonwealth. Before turning our attention to the details of Virginia's accountability plan and its impact on educational leadership, it is useful to understand the larger national context surrounding Virginia's reform efforts. This chapter serves as an introduction to the national context of accountability reform within which Virginia's accountability plan is embedded. We will review the history of accountability reforms in American education. We then turn to state responses to current accountability reforms sweeping the nation, and finally, we look at the challenges presented by the current standards and assessment reforms.

A BRIEF HISTORY OF THE ACCOUNTABILITY MOVEMENT

The accountability movement has gone by various names in its evolution over the past 25 years. It has been referred to as the standards and accountability movement, measurement-driven or assessment-driven reform, performance-based accountability, or minimum competency testing (MCT). Understanding the accountability movement may be enhanced by an understanding of the values influencing reform trends in American educational history. In their 1989 study of political culture and state educational policy, Marshall, Mitchell, & Wirt (1989) reported three significant findings that are useful for our analysis of accountability reform. First, they argued that educational policy was largely a reflection of values which change and compete in different historical eras. Fundamental values, such as efficiency, equity, quality, and choice, undergird most of American educational policy. They asserted that the values of efficiency and quality were predominant values influencing national educational policy and reform from the 1920s through the 1950s. Equity arose as a predominant value in the 1950s through the 1970s. Quality also began to dominate the educational policy landscape in the post-*Sputnik* period, which led to the "excellence," "achievement," and "competency" reforms of the 1970s and 1980s. The value of choice has risen to prominence in the reform debate in the 1980s and 1990s.

Efficiency is a deeply held American value. Marshall et al. (1989) found that in the 1980s, policy makers prioritized quality and efficiency as the top two reform values. Efficiency has a machinelike quality (Marshall et al., 1989). It is focused more on means than ends. Marshall et al. asserted that there are two forms of efficiency: (1) "the economic form, minimizing costs while maximizing gains to optimize program performance" (p. 136); and (2) the accountability form, whereby superiors mandate the means to oversee and control subordinates' exercise of power and responsibility. Quality and efficiency are mutually reinforcing values. Once uniform high standards are selected, they must be administered in the most efficient manner using accountability mechanisms.

Second, Marshall et al. (1989) found that the national political culture, reflecting periodic consensus about these values, influences state policy-making agendas. The national culture exerts a significant influence on the types of policy goals and mechanisms states employ for education reform. In addition, they found that in the 1980s educational quality began to supersede other values. "So powerful has been this nation-wide reform current that differentiating political cultures of the states can explain little difference in what happened" (p. 170). During this period, student testing and program definition (controlling program planning and accreditation, specifying what schools must teach) were high-priority policy mechanisms nationally. In the student testing domain, the top priority expressed by policy makers in the six-state study was the specification of test format or content. In the domain of program definition, highest priority was assigned to setting high standards. Setting higher standards included "specifying accreditation procedures, defining promotion and graduation requirements, or otherwise holding districts responsible for implementing particular program elements" (p. 82).

Third, while Marshall et al. (1989) asserted that state policy agendas are influenced by particular national reform ideas, they found that state political culture acts as a filter for implementation of national reforms and policies. States implement national reforms in various, and often divergent, ways (Cohen, 1996). Cooley and Thompson (1990) found that states in the South have been the most influenced by and responsive to recent national reform movements.

Various value-based reform movements have ebbed and flowed over the course of American history. To a certain extent the accountability reforms we are experiencing presently are related or conditioned by previous reform movements. The current accountability reform movement can be seen as a convergence of previous streams of reform, including measurement-driven or assessment-driven reforms beginning at the turn of the century and recurring in the 1960s and 1970s, the accountability reforms of the 1970s, the excellence and standards movements of the 1980s, and the movement for systemic reform of the early 1990s. The following sections examine the evolution of these reforms into the current accountability movement of the 1990s.

ORIGINS OF EDUCATIONAL ACCOUNTABILITY AND TESTING

Two developments in the history of educational testing have had a significant influence on the accountability movement: the development of intelligence testing and the development of achievement testing. Both contributed to educational processes that either reinforce the status quo or promote the interests of powerful external groups (Corbett & Wilson, 1991). Resnick (1980) suggests that achievement testing has experienced two waves of popularity in the United States: the first occurred from the mid-1800s to 1930 with the second wave beginning in the 1960s and intensifying ever since. It is the area of achievement testing for accountability purposes that is the focus of this section.

Pre-*Sputnik*

The current accountability movement in public education has historical antecedents dating back to 210 B.C. with the establishment of a civil service examination by the Han (Madaus, 1990). In Europe, during the 18th century, the development of ranking systems, where individuals could be classified or ranked according to their performance on examinations allowed bureaucrats to accumulate and aggregate student performance data. Bureaucrats soon realized that aggregated data could be ranked, classified, and normed (Hoskins, 1968).

While these European developments were occurring, the United States was also undergoing significant developments in the area of testing. Educational assessment and standards long have been driven by political motivations. Horace Mann explored new ways to hold teachers and administrators accountable for student performance (Sacks, 1999). In 1845, he persuaded local Boston school committees to administer uniform written tests instead of the oral examinations, which were more typical for the time period (Office of Technology Assessment [OTA], 1992). Mann, in a letter to his confidant, Samuel Gridely Howe, wrote:

> Some pieces should be immediately written for the papers. . . . All those abominable blunders . . . punctuation, capitalizing and grammar are the direct result of imperfect teaching. Children will not learn such things by instinct. They will not fail to learn them, under proper instruction. . . . One very important and pervading fact in proof of this view of the case, is the great difference existing between schools, on the same subject, showing that children could learn, if teachers had taught. (as cited in Madaus & Kellaghan, 1993, p. 7)

The uniform written test format introduced by Mann soon spread to the remainder of the country and remained the predominant mode of testing for the later half of the 19th century and the early part of the 20th century.

Educational accountability received a further push at the turn of the 20th century with the development of the industrial revolution and the era of scientific management. Businesses and corporations became fixated on the "measurability, standardization and classification of individuals. Schools played a similar role in converting the disorder of large groups of heterogeneous immigrants into an ordered citizenry" (Sacks, 1999, p. 23). Uniformity was the goal. Testing became the tool for sorting and categorizing the citizenry. Callahan, in *Education and the Cult of Efficiency*, wrote: "By 1915 there were specified 'efficiency bureaus' set up in major cities where 'educational efficiency experts' worked full time developing rating procedures to measure teachers' performance and apply the principles of scientific management to education" (Sciara & Jantz, as cited in Hansen, 1993, p. 12).

Edward Lee Thorndike was to a large extent the individual responsible for the popularization of achievement testing (Corbett & Wilson, 1991). Adapting new statistical procedures that reflected capitalism's commitment to standardization, precision, clarity, and quantification (Staudenmaier, 1985), Thorndike and his students initiated the scientific study of educational achievement. Thorndike believed that anything that existed could be counted, and much of his professional career was focused on assessment. With the implementation of subject-matter tests, Thorndike and his colleagues were able not only to influence what was taught and how it was taught, but also establish the criteria for evaluating and standardizing the process (Cronbach, 1975). Tests and their results provided educators with the mechanism to classify students and further standardize the schooling process (Cronbach, 1975).

The 1960s and 1970s: Accountability Movement Phase II: Post-*Sputnik* Era

The field of educational achievement testing began to change following the launching of *Sputnik* in 1957. International competition served as the impetus for national criticism of American schools and the second wave of educational accountability and testing in the United States. This second wave of account-ability reform was characterized by an important shift in power over educational policy making from local educators to state policy makers. This shift was accom-panied by an increased concern for school accountability by policy makers. Bow-ers (1991) argues that by 1965 three influences were beginning to affect state and local testing programs: the accountability movement of the 1960s and 1970s, the Elementary and Secondary Education Act of 1965, and the National Assessment of Educational Progress (NAEP) started in the late 1960s.

In the 1960s, testing programs began to be shaped by changing legislative and accountability mandates. The U.S. Office of Education (now the U.S. Department of Education) sponsored Project TALENT, which applied student performance on objective tests against variables such as class size, teacher qual-ifications, student socioeconomic level, and levels of school expenditures. Although not intended for accountability purposes, Project TALENT findings were cited by Francis Keppel, the U.S. Commissioner of Education at the time, when he testified in support of the Title I component of the 1965 ESEA (Wynne, 1972). Keppel reiterated the findings that the achievement of students from eco-nomically disadvantaged environments fell below that of students in the same grade level who came from more advantaged environments. The intentions of the ESEA were to increase quality and equity, and the legislation was accompanied by an accountability component requiring evidence of effectiveness in terms of norm-referenced standardized tests. This provision allowed for comparisons of schools and comparison to a national norm (Sacks, 1999). The ESEA "effec-tively mandated states to employ standardized tests" in order to receive federal aid (Sacks, 1999, p. 74).

In 1966, the Coleman Report (Coleman et al., 1966), indicated that varia-tions in teacher qualifications, per pupil expenditures, and other objective vari-ables in public schools did not account for much of the variation in the cognitive abilities of American schoolchildren. As a result of this report, critics of public education began to use test scores as an indicator of school failure (Airasian, 1987; Bowers, 1991).

By 1968, "74 different state testing programs were operating in 42 states. . . . However, only 17 states used the results of their tests to help evaluate and guide instruction and only 13 used the results to measure student progress in academic subjects. State testing programs at the time were primarily designed to help teachers with individual student progress" (Dyer & Rosenthal, 1971, as cited in Bowers, 1991, p. 52). Test results were not released to the public nor were they used for the purpose of comparing school or teacher performance.

The Coleman report also served as the basis for a key speech on educa-tional policy ("Message on Education Reform") delivered by President Nixon in 1969 to the American public. Nixon has been credited with ushering in a new era of accountability (Wynne, 1972). Prior to his speech, the first nationwide, congressionally mandated, National Assessment of Educational Progress (NAEP) was launched. Also known as the Nation's Report Card, the NAEP had a tremendous influence on educational accountability by reporting student achievement performance based on a representative sampling of students in grades 4, 8, and 12 in the areas of reading, writing, mathematics, science, history, geography, the arts, and other subject areas. The Nation's Report Card has continued to provide information about student performance and instructional factors related to performance to policy makers at the national, state, and local levels on the condition of American education. More recently, international comparisons (Third International Math and Science Study; Third International Math and Science Study-Revised) have highlighted the conditions of the American educational system with findings indicating that American students, as a whole, do not perform as well as do students in other industrialized nations—Japan, West Germany, and Sweden (NCES, 1999/2001).

Declining college entrance scores, comparisons with international competitors, national economic decline, and perceptions of undisciplined youth culture precipitated a national wave of criticism that spurred the accountability movement in the 1970s and led to the minimum competency testing movement (MCT) and a shift of accountability focus to the student. Leon Lessinger, recognized as one of the most influential advocates of accountability of the early 1970s, proposed in his book, *Every Kid a Winner* (1970), the idea of a "certified diploma," used to certify the specific tasks that a student is able to perform (Kirst, 1990). Lessigner's model focused accountability on outcomes, and attached costs to them (Hansen, 1993). The goal was to apply principles of engineering to education for greater control and measurability of the educational process (Hansen 1993). This initiative, with its emphasis on performance contracts and educational outcome audits, resulted in establishing minimum competency requirements in many states and to the expansion and proliferation of statewide testing programs (OTC, 1992).

Minimum competency tests were legislatively and "legally mandated testing programs . . . which established minimum levels of achievement required for all students" (Pipho, 1980, as cited in Bowers, 1991, p. 56). These tests, which gained popularity in the late 1970s (33 states in 1978), were linked to high school graduation. The goals of the MCT movement were to certify student mastery of basic skills and make the diploma more meaningful; encourage students to obtain skills; identify students for remediation; pressure schools and teachers to teach basic skills; assist employers to identify potential employees with basic skills; govern from grade to grade; and improve the curriculum (Bowers, 1991).

Between 1963 and 1974, at least 73 accountability laws were passed. By 1972, 23 states had passed joint resolutions or legislation featuring some form of accountability, 13 of which required measuring the level of pupil performance by some form of state testing or assessment. By 1973, the number had risen to 33, with still others considering action. (Bowers, 1991, p. 55)

These laws had certain common features such as comprehensive planning, program evaluation, assessment of student performance, educational goals and performance objectives, and management information systems. "Nearly every state specified some form of assessment and testing" (Bowers, 1991, p. 55). State assessment programs aimed at accomplishing a number of objectives, including

> evaluating the efficiency and effectiveness of educational programs (especially basic skills); providing information to legislators, school boards, and the public to allow comparison of a school district's performance with that of another district with its expected performance; providing information useful in allocating resources; and determining teacher and administrator effectiveness. (Bowers, 1991, p. 55)

Massive implementation problems eroded enthusiasm for the accountability initiatives of the 1990s. Funding problems were encountered, and legal challenges were made. Testing programs persisted despite these problems. As of the mid-1980s, 42 states required local school districts to test students at one or more points between grades 1 and 12, and 30 states used tests to compare results against state standards. Nearly half the 50 states required students to pass a test to receive a diploma (Bowers, 1991).

The Accountability Movement: Excellence and Efficiency in the 1980s and 1990s

A new interest in educational accountability was sparked by the release in 1983 of *A Nation at Risk* (National Commission on Excellence in Education [NCEE], 1983). The report asserted that,

> Standardized tests of achievement . . . should be administered at major transition points form one level of schooling to another. . . . The purposes of these tests would be to: (a) certify the students' credentials; (b) identify the need for remedial intervention; and (c) identify the opportunity for advanced or accelerated work. The tests should be administered as part of a nationwide (but not federal) system of State and local standardized tests. (p. 29)

Inadequate preparation of high school graduates for the workplace, increased school dropout rates, and low achievement by American students relative to their international peers were cited in *A Nation at Risk* as causes of the decline of the United States as a world power (Airasian, 1993; Marcoulides & Heck, 1994). The report solidified the efficiency and accountability trends of the 1960s and 1970s, effectively "nationalized the call for high standards," and ushered in a new era of excellence and accountability.

Bowers (1991) notes that in the late 1980s and early 1990s the trend of statewide testing took a turn when the threat of state intervention in deficient schools and school districts was introduced. *A Nation at Risk* (NCEE, 1983) called for more testing, but it also called for consequences attached to test scores, recommending that educators and elected officials be held responsible for providing the leadership necessary to accomplish the reform agenda. The report was a clarion call for tying student performance to instruction and assigning the responsibility for improvement in student performance to those most responsible for educating American's children.

The Reagan administration promoted policies that returned some authority for education policy (among other policy domains) back to the states. By the mid-1980s the states replaced the federal government as the primary source of educational reform initiatives. Marshall et al. (1989) wrote:

> In the 1980s demands for action fell on the state policy actors and agencies. They had been strengthened by previous experience with federal programs, directed by the Reagan's "new federalism," and stimulated by the demand for reform in *A Nation at Risk*. All of these changes mean that there is a great need to understand the state policy system, for it is the arena with the greatest capacity and responsibility for reforming education. (p. 4)

As the national agenda shifted from equity to excellence and efficiency in the 1980s, several successive waves of reform swept the nation. Marsh and Crocker (1991) assert that as states took a more central role in directing education reform, multiple reform efforts emerged as a series of waves focusing on excellence in curriculum and instructional practices. While much of this movement supported ongoing local change efforts, it also set in motion a series of four "waves" of educational reform.

The first wave involved higher standards, including more stringent high school graduation requirements and more academic courses for students. The second wave emphasized the qualities of a more traditional high school, marked by better course offerings, higher curricular standards, and educational program quality standards. These early waves of state-mandated reform were followed by a third wave that emphasized curriculum integration across content areas, higher order thinking skills, and interpersonal small group skills. The fourth wave of reform focused on the development of teacher professionalism, site-based management, restructured schools, parental choice, and system incentives.

These waves reflected tensions between two distinct approaches to reform: the systemic or state-driven approach and the school-by-school approach. In 1986 the National Governors Association proposed combining school-restructuring reforms with performance accountability. In this proposal, states would reduce rules and regulations and give schools more decision-making authority, but schools had to agree to measure and report performance levels (Firestone, Fuhrman, & Kirst, 1991).

A further shift in the standards and accountability reform movement occurred in the late 1980s and continued through the early 1990s. Policy makers became increasingly frustrated with the lack of results from the various reforms of the 1980s, reforms that focused primarily on improving inputs to the system. Emphasis on educational inputs was supplanted by a focus on student outcomes as measured by standardized tests. In 1988 Congress sharpened the accountability component of Title I by requiring schools to develop program improvement plans with defined outcomes measured by standardized student test scores (Sacks, 1999). The following year President George Bush convened the nation's governors in Charlottesville, Virginia, for an "Education Summit" to discuss the condition of American education and to draft goals and ways to measure progress toward the goals. This summit catalyzed a new wave of educational reform driven by accountability and assessment (Gordon, 1995).

The National Governors' Association's Committee on Education Goals proposed six general goals for improvement of the American educational system through a national examination (National Education Goals Panel, NEGP, 1991). The U.S. Department of Education published *America 2000: An Education Strategy* in 1991. This document embraced the six general goals of the NEGP, but instead of advocating only one exam, the Department of Education advocated a system of examinations. At the same time, the Department of Education also awarded grants to professional organizations to develop academic standards. Major accountability initiatives also were started in several states such as Arkansas, California, Kentucky, Maryland, South Carolina, and Vermont (Gordon, 1995).

The reauthorization of the ESEA served as a pivotal point in the standards and accountability movement. In 1994, the "Goals 2000: Educate America Act" was formally enacted by Congress and signed by President Clinton (Wheelock, 1995). This act emphasized that all students can learn and that schools should ensure that students demonstrate what they have learned in specific subject areas. One of the intentions of the bill was to promote a unified approach to standards and accountability for all students, merging state standards and accountability reforms with Title I standards and accountability reforms. The law required states receiving federal education funds to set high academic standards, develop and align their system of state assessments with those standards, and establish accountability systems to ensure that students were meeting the standards (U.S. Department of Education, 2001).

Under Title I provisions, state testing systems, at a minimum, had to include testing in math and reading/language arts. States were required to test at least one grade a year in each of three bands: grades 3–5, 6–9, and 10–12. Assessments were expected to be aligned with state standards and employ multiple measures to assess higher order thinking skills and "meet professional standards for technical quality" (U.S. Department of Education, 2001, p. 22). States also had to include students with disabilities as well as limited English proficient (LEP) students in the testing programs. Test results were to be disaggregated by gender, ethnicity, special education status, and LEP status as well as socioeconomic status. The U.S. Department of Education, using a peer review system, was responsible for approving states' assessment systems.

The reauthorization of the Title I component of the ESEA aimed to create a "culture of accountability and improvement" by the 2000–2001 school year (U.S. Department of Education, 2001, p. 24). States were required "to develop accountability systems to reward successful schools, identify low performing schools and districts in need of improvement, and take corrective action in continuously failing schools" (p. 24). Performance was to be publicly reported and data was to be provided to local practitioners for the purpose of student improvement. Each state was to develop a standard in order to determine yearly progress for districts and schools. Failing schools were expected to receive state assistance after 2 years and more significant corrective action if failing after 3 years (U.S. Department of Education, 2001). The intention of federal policy-makers was to use Title I accountability requirements as a vehicle to create more uniform state systems of standards and accountability.

By the mid-1990s it could be asserted that the national educational agenda was being driven by concerns for systemic accountability. While various elements of accountability had been percolating since the 1970s, they were not focused on a coherent national vision. *A Nation at Risk* (NCEE, 1983) brought together concerns for excellence, in the form of higher standards, and efficiency, in the form of measurement-driven reform. The current accountability movement, with its emphasis on systemic change, student performance, and sanctions or consequences for "underachieving" schools, is the result of the confluence of these various streams of educational reform. As accountability reforms have evolved, however, so too have their definitions.

THE NEW STANDARDS AND ACCOUNTABILITY MOVEMENT: DEFINITIONS AND COMPONENTS

One difficulty with the accountability movement concerns the many meanings of the term (Ahearn, 2000). Various definitions include: (1) "a process by which school districts and states (or other constituents such as parents) attempt to ensure that schools and school systems meet their goals" (Newman, King, & Rigdon, 1997, as cited in Ahearn, 2000, p. 9); and (2) "a systemic collection, analysis and use of information to hold schools, educators, and others responsible for student performance" (Husain, 1998, as cited in Ahearn, 2000, p. 9). Others have tied accountability to evaluation and assert that in present iterations accountability is used for control, rather than improvement (Ahearn, 2000).

> As a concept, accountability included (a) gathering and providing information, (b) explaining results to specified individuals or groups, (c) establishing standards of performance, (d) maintaining a strong relationship between an authority and the person or group being held accountable, and (e) developing trust, responsibility, and discretionary authority (Fenstermacher, 1979). . . . However in all the definitions, measurability of outcomes was essential and obvious. . . . Accountability became interchangeable with metaphors such as measurements, student outcomes, and behavioral objectives. (Bowers, 1979, p. 53)

Thus by the 1980s, for the public and legislators, "accountability had become equivalent to assessment programs, which were equivalent to testing programs" (Bowers, 1991, p. 53).

The components, as well as the definition, of accountability have varied. Newmann, King, and Rigdon (1997) assert that accountability systems include four parts: information about performance, standards for judging its success, significant consequences, and designation of an agent that does the judging and distribution of consequences (as cited in Ahearn, 2000, p. 9). Elmore, Abelman, and Fuhrman (1996), on the other hand, state that the new accountability model is based on three major components:

> a primary emphasis on measured student performance as the basis for school accountability; the creation of relatively complex systems of standards by which data on student performance are compared by school and by locality; and the creation of systems of rewards and penalties and intervention strategies to introduce incentives for improvement. (p. 65)

The Education Commission of the States (ECS) (1999) argued that accountability systems consist of: (1) standards and assessments, (2) multiple indicators or a performance reporting system, (3) rewards, and (4) sanctions. Fuhrman (1999) noted that current accountability reforms vary from traditional systems in 6 ways:

> District/school approval is being linked to student performance rather than compliance to regulations; accountability is focusing more on schools as the unit of improvement; continuous improvement strategies involving school-level planning around specific performance targets are being adopted; new approaches to classroom inspection are being developed; school-level test scores are being publicly reported; and more consequences are being attached to performance levels. (p. 1)

STATES AND THE STANDARDS, ACCOUNTABILITY AND TESTING MOVEMENT

Since 1994 most states have actively responded to the accountability movement (Goertz & Duffy, 2001; U.S. Department of Education, 2001). At the same time, federal policy has been developing to support state-led accountability reform. State accountability initiatives show signs of uniformity as well as diversity. It is clear, though, that no one best approach has been identified.

In the first wave of reforms, states enacted educational reforms using familiar policy mechanisms. For instance, Georgia relied heavily on mandates, and California tied accountability to incentives (Firestone et al., 1991). According to some observers, most state reform packages lacked coherence (Firestone et al., 1991; Fuhrman, 1993).

Examining the pattern of state responses to the national accountability movement over the past 6 years, two trends are noteworthy. First, states have attended to certain elements of the accountability movement while ignoring others. For instance, in the process of implementing Title I accountability reforms, some states have ignored federal calls for uses of multiple measures of student and school success, and capacity-building related to professional support for teachers and academic support for low performing students (Independent Review Panel, 2001). Second, states have varied significantly in the interpretation, development, design, and implementation of accountability systems. State content standards, performance standards, and assessment systems vary considerably (Elmore, Abelman, & Fuhrman, 1996; Goertz & Duffy, 2001; Independent Review Panel, 2001; U.S. Department of Education, 2001). Additionally, ECS (1999) reported that the existence of various components in a state accountability system did not ensure that the components were aligned into a coherent accountability package. Components of the accountability systems have come

> in fits and starts rather than in logical sequence of developing standards and aligning assessments first. States may implement some components by law and others by regulation. Often components of state systems are not aligned because they were implemented years apart and for different purposes. (Stapleman, 2000, p. 4)

An understanding of the diversity of state responses to accountability has been gained through a set of recent studies of state responses to accountability reforms (Goertz & Duffy, 2001; Independent Review Panel, 2001; U.S. Department of Education, 2001). These studies, summarized below, track state responses to 1994 ESEA directives for the development of uniform state accountability systems.

Standards

By the year 2000, almost all states had developed content standards (Goertz & Duffy, 2001; Independent Review Panel, 2001; U.S. Department of Education, 2001). In addition, all states except Iowa had developed new content standards (Ahearn, 2000) and, by 2001, Iowa had submitted "evidence of its content standards currently under review by the U.S. Department of Education" (U.S. Department of Education, 2001, p. 20). However, there has been significant variation with regard to state content standards (especially in social studies and history), their development, and implementation. Some states have developed standards that promote basic skills while others have focused on higher order thinking skills. States have taken a variety of approaches to developing standards, some highly centralized and others with more local direction. The way in which standards were developed also has varied in terms of the participation of various stakeholders, the degree of specificity of the standards, and the role of the locality in standards setting (Independent Review Panel, 2001, U.S. Department of Education, 2001).

Assessment Systems

The issue of standards typically has been tied to the issue of measurement. The language of assessment has dominated the recent discourse on standards (Murphy & Doyle, 1998; Strike, 1998). As of the year 2000, 48 of the 50 states have some type of state specified assessment program in place in which assessment results are used as an indicator of school performance (Ahearn, 2000; CCSSO, 2000; Goertz & Duffy, 2001). Two states, Iowa and Nebraska, allow school districts to specify assessment forms.

According to the 1994 reauthorization of ESEA Title I, state assessment systems must include alignment with state standards, performance standards, and testing in at least one grade at three levels. They must also include the use of multiple measures and accommodate Limited English Proficient students as well as students with disabilities. Assessment was expected to be of significant technical quality, and states were expected to disaggregate test results by gender, race/ethnicity, LEP and special education status, and socioeconomic status. By the beginning of 2001 only 11 states had reached fully approved status, 6 states had received "conditional approval," 14 states had received a "timeline waiver," 3 states were under a "compliance agreement," and 18 states had their assessment systems under review by the U.S. Department of Education (U.S. Department of Education, 2001, p. 23). Almost all states reported using their assessment results to improve instruction; 41 states reported using them for school accountability, 27 for student accountability, and 5 for staff accountability (CCSSO, 2000). By the beginning of 2001, a significant number of states had not aligned their state tests with state standards as required by ESEA (Independent Review Panel, 2001).

At the beginning of 2001, there was significant variation in the types of tests used by states. Seventeen states used only criterion-referenced tests (CRTs), 2 states used only norm-referenced tests (NRTs), and 29 states used a mix of criterion-referenced and norm-referenced tests in their assessment program. Of the 29 states using a mix, 4 states used NRTs as the primary mechanism, 10 states used NRTs and CRTs in different grades, 8 states used NRTs and CRTs in the same grade, and 6 states used CRTs combined with NRT questions for comparability (Goertz & Duffy, 2001). The types of tests they use may be traditional skills-based and multiple-choice format tests, performance assessments, or a combination of both.

States varied in their approach to testing special education students and students with limited English proficiency. Twelve states had an alternative assessment program implemented for these students, while 35 states were in the process of developing these alternative assessment procedures (Goertz & Duffy, 2001). The same can be said of the variability shown by states in the implementation of testing requirements and procedures for Limited English Proficient students.

States are having significant difficulty developing and setting performance levels for their assessment systems (Independent Review Panel, 2001). All states reported they had achieved the federal requirement to develop performance levels for state tests by the year 2001, but these varied significantly in form. For instance, 37 of the states reported they used four or five different performance levels, but 2 states reported using only two performance levels. Twenty-eight states had their performance level system approved by the U.S. Department of Education. The setting of the cut scores has been highly variable and very political, and the language used to denote these levels has not been uniform among the states (Goertz & Duffy, 2001).

The stakes ascribed to the tests by various states vary from none or low stakes to high stakes. States have taken varied approaches to the use of test results. In 1996–1997, 18 states required students to pass a standardized test in order to graduate. In 1999–2000, 19 states had such a requirement (Gratz, 2000). By 2008, 28 states will have such a requirement for graduation (Goertz & Duffy, 2001). Some states note test results on student transcripts and/or diplomas. Some states report end-of-course test results on transcripts. Some states had no consequences tied to test results. Ten states required end-of-course tests, five of which used these results as graduation requirements and four reported the results on student transcripts (Goertz & Duffy, 2001).

Reporting Systems

All 50 states produce or require local school districts to publish performance reports or report cards. Forty of the states produce school report cards (Goertz & Duffy, 2001; U.S. Department of Education, 2001). The measures included in these reports vary, however. Generally speaking, states reported using both cognitive and noncognitive indicators but varied in which specific indicators were included.

Accountability Systems

States varied also in the nature, development, and implementation of their accountability systems. According to Goertz and Duffy (2001) there are three categories of accountability systems across the states: accountability systems that use reporting of indicators as the primary accountability mechanism (13 states), locally defined accountability systems (7 states), and state-defined accountability systems (33 states). From these data one can assert that only 33 states have taken a systemic approach to accountability. However, even within these 33 states, there is a significant amount of variability in terms of system design and implementation. For instance, of the 33 states with state-defined accountability systems, there is variability in the type of test used. Twenty states use CRTs, 6 states use NRTs, and 7 states mix test format (Goertz & Duffy, 2001).

As an indication of further variety in accountability systems, states use student achievement results and noncognitive indicators in various mixtures: as part of their performance index, as discrete measures, and as preliminary or secondary indicators of school performance (Goertz & Duffy, 2001). States have taken various approaches to determining what indicators should be used to determine if sanctions are required; some use test scores only and look at the absolute score while others look at growth in scores across time. Still others use composite indices that include factors like SES, dropouts, graduation rates, and so on, to produce a score. Of the 33 states with state-defined accountability systems, 19 states employ noncognitive indicators to measure school performance. Fifteen states report attendance rates, 12 states report drop-out rates, and 6 states report graduation rates. Many of the states rely on standardized tests results as the single indicator to assess school performance (Independent Review Panel, 2001).

Because there is no comprehensive federal mandate on accountability, states have varied significantly in the setting of their performance measures; some set expected performance levels (like basic/proficient), some set a percentage of students required to meet a level, and some establish short time periods within which schools have to meet the performance measure (U.S. Department of Education, 2001). This makes it impossible to make comparisons across states. States use different standards, different tests, and different cut scores on their tests (Goertz & Duffy, 2001). Of the 33 states with a state-defined accountability system, 14 states use an absolute cut score to define school progress, 5 states use relative growth based on past school performance, 6 states focus on narrowing the achievement gap in order to reduce the percentage of low scorers, and 8 states use a combination of absolute and relative performance to measure progress (Goertz & Duffy, 2001).

In terms of consequences, most states focus on the school as the unit of analysis. Sixteen states use the school as the locus of accountability, 4 states use the school district, and 13 states use both the school and district as the focus of accountability (Goertz & Duffy, 2001; U.S. Department of Education, 2001). Fuhrman (1999) reported that 31 states had adopted sanction provisions as of the late 1990s. Most states have focused on sanctions rather than rewards (ECS , 1999, Goertz & Duffy, 2001). Some states have attached significant consequences for students in terms of graduation and promotion; others have attached the stakes primarily to schools in terms of probation, warnings, loss of accreditation, funding consequences, regulatory waivers, and dissolution (takeover, reconstitution, closure) (Ahearn, 2000). Other states assign consequences to the district. Some states have taken a nonpunitive approach to accountability instead of focusing on punishing schools for failure to reach outcome measures. These states have emphasized school capacity-building and technical assistance. States have also taken a variety of approaches to accountability monitoring, including inspections of input, process, and outcome measures (Ahearn, 2000). States vary in terms of the inclusion of market-oriented choice and charter school options as part of the accountability reform. As of 1999, 34 states had charter school laws on the books (Ahearn, 2000).

Thirty-three states identify low performing schools and then provide assistance such as school improvement planning, funding, and technical assistance (Goertz & Duffy). However, the criteria used for such identification are uneven across the states (Independent Review Panel, 2001). Eight states have polices ending social promotion. Only 22 states have aligned their accountability systems to include Title I and non–Title I schools, and 28 states have a dual system of accountability for these classes of schools (Goertz & Duffy, 2001).

Perhaps the most important issue concerning state responses to accountability reforms has been their selective attention to certain accountability components over others. In the face of federal mandates to develop accountability systems, many states have attended to issues such as the setting of standards, and developing assessment systems and consequences based on student performance, while paying less attention to professional support for teachers and academic support for low-performing students (Independent Review Panel, 2001, p. 11).

ISSUES ASSOCIATED WITH ACCOUNTABILITY SYSTEMS

States have encountered difficulties designing and implementing accountability systems. Elmore et al. (1996) found that states in the midst of systemic accountability reforms experienced significant challenges in terms of design, implementation, and politics. Design issues included the signals that these systems send to schools and districts about acceptable performance, technical complexity of the systems, and public confidence. Implementation issues included: the unit of analysis for incentive systems, problems with the operation of incentives, perceptions of fairness, and the continual tinkering and changing of system designs as a result of implementation problems. Political issues included constituency pressure, resource constraints, institutional capacity, political stability, public and educator understanding, and the persistence of traditional input and process standards (Elmore et al., 1996).

States have experienced "numerous political, technical, and resource issues in devising reliable ways to measure student and school performance, identifying schools in need of improvement and assisting and intervening to improve low-per-forming schools" (U.S. Department of Education, 2001, p. 25). Many states and districts have lacked the capacity to provide support to low-performing schools. Banks (1994) argues that there is a growing body of research-based evidence that high-stakes accountability hurts instruction (see also Smith & Rottenberg, 1991). Researchers have cited problems arising from top-down accountability mandates such as: a state focus on scores rather than capacity for improvement (Dornan, 1993, as cited in Banks, 1994); and, "attempts to raise scores through means other than instructional improvement" (Banks, 1994, p. 26). Researchers consequently question the assumption that stricter accountability requirements or compliance behavior necessarily lead to improvements in education (Banks, 1994; Hansen, 1993; Noble & Smith, 1994).

Issues Associated with Equity

Another criticism has been that the accountability movement has not addressed issues of equity (Ahearn, 2000; Berliner & Biddle, 1996; Gordon; 1995; Massell, Kirst, & Hoppe, 1997). Accountability systems have the potential to create greater disparities than currently exist. Gratz (2000) asserts that low-income and minority students have been adversely affected by the high-stakes accountability system. States differ concerning which students they test and how they test students with special needs. The development of alternative forms of assessment is still in progress, and states face challenges in terms of test validity. Very few states address the gap between high- and low-performing groups. This has also raised issues concerning opportunities to learn. Do all students have access to the same quality of learning in order to be on an equal footing when mastering high standards? Do they have equal access to high-quality teachers, materials, equipment, and facilities?

Issues Associated with School Capacity

Another criticism of the accountability reforms is the lack of attention to input variables affecting the processes of education that lead to variable outcomes in test scores (Elmore & Fuhrman, 1995). States have not always provided teachers with the professional development necessary to enable students to meet high standards (Independent Review Panel, 2001). Several researchers have called for greater atten-tion to school delivery standards (Porter, 1993) and opportunity-to-learn standards (Elmore & Fuhrman, 1995). The National Association of State Directors of Educa-tion offers a model for accountability that includes accountability for inputs and processes; accountability for system standards; and accountability for individual student learning (Ahearn, 2000). Critics argue that accountability reformers should focus on opportunity to learn standards and the impact of unequal resources on stu-dent performance. Accountability can have desired effects if adequate resources are made available to remediate defects in the system (Hansen, 1993).

TWO EXAMPLES OF STATE RESPONSES

As an example of the variation in state responses to accountability reform, Elmore et al. (1996) compared Mississippi to Kentucky in terms of the design, implementation, and politics of accountability systems. Mississippi's system focused on state accreditation of school districts. The state uses a variety of norm-referenced and criterion-referenced tests to determine accreditation status of districts, which consists of five levels. Levels 1 and 2 are considered inadequate. Indicators of success include student performance on national college entrance exams, graduation rates, and college enrollment. Accreditation levels are tied to norm-referenced tests and a composite index. Some incentives are given to those districts at levels 4 and 5. The state provides assistance to districts at level 1 (Elmore et al., 1996).

Kentucky's accountability system holds schools, not districts, accountable. Standards have been established in content areas and in noncognitive achievement. Student performance is measured in grades 4, 5, 8, 11, and 12. The state established a baseline average performance score in 1991. Schools are evaluated every 2 years, and financial rewards are used as incentives. Schools that score above baseline but below the expected growth outcomes must develop improvement plans. Schools below baseline levels develop school improvement plans and receive financial and technical assistance. Schools at the lowest level are labeled "in crisis" and receive assistance. Their staffs are put on probation, and students are given the right to transfer to another school (Elmore et al., 1996).

EXPLAINING PATTERNS IN THE VARIATIONS ACROSS STATES

There has been significant variation in the responses of states to accountability reform. Some states have jumped on the bandwagon earlier than others. Some states have moved quickly toward full accountability systems while others have lagged behind. What explains a particular state's disposition toward accountability reforms? Variation in state responses can be partially explained by differences in "state demographics, political culture, educational governance structures and policies and educational performance" (Goertz & Duffy, 2001, p. 34). ECS (1999) conducted an analysis of the frequency of accountability components by type of state authority to control the schools (centralized, moderately centralized, and decentralized decision-making). States with centralized systems of governance (including Virginia and most states in the South) have a greater tendency to adopt complete accountability systems (Cooley & Thompson, 1999; ECS, 1999).

The ECS (1999) report also indicated a relationship between the education governance system in a state and state adoption of a complete accountability system. Governance systems are comprised of various relationships between the Governor and Chief State School Officer and the State Board of Education.

Complete systems of accountability are more likely in states that are centralized and have a tightly controlled governance structure. Variability among state accountability reforms also is related to how reforms were adopted, whether by statute or regulation. The report further noted differences in state accountability policies arising from the alignment of system components and the presence or absence of rewards (ECS, 1999, p. 22). Some researchers have concluded that there are 50 different stories of accountability reform (Goertz & Duffy, 2001).

MULTIPLE INTENTIONS, POLITICS, AND DYSFUNCTIONAL EFFECTS OF ACCOUNTABILITY REFORM

Accountability and testing have been driven less by educational consider-ations than political motives (Ahearn, 2000; Education Week, 1999; Sacks, 1999). Most accountability reforms occur within a politically turbulent context, characterized by pressure for quick fixes.

Policies, born of political compromise and negotiation, reflect various val-ues, assumptions and beliefs (Rein, 1976). In top-down reform efforts, the con-flicts and ambiguities embedded in policies frequently are encountered during the implementation phase of the policy (Hall & McGinty, 1987; Rein, 1976). The accountability reforms of the 1980s and 1990s are no different in this regard. Accountability reforms are replete with multiple and divergent assumptions, beliefs, and principles (Independent Review Panel, 2001; Noble & Smith, 1994; Sheldon & Biddle, 1998). As these multiple and divergent assumptions and beliefs operate on the process of reform, policy intentions are transformed (Hall & McGinty, 1987). The result often includes unintended negative effects for schools, teachers, and students.

The accountability movement is based on certain fundamental assumptions about human nature, teaching, and learning (Noble & Smith, 1994; Sheldon & Bid-dle, 1998). Advocates of accountability assume that educators are "not sufficiently focused on the bottom-line of student performance" (p. 165), so higher standards are necessary, as well as assessments of results using standardized tests and conse-quences for students, teachers, and schools (Sheldon & Biddle, 1998). Account-ability systems often seem to be based on a fundamental distrust of educators.

Furthermore, proponents of accountability assume that meaningful educa-tional improvements can be effected through legislatively mandated accountabil-ity. They also believe that the most appropriate focal point for accountability dri-ven reform is the individual school (Independent Review Panel, 2001).[1] In addition, they indicate that American education and the policy that influences it is fundamentally rational and systematic. These assumptions reflect a top-down view of educational change and reform.

Many of these assumptions have been challenged by research on high-stakes testing reforms and accountability reforms. Gratz (2000) argues that recent support for standards and accountability reforms have emerged from divergent interests, such as attempts to alter teacher expectations, promote equity, and produce skilled workers.

Several researchers have found that the multiple and often conflicting policy intentions of accountability reforms get worked out in dysfunctional ways as policies make their way from the state house to the classroom (Ahearn, 2000; Banks, 1994; Noble & Smith, 1994). For instance, in a study of standards and assessment reform in Arizona, Noble and Smith (1994) found there were multiple interpretations of the goals of standards-based reforms held by various policy-makers involved in the design and implementation of measurement-driven reform (MDR) policies. The Arizona case is illustrative of attempts by policy-makers with multiple beliefs and intentions to define and implement measurement-oriented reforms. Arizona reformers attempted to combine constructivist-based instructional improvement with accountability through a behaviorist-driven high-stakes performance assessment reform, resulting in several dysfunctional side effects and the eventual termination of the testing program (Noble & Smith, 1994). The assumptions of the accountability component conflicted with the goals of instructional reform aimed at achieving higher standards. Embedded in the Arizona accountability reforms were divergent goals and assumptions about teaching and learning. Noble and Smith (1994) found that reforms designed to change instructional practice did not mix well with reforms intended to achieve accountability. Mandates can detract from the type of environment necessary to build capacity and foster real change in teacher practice (Noble & Smith, 1994). The political nature of the accountability movement can result in significant levels of ambiguity and instability for educators who must implement the reforms.

Gratz (2000) argued that the positive intentions underlying the accountability movement are being distorted by poor implementation and political opportunism. In this political environment, policy makers have transformed accountability systems and assessments from formative tools used by schools and districts to determine readiness for learning, to diagnose learning problems, to place students, and to inform teachers, students, and parents about student achievement, into summative tools used to inform policy makers and the public about the status of student achievement in a school district or state, to establish statewide minimum competencies for high school graduation, and to identify successful and unsuccessful schools and school districts. Tests have become powerful political tools whose results are used to shape educational policy and practice (Gratz, 2000; Suarez & Gottavi, 1992).

THE DYSFUNCTIONAL AND FUNCTIONAL EFFECTS OF ACCOUNTABILITY REFORMS

The results of attempts to design and implement accountability policies based on multiple and conflicting beliefs, values and assumptions, in highly political contexts, are often dysfunctional at the school level. Ambiguous and divergent goals, political control, and hasty implementation of accountability systems can lead to unintended consequences.

Schools are responding to accountability mandates in both functional and dysfunctional ways. Functional responses include upgrading and aligning curricula, increasing faculty collaboration and data-driven planning, and providing extra help to low-performing students. Dysfunctional responses include excessive homework, abolishing recess, cheating on tests, transferring pressure to students, flunking more students, teaching to the test, and trying to eliminate low performers. In some instances where a designated percentage of students must pass tests in order for a school to obtain accreditation, teachers focus on "bubble kids"—ignoring students at the low end of the performance spectrum. Additional harmful side effects include increased stress on young children as homework is increased, free play reduced, and recess eliminated (Gratz, 2000). Gratz also points out that accountability systems using test scores as a mechanism for promotion can cause severe problems with dropouts. High-stakes tests, and the environments they create, stifle student motivation and interest in learning (Sheldon & Biddle, 1998). In a report to Congress on high-stakes testing, the National Academy of Sciences warns that when tests are used inappropriately, "especially in making high-stakes decisions about individuals, [they] can undermine the quality of education and equality of opportunity" (Heubert & Hauser, 1999, p. 4).

Some researchers (Hansen, 1993; Sheldon & Biddle, 1998) claim that sanctions alone will not change low-performing schools and that there is little evidence that punitive consequences lead to improved outcomes. Sanctions such as reporting test results in the media, loss of accreditation, loss of state funding, state takeovers, and closing or reconstituting schools, can motivate but may also have unintended consequences, especially for poor and minority schools. Hansen (1993) finds no evidence that a focus on the individual school in statewide accountability initiatives has led to significant improvements in student performance. He concludes there is weak evidence at best for the efficacy of mandated accountability reform but does indicate that accountability reforms may be useful for generating the data necessary for self-examination and school improvement decisions by local school personnel. As a result of these problems with accountability, many states that instituted high-stakes accountability systems are reevaluating those policies (Steinberg, 2000). There have even been calls for the accountability of accountability systems (Lane, Parke, & Stone, 1998; Porter, 1993; Sirotnik & Kimbal, 1999; Stapleman, 2000), including various standards by which accountability reforms can be evaluated.

Some researchers contend, on the other hand, that there have been significant positive results from accountability reforms (Edusource, 1998; Elmore et al., 1996; Fuhrman, 1999). For example, schools are using data to make instructional improvements. Fuhrman (1999) reported:

New accountability systems that are well-designed (with fair, comprehensible, meaningful and stable features) are associated with improved student achievement when adequate capacity . . . is present in schools or can be provided by an outside partner. Generally, teachers find the new systems motivating. But in the absence of explicit attention to capacity, the new systems are insufficient approaches to improving student achievement. (p. 10)

Similarly, the U.S. Department of Education has concluded that state and Title I accountability requirements have helped states, districts, and schools to focus on improving school quality and performance. They cite preliminary research that attributes improvements in teacher practices and student performance to accountability reforms (U.S. Department of Education, 2001).

CONCLUSION

States are changing their educational systems in a national context of accountability reform promoted by various federal and national actors. As we conclude this chapter, the U.S. Congress is considering a revision of the ESEA, which would for the first time tie federal aid to student outcome performance, as well as require state testing of all third through eighth graders annually (Fletcher, 2001). Advocates of systemic reform assume that by addressing standards and assessment in a coherent manner, improvements in student outcomes will automatically result. With the threat of sanctions at the student and school level, unresponsive principals and teachers will teach the prescribed curriculum, students will be motivated to learn it, and tests will measure their mastery of facts. In reality, however, accountability reforms are being driven by political rather than rational or professionally defined educational concerns. At the symbolic level, state responses have been fairly uniform: most states are doing something to respond to calls for standards and accountability. At the substantive level, variation rather than uniformity characterize state reforms.

It is not surprising that states have interpreted and implemented national accountability reforms in different ways. This would be expected because: (1) the federal legislation motivating the movement is vague and ambiguous, and reflects multiple intentions and values; (2) states vary in terms of their political cultures, histories, governance structures, demographics, and preferences for policy mechanisms (ECS, 1999; Goertz, & Duffy, 2001; Marshall et al., 1989); and (3) in those states leading the implementation charge, accountability reforms have been politically motivated. What is at issue, then, is how to judge these adaptations: Are they functional or dysfunctional in terms of effects on classroom practice?

State contexts of reform are extremely important in determining the translations of those reforms and their subsequent effects on educational practice and outcomes (Fuhrman, 1988; Hall & McGinty, 1997; Marshall et al., 1989). The coupling of national accountability reforms and classroom practice may vary depending on the state, loosely coupled in some state and local contexts and tightly coupled in others. In studies of the implementation of the first wave of reforms, researchers found that "local response was remarkably uniform, with little apparent local resistance" (Odden, 1991, p. 302). There was significant implementation of state reform programs with little adaptation by school districts. Odden, citing Yudoff (1984), reminds us that "the education system responds swiftly when there is a consensus for educational change on the part of political leaders outside of education" (p. 303). In the case of accountability reform there has been congruence between the various levels of the intergovernmental system of education in terms of political symbolism, but divergence at the substantive level. This is readily visible in the types of tests, indicators, and consequences used.

Perhaps what we are experiencing in the new national accountability movement is reminiscent of an earlier confluence of the values of quality and efficiency that Marshall et al. (1989) argue influenced the turn-of-the-century educational policy. Then, the education experts were solidly in charge of deciding both the ends and the means of educational reform. In this new accountability era, professional influence has been replaced with political control; local control replaced by state control. The mechanisms by which to efficiently pursue educational quality have been wrested from the hands of education professionals and seized by politicians.

Marshall et al. (1989) argues that a state's political culture disposes it to certain types of values that influence both the speed and intensity with which the state pursues or resists a national policy idea. Despite the strong influence of the national reform agenda on state reform policies, state political cultures influence how reforms are translated into policy. These include decisions about policy mechanisms and design characteristics reflecting unique political realities, "such as the balance of power between state and local districts" (Fuhrman, 1989, p. 73).

Tacheny (1999) argues that accountability is not a system or a thing, but a value, one developed though relationships into a motivating force that guides daily practice. To be successful, the accountability movement must inspire people. Tacheny summarizes the local meaning of accountability: "The words and actions of key leaders within the education system including principals, teacher mentors, and department heads, as well as central office administrators and elected officials will set the example of what accountability truly means in schools" (p. 62). A reasonable way to approach accountability, argue Sheldon and Biddle (1998), is to base reforms on trust in students and teachers, assuming that most students want to learn and most teachers want to teach. Trust, however, appears to be in short supply in the current reform era.

NOTE

1. According to an independent review of a U.S. Department of Education evaluation of state responses to Title I mandates (Independent Review Panel, 2001), policy makers have based accountability reforms on a set of assumptions, beliefs, and principles that should be scrutinized (Independent review Panel, 2001). The first assumption is that educators and the public can agree on content standards. Reformers also assume that standards can be focused and coherent and that multiple stakeholders can blend different perspectives that send unambiguous messages to teachers. Reformers believe that aligning all elements of the educational system with high content standards will generate improvements in student learning and that students of all backgrounds can do more challenging work when given high-quality curriculum and instruction. Accountability reformers assume that a new curriculum can incorporate both basic skills and higher-order thinking skills. It is assumed that students can master these new standards if teachers are well prepared and have mastered content. The improvement of teacher quality can result from investments in high-quality professional development. Reformers also assume that exchanging flexibility for accountability can drive improvements in student learning, but this is dependent on the alignment of high standards, assessments, well-trained teachers, and targeted resources. In addition, reformers believe that large-scale assessments can accurately measure student progress toward meeting standards. Traditional assessments do not gauge what students can do with basic skills. They must be redesigned to measure student progress and school performance. There is also an assumption embedded in accountability reforms that assessments can serve multiple purposes.

REFERENCES

Ahearn, E. M. (2000). *Educational accountability: A synthesis of the literature and review of a balanced model of accountability*. Final Report. National Association of State Directors of Special Education, Alexandria, VA (Eric Document Reproduction Service No. ED 439573.)

American Educational Research Association. (1991, June). AERA speaks out against national test. *OIA Info Memo*, pp. 3–5.

Airasian, P. W. (1987). State-mandated testing and educational reform: Context and consequences. *American Journal of Education, 95*(3), 392–412.

Airasian, P. W. (1993). Policy-driven assessment or assessment-driven policy? *Measurement and Evaluation in Counseling and Development, 26*(1), 22–30.

Banks, K. E. (1994, April). *Assessment's conflicting purposes, conflicting politics: Impact on local school systems*. Paper presented at the Annual Meeting of the American Educational Research Association, New Orleans, LA. (Eric Document Reproduction Service No. ED 374 572.)

Barton, P. E. (1999). Too much testing of the wrong kind; too little of the right kind in k–12 education. Educational Testing Service. Princeton, NJ. Author. (ERIC Document Reproduction Service No. ED 430 052.)

Berliner, D. C., & Biddle, B. J. (1996). Standards amidst uncertainty and inequality. *The School Administrator, 53* (5), 42–46.

Bowers, J. J. (1991). Evaluating testing programs at the state and local levels. *Theory into Practice, 30*(1), 52–60.

Cohen, D. K. (1996). Standards-based school reform: Policy practice, and performance. In H. F. Ladd (Ed.), *Holding Schools Accountable* (pp. 99–127). Washington, DC: The Brookings Institution.

Cohen, D. K. (2000). Instructional policy and classroom performance: The mathematics reform in California. *Teachers College Record, 102* (2), 294–343.

Coleman, J. S., Campbell, E. Q., Hobson, C. J., McPartland, J., Mood, A., Weinfeld, E. D., & York, R. L. (1966). *Equality of educational opportunity.* Washington, DC: U.S. Government Printing Office.

Cooley, V. C., & Thompson, J. C. (1990, October). *A study of the fifty states to determine the effect of educational reform on seven educational improvement areas.* A paper presented at the Twelfth Annual Meeting of the Mid-Western Educational Research Association, Chicago, IL. (ERIC Document Reproduction Service No. ED 325494.)

Corbett, H. D., & Wilson, B. L. (1991). *Testing, reform, and rebellion.* Norwood, NJ: Ablex Publishing.

Council of Chief State School Officers. (1998). *State education accountability reports and indicator reports: Status of reports across the states.* Washington, DC: Author.

Council of Chief State School Officers. (2001). *Key state education policies on K–12 education: 2000.* Washington, DC: Author.

Cronbach, L. J. (1975). Five decades of public controversy over mental testing. *American Psychologist, 30* (1), 1–14.

Education Commission of the States. (1999). *Education accountability systems in 50 states.* (ECS Report No. SI-99–8.) Denver, CO: Author. (ERIC Document Reproduction Service No. ED428 455.)

Education Week (1999, January). *Quality counts 1999: Rewarding results, punishing failure.* Bethesda, MD: Author.

Edusource (1998, June). *Shifting focus to learning: California's accountability debates.* Palo Alto, CA: Author.

Elmore, R. F., Abelman, C. H., & Fuhrman, S. H. (1996). The new accountability in state education reform: From process to performance. In H.F. Ladd (Ed.), *Holding schools accountable: Performance-based reform in education* (pp. 65–98). Washington, DC: Brookings Institution.

Elmore, R. F., & Fuhrman, S. H. (1995). Opportunity to learn standards and the state role in education. *Teachers College Record 96* (3), 1–26.

Firestone, W. A, Fuhrman, S. H., & Kirst, M. W. (1991). State educational reform since 1983: Appraisal and the future. *Educational Policy 5*(3), 233–250.

Fletcher, M. A. (2001, May 29). School accountability remains tough task. *Washington Post*, p. A2.

Fuhrman, S. (1989). State politics and education reform. In J. Hannaway and R. Crowson (Eds.), *The Politics of reforming school administration: The 1988 yearbook of the Politics of Education Association* (pp. 61–75). New York: Falmer Press, 1989.

Fuhrman, S. (1999). *The new accountability.* (CPRE Policy Brief No. RB-27.) Philadelphia, PA: University of Pennsylvania, Consortium for Policy Research in Education.

Goertz, M. E., & Duffy, M. C. (2001). *Assessment and accountability systems in the 50 states: 1999–2000.* (CPRE Research Report No. RR-046.) Philadelphia, PA: University of Pennsylvania, Consortium for Policy Research in Education.

Gordon, E. W. (1995). The promise of accountability and standards in the achievement of equal educational opportunity. *Teachers College Record, 96*(4), 751–756.

Gratz, D. B. (2000, May). High standards for whom? *Phi Delta Kappan, 81*(9), 681–687.

Hall, P. M. & McGinty, J. W. (1997). Policy as the transformation of intentions: Producing program from statute. *The Sociological Quarterly, 38*(3), 439–467.

Hansen, J. B. (1993). Is educational reform through mandated accountability an oxymoron? *Measurement and Evaluation in Counseling and Development, 26*(1), 11–21.

Harrington-Lueker, D. (1998). Now local school districts are responsible for results. *The American School Board Journal, 185*(6), 17–21.

Hoskins, K. (1968). The examination, disciplinary power and rational schooling. *History of Education, 8*, 135–146.

Heubert, J. P., & R. M. Hauser (Eds.). (1999). *High stakes: Testing for tracking, promotion and graduation.* National Academy of Sciences-National Research Council, Washington, DC. (Eric Document Reproduction Service No. ED 439151.)

Independent Review Panel, National Assessment of Title I (2001). *Improving the odds: A report on Title I from the Independent Review Panel.* Washington, DC: Council for Basic Education.

Kirst, M. (1990). *Accountability: Implications for state and local policymakers.* Washington, DC: U.S. Department of Education, Office of Educational Research and Improvement.

Lane, S., Parke, C. S., & Stone, C. A. (1998). A framework for evaluating the consequences of assessment programs. *Educational Measurement: Issues and Practice, 17*(2), 24–28.

Lessinger, L. M. (1970). *Every kid a winner: Accountability in education.* Chicago, IL: Science Research Associates.

Linn, R. L. (2000). Assessments and accountability. *Educational Researcher, 29*(2), 4–16.

Madaus, G. F., & Kellaghan, T. (1993). Testing as a mechanism of public policy: A brief history and description. *Measurement and Evaluation in Counseling and Development, 26* (1), 6–10.

Madaus, G. F. (1990). *Testing as a social technology: The inaugural Boisi lecture in education and public policy.* Boston, MA: Center for the Study of Testing, Evaluation, and Educational Policy, Boston College.

Marcoulides, G. A., & Heck, R. H. (1994). The changing role of educational assessment in the 1990s. *Education and Urban Society, 26* (4), 332–339.

Marsh, D. D., & Crocker, P. S. (1991). School restructuring: Implementing middle school reform. In A. R. Odden (Ed.), *Education Policy Implementation* (pp. 259–278). Albany: State University of New York Press.

Marshall. C., Mitchell, D., & Wirt, F. (1989). *Culture and education policy in the American states.* New York: Falmer.

Massell, D., Kirts, M. W., & Hoppe, M. (1997). *Persistence and change: Standards-based systemic reform in nine states.* (CPRE Policy Briefs, No. RB-21.) Philadelphia, PA: Consortium for Policy Research in Education, University of Pennsylvania.

National Center for Educational Statistics (NCES). (1999/2000). Third International Math and Science web site: *www.nces.ed.gov/timss*.

National Commission on Excellence in Education. (1983). *A nation at risk: The imperative for educational reform*. Washington, DC: U.S. Department of Education.

National Education Goals Panel. (1991). Measuring progress toward the national education goals: Potential indicators and measurement strategies. Washington, DC: U.S. Government Printing Office.

Noble, A. J., & Smith, M. L. (1994). Old and new beliefs about measurement-driven reform: "Build it and they will come." *Educational Policy, 8*(2), 111–136.

Odden, A. R. (1991). New patterns of education policy implementation and challenges for the 1990s. In A. Odden (Ed.), *Education Policy Implementation* (pp. 297–328). Albany: State University of New York Press.

Office of Technology Assessment, U.S. Congress. (1992). *Testing in American schools: Asking the right questions*. (Report No. OTA-SET-519.) Washington, DC: U.S. Government Printing Office.

Porter, A. C. (1993). School delivery standards. *Educational Researcher, 22*(5), 24–30.

Ramirez, A. (1999). Assessment-driven reform: The emperor still has no clothes. *Phi Delta Kappan, 81*(3), 204–208.

Rein, M. (1976). *Social science and public policy*. New York: Penguin Books.

Resnick, D. P. (1980). Minimum competency historically considered. *Review of Research in Education, 8*. Washington, DC: American Educational Research Association.

Sacks, P. (1999). *Standardized minds: The high price of America's testing culture and what we can do to change it*. Cambridge, MA: Perseus Books.

Sheldon, K. M., & Biddle, B. J.(1998). Standards, accountability, and school reform: Perils and pitfalls. *Teachers College Record, 100*(1), 164–180.

Sirotnik, K. A., and Kimball, K. (1999). Standards for standards-based accountability systems. *Phi Delta Kappan, 81*(3), 209–214.

Smith, M. L., & Rottenberg, C. (1991) Unintended consequences of external testing in elementary schools. *Educational Measurement: Issues and Practice, 10*, 7–11.

Smith, M. L., Edelsky, C., Draper, K., Rottenberh, C., & Cherland, M. (1990). *The role of testing in elementary schools* (CSE Tech Rep. No. 321.) Los Angeles: University of California, Center for Research on Evaluation, Standards, and Student Testing.

Smith, M. L., Heinecke, W. F., & Noble, A. J. (1999). Assessment policy and political spectacle. *Teachers College Record, 101* (2), 157–191.

Stapleman, J. (2000). *Standards-based accountability systems*. Policy Brief. Aurora, CO: Mid-Continent Regional Educational Lab. (Eric Document Reproduction Service No. ED440979.)

Staudenmaier, J. M. (1985). *Technology's storytellers: Reweaving the human fabric*. Cambridge, MA: MIT Press.

Steinberg, J. (2000, December 22). Student failure causes state to retool testing programs. *New York Times*, A1.

Suarez, T. M., & Gottovi, N. C. (1992). The impact of high-stakes assessments on our schools. *NASSP Bulletin 76*(545), 82–88.

Tacheny, S. (1999). If we build it, will they come? *Educational Leadership, 56*(6), 62–65.

Texas Education Agency. (1990). *Texas educational assessment of minimum skills and Texas assessment of academic skills: Annual report.* Austin, TX: National Computer System.

Texas Education Agency. (1994). *Texas student assessment program technical digest for the academic year 1993–1994.* Austin, TX: National Computer System.

Texas Education Agency. (1996). *The development of accountability systems nationwide and in Texas* (Pub. No. GE6–601–07). Austin, TX: Author.

Texas Education Agency. (1999). *Accountability manual* (Pub. NO. GE6–602–02). Austin, TX: Author.

U.S. Department of Education. (1991). *America 2000: An education strategy.* Washington, DC: Author.

U.S. Department of Education, Planning and Evaluation Service. (2001). *High standards for all students: A report from the National Assessment of Title I on progress and challenges since the 1994 reauthorization.* (U.S. DOE Publication No. 2001–15.) Washington, DC: Author.

Wheelock, A. (1995). *Standards-based reform: What does it mean for the middle grades?* NY: Edna McConnell Clark Foundation. (ERIC Document Reproduction Service No. ED 389 772.)

Wynne, E. (1972). *The politics of American education.* Berkeley, CA: McCutchan.

Chapter Two

THE EVOLUTION OF EDUCATIONAL ACCOUNTABILITY IN THE OLD DOMINION

DANIEL L. DUKE
AND
BRIANNE L. RECK

Lovers of classical fiction are likely to find reading about policy initiatives frustrating. They are accustomed to stories with distinct beginnings and endings. Determining when policies are born and when they cease to exist, however, is very difficult. Policies frequently begin with public ideas that form slowly over time. In many cases, a particular policy initiative can be traced to a variety of precursors, making it hard to determine a precise point of origin. Because policy is formulated in the crucible of politics, pinpointing a policy's parentage also can be fraught with problems. If the policy eventually is regarded as successful, all parties are likely to claim it. If the policy fails, each party may disown it or blame others for subverting it. Policies also have a habit of changing character over time. They can be amended, revised, and ignored. Some policies are modified so significantly that they hardly resemble their original form. The evolutionary nature of policy makes it difficult to decide when one policy has died and another policy has been born. Does a thoroughly revised policy constitute a new policy, or simply a "reborn" version of the original? At what point can it be said that a particular policy initiative has ended?

This chapter describes the development and evolution of Virginia's accountability plan, a four-part policy initiative consisting of Standards of Learning (SOL), statewide standardized tests, Standards of Accreditation (SOA), and School Performance Report Cards. The SOL constitute the curriculum content that all Virginia students are expected to know in order to receive a high school diploma. To determine whether these standards are met, barrier tests are given to students in elementary, middle, and high school. The SOA serve as the mechanisms for holding schools accountable for student performance on the state SOL tests. Parents and communities are apprised of local schools' success by annual report cards. The elements of the accountability plan were adopted by the Virginia Board of Education between June of 1995 and December of 1997.

The first part of the chapter traces the rise of educational accountability in Virginia during the 1970s, 1980s, and early 1990s. It shows how early initiatives paved the way for the four-part accountability plan. Next comes a discussion of the adoption of revised Standards of Learning and statewide tests. Succeeding sections examine the adoption of Standards of Accreditation and School Performance Report Cards, the immediate postadoption period when Richmond began to receive challenges to the accountability plan, and the subsequent period during which state leaders acknowledged the need for adjustments. The chapter concludes with reflections on the process of institutionalizing educational accountability in the Old Dominion.

FIRST STEPS TOWARD ACCOUNTABILITY

The 1968 amendment to the Virginia Constitution mandated public schools of "high quality" and required the development of Standards of Quality (SOQ). In his annual report for 1971–1972, the State Superintendent for Public Instruction wrote:

> In accordance with the requirements of the State Constitution, standards of quality for the public schools were approved by the state Board of Education in August 1971 and were submitted to the General Assembly. As revised by the General Assembly the legislation contains: standards for personnel, instructional materials (including educational television), education programs, and system wide planning and management; and performance objectives for the state and for local school divisions, and planning and management objectives for schools and instructional personnel. The Board of Education was directed to adopt rules and regulations needed to achieve the objectives. (Virginia Department of Education, 1972)

Borrowed from business and industry, the concept of standards, particularly standards of "quality," captured the imagination of policy makers. The enactment of state standards required local divisions to appoint Standards of Quality committees to promote an understanding of the SOQ within their school systems and communities, to determine the status of their school divisions with respect to the standards, and to support the work of eight statewide committees established to develop forms and guidelines to assist all divisions in planning and implementing programs to meet the standards. Ensuring a more uniform educational experience for students across the Commonwealth also required attention to the unequal distribution of financial resources among school divisions and a willingness on the part of localities to cede some of their power to the state. The purposes of education and the roles of local and state policy-making bodies came under increasing public scrutiny during the 1970s and 1980s.

Proposed in 1971, the first Standards of Quality (SOQ) for public education were enacted in 1972, during the administration of Republican Governor Linwood Holton. This was one of the earliest attempts by the state to impose uniformity on local divisions, and the first SOQ were met with some suspicion, particularly by school systems with limited resources. While state assistance was promised, it was not immediately forthcoming.

The first Governor's Schools Program was established in 1973, signaling the interest of policy makers in providing quality educational opportunities for those identified as the Commonwealth's best and brightest students. In 1976, the entry age for schools was lowered to five, and by 1979 the state had implemented both an elementary-level basic-skills curriculum and high school competency tests. These programs were precursors to later, more sophisticated attempts to press for educational standards and accountability. A tightening economy and eventual recession spurred public demands for accountability and forced educators to share how they were allocating resources and to what effect.

During the Reagan and Bush administrations, the idea that public education was in decline received support at the highest levels of government. Not only were American students and their schools "at risk," but the nation's economic well-being and ability to compete on the international scene had been jeopardized as a consequence of failing schools (Tyack and Cuban, 1997, p. 34). Provoked to act by the publication in 1983 of *A Nation at Risk*, an alliance of educators and politicians launched a campaign to restructure schools and restore America's economic dominance.

Several years before this national campaign, Virginia took another major step toward educational accountability with the first "Standards of Learning" (SOL). Touted as a program that combined the "best features" of the Basic Learning Skills and Graduation Competency programs, the SOL initiative sought to define the skills and knowledge students were expected to acquire from the time they entered school until the time they graduated. The State Superintendent for Public Instruction's report for 1979–1980 noted that the SOL would form the basis for student assessment in Virginia and allow the Standards of Quality to be measured (Virginia Department of Education, 1980, pp. xiii–xv). The State Superintendent acknowledged the effects of the "back-to-basics" movement and its impact on Virginia's public schools in his announcement regarding the first SOL:

> Within recent years, greater attention has been given to the so-called "basics"— reading and mathematics. Several years ago Virginia began a Basic Learning Skills Program for the elementary grades and a Graduation Competency Program for high school students. To broaden response to public demands, the state, during the 1979–80 fiscal year, launched a new program called "Standards of Learning," which emphasizes instruction in mathematics and language arts from kindergarten through grade 12. (Virginia Department of Education, 1980, pp. xiii–xiv)

The original SOQ and SOL were the foundations on which successive administrations would build the current accountability, accreditation, and assessment programs. The standards were field-tested in 25 localities during 1981, and workshops to introduce and support the implementation of the SOL were held throughout the state during 1981 and 1982. At this time, concerns about control of education at the local level, particularly control of funding, began to emerge among state politicians and local school boards (Virginia Department of Education, 1981, pp. xi–xii). With the SOL the state appeared to be moving toward greater control over what once had been primarily the province of local school divisions, just as it had with the institution of competency testing for high school students in 1979. The codification of the Standards of Quality in 1984 was seen as yet another step toward centralization of control over public schools.

The Virginia Constitution vests in the General Assembly the authority to approve educational policy and funding for a biennium. The state Board of Education is supposed to enact regulations each year to enable legislative policies to be implemented. Some legislators feared that the state Board would revise the SOQ and SOL without obtaining the approval of the General Assembly. The effect of these regulatory changes could be regarded as a form of de facto policy-making.

THE PUSH FOR ACCOUNTABILITY AND EXCELLENCE

Gerald L. Baliles, a Democrat, became governor in 1986. He sounded the call for a new round of reforms and established the Governor's Commission on Excellence in Education in March of 1986. In the commission's swearing-in ceremony the governor urged the 18-member committee to be "bold and creative" in recommending reforms, and said that "hot potatoes, sacred cows and turf questions are not off limits" (Baker, March 26, 1986, p. B-7). The committee's report, published later that year, stated that, while some progress had been noted as a result of earlier reforms, "for whatever reason, some of Virginia's schools are not presently able to prepare students for gainful employment or higher education" (Commission on Excellence in Education, 1986). In the same report, Baliles stated, "We must put Virginia in the first rank of states in the quality of education . . . not because of pride, but for the well-being of all Virginians—and yes, because of jobs." The approach that the administration took, based on the recommendations of the Commission, was to "raise the bar" for teachers and for students in the Commonwealth.

In July 1988, as a result of the commission's recommendations, the State Board of Education adopted new Standards of Quality, later incorporated into state law, that called for a performance indicator for Virginia's public schools (Glass, April 28, 1995, p. B-1). The resulting instrument, the Literacy Passport Test (LPT), was comprised of basic literacy measures in reading, writing, and arithmetic. The adoption of the LPT program marked the first time the state linked a state test to student promotion.

Phased in over a 7-year period, the LPT was designed to be administered to all students in grade 6. Those who met the established criteria for passing were eligible to move forward. Remediation, including summer school, was provided for students who failed one or more portions of the LPT. Retesting occurred in grade 7 and, if necessary, in grade 8. Passing all three tests was required for promotion to grade 9. The regulations later were amended to allow students to enroll in high school classes even if they had not passed the LPT. The opportunity to earn credit toward graduation, however, was denied these individuals until all three portions of the LPT had been passed. The state had stepped in for the first time to set a standard for graduation beyond credit accumulation in particular subjects.

At this time the bar was raised for Virginia teachers as well. Among the recommendations included in the Commission on Excellence in Education's report was an overhaul of teacher preparation and certification. The Commission determined that an undergraduate degree in an arts and sciences discipline rather than in education would be required for all teachers educated in Virginia. They recommended that the state "limit education course requirements to 18 semester hours," and revise certification requirements to reflect these changes (Commission on Excellence in Education, 1986). The need to retain qualified teachers was also addressed by the Commission as it suggested that the state provide financial incentives to school divisions for developing and implementing ways to keep effective teachers in the classroom. Despite Republican objections to federal interference in state affairs, the Committee endorsed the notion of national certification of teachers to "raise the professional standing of teachers" (Commission on Excellence in Education, 1986).

The recommendations of the Commission on Excellence in Education received qualified support from the public and the education profession. Brenda Cloyd, president of the 43,000-member Virginia Education Association, indicated that her organization had "no real objection to the passport" (Baker, November 8, 1986, p. C-1). Cathy Belter, president of the Virginia Parent-Teachers Association, concurred, but expressed fear on the part of parents whose children were struggling in school that they could be adversely affected by the LPT. The VEA registered concern about limiting the number of education courses taken by prospective teachers (Baker, November 8, 1986, p. C-1).

If there was a major source of contention over education in the late eighties, it involved family life education and teaching about human sexuality. During 1988 the state legislature voted funding in the amount of $4.7 million to establish a "family life" program in public elementary and secondary schools. The proposal was opposed by some religious groups and political conservatives, and the Governor was able to secure the support of several key conservative legislators only after he backed away from the State Board of Education's decision to link school funding to school divisions' compliance with the mandated state guidelines for family life education. The Baliles administration assured local school systems that they would be fully reimbursed even if they drafted their own "family life" curricula (Melton, February 22, 1988, p. D-1). State superintendent John Davis's letter indicating that the standards were " 'not an absolute determination' of when sex education should be taught to young people" appeared to mollify parents and lawmakers who opposed the state mandates (Melton, February 22, 1988, p. D-1). The message seemed to be that at least some state standards were more advisory than regulatory in nature, and that local control of curriculum remained a guiding principle for state policy makers.

Financial disparity among districts surfaced as a major educational issue in the 1989 gubernatorial campaign. Democratic candidate L. Douglas Wilder's proposed policy initiatives focused on what he called the "three Ds: drugs, dropouts and disparity" (Jenkins, September 16, 1989, p. B-5). Among his proposals were early education programs for children from disadvantaged backgrounds, special educational centers that were separate from regular schools for students with drug problems, and a reduction in class sizes, particularly in "poor areas" (Jenkins, September 16, 1989, p. B-5). His embracing of such programs was supplanted after his election, however, by an accountability program based on outcome-based education.

A SETBACK ON THE ROAD TO ACCOUNTABILITY

The last decade of the twentieth century occasioned an unprecedented discussion of national education goals. The Education Summit in Charlottesville, Virginia, in the fall of 1989 brought together President Bush and the nation's governors. Two days of meetings produced agreement on six national education goals, which Bush then presented in his State of the Union Address. The governors also committed to engage in restructuring their state education systems and to develop methods to measure student performance in order to monitor the effectiveness of their reform efforts (Klein, September 16, 1990, p. A-10).

In Virginia, concern focused on improving schools at a time of economic retrenchment. Superintendents from school divisions across the state worried that the Wilder administration's push for educational reform was under-funded. Their fear was that reforms might result in new mandates that would drain resources from existing programs (Ruberry, May 3, 1990, pp. A-1, A-12). During September of 1990 a coalition representing 38 of the state's 135 school divisions decided to file suit against the state to address what they saw as a need for a more equitable system for addressing funding disparities in the Commonwealth (Walker, September 18, 1991, p. 1). While the suit was eventually dismissed, it brought attention to the difficulties faced by less affluent districts in their efforts to meet the requirements of the Standards of Quality and Standards of Learning

The Wilder administration's package of reforms was referred to as the World Class Education Program. The "Common Core of Learning" served as its centerpiece and constituted a set of educational "outcomes" designed to make graduates of Virginia schools competitive in the global marketplace. Wilder's program reflected the push for higher learning standards and accountability that emerged from the Education Summit.

The Common Core of Learning soon ran afoul of two groups in Virginia. According to Superintendent of Public Instruction Joseph A. Spagnolo, Jr., the Wilder plan promised to establish objectives for local school systems that would "meet or exceed the world's highest standards for student achievement" and ensure that graduates of Virginia's public high schools would have "basic skills of communication and computation, thinking skills including problem solving, self-esteem, sociability, self-management, integrity and honesty" (Bradley, September 26, 1991, p. 17). The announcement contained the seeds of the effort's demise. Conservative religious groups soon registered opposition to the Common Core of Learning because it included affective and normative outcomes. Superintendents and school boards later objected to the program because they viewed it as an attack on local control. In the face of this opposition, the Wilder administration was compelled to abandon the Common Core of Learning.

The decision was seen by some observers as a political decision having more to do with Governor Wilder's desire to run for the U.S. Senate in 1994 than his commitment to local control of education ("Virginia's World-Class," *Washington Post*, September 17, 1993, p. A-22). Wilder abandoned his own initiative and agreed with critics who complained that the State Board of Education's proposals would have restricted the power of local school boards and emphasized the teaching of vaguely defined values at the expense of academics:

> Make no mistake: I do not now, nor have I ever endorsed changing Virginia's education standards to encompass values-based education in our Commonwealth. . . . Knowledge and proficiency of basic skills must remain the basis for education in our Commonwealth. (Harris, November 18, 1993, pp. C-1, C-2)

Ironically, many of the people who objected to the inclusion of values-based and affective outcomes in the Common Core of Learning were among those who supported legislation in the late 1990s requiring formal character education in public schools and a required moment of silence at the start of each school day.

THE COMING OF NEW STANDARDS OF LEARNING

Interest in curriculum standards, as the preceding discussion indicates, did not commence when the Republicans captured the governorship in November of

1993. On the national level, the Clinton administration had been touting the importance of higher learning standards since its early days. Soon after George Allen assumed office in Virginia, President Clinton signed into law the Goals 2000 Educate America Act (March 31, 1994). The wide-ranging bill, which traced its origins to President Bush's 1989 Education Summit in Charlottesville, Virginia, called for substantial monetary incentives for states that voluntarily agreed to develop educational reforms. The reforms had to include standards for curriculum, student performance, school funding, and teacher preparation.

While Governor Allen made a political point of keeping Virginia from initially participating in the Goals 2000 program, he and his supporters did not reject the idea of higher learning standards. Although they had strongly resisted the Wilder administration's efforts to develop curriculum standards in the form of world-class outcomes, they embraced the notion of challenging standards of learning. Their quibble, they explained, was not with the *idea* of outcomes, but with the specific outcomes that had been included in the previous administration's inventory.

One of Governor Allen's first acts was to create the Champion Schools Commission, chaired by his Secretary of Education, Beverly Sgro, and his State Superintendent of Public Instruction, William C. Bosher. The Executive Order that established the Commission asked for recommendations regarding four objectives: (1) the creation of higher academic standards, (2) the development of accountability through testing, (3) provisions for greater parent involvement in their children's education, and (4) reduced school violence and drug use (Virginia Department of Education, 1994, p. v). The 49-member group included several members of the Virginia General Assembly and the state Board of Education.

Before the Commission received its charge, however, the state Department of Education already had selected four of the largest school divisions in Virginia—Fairfax County, Virginia Beach, Prince William County, and Newport News—and asked them to assist in revising existing Standards of Learning in the core areas of mathematics, science, language arts, and social studies. In the process of generating revisions, each division solicited input from teachers, parents, and other community members. Writing teams from each division submitted their revised standards to State Superintendent Bosher in the early fall of 1994.

What happened next became a source of considerable controversy (Farmer, June 18, 1995). The Champion Schools Commission, it turns out, had been receiving suggestions directly from "school division leaders" regarding desired changes in state curriculum standards. As a result, the Commission developed its own set of desired revisions. Bosher assigned writing teams to "meld the school districts' revisions with the commission's" (Farmer, June 18, 1995, p. A-8). Many of the educators from the four school divisions who had worked hard to draft revised standards felt betrayed. They had received no indication that their efforts would be merged with other revisions before being formally presented to the Commission. An article in the *Richmond Times-Dispatch* summed up the criticism, which focused on the process itself as well as the standards in social studies:

> Some critics contended that the proposals were rewritten to suit the political ideology of Allen and his appointees on the conservative Champion Schools Commission. The revised standards, they said, reflected a narrow view of government and history.
>
> The standards lacked academic rigor, critics contended, and some contained unrealistic expectations for students in kindergarten through third grade. (Farmer, June 18, 1995, p. A-8)

During March and April of 1995, 10 public hearings on the proposed revisions to the Standards of Learning were held across the state. Approximately 5,000 individuals expressed their opinions, with the greatest amount of concern being registered about standards in social studies and language arts. A frequently heard complaint was that standards for elementary students in these two areas focused too much on isolated facts and not enough on understanding what the facts meant (Farmer, June 18, 1995, p. A-8). Under the old standards, for example, kindergarten students were expected to "identify and describe personal feelings." Items of this kind were replaced in the proposed standards by standards such as "recognize patriotic symbols, such as flags and monuments of Virginia and the United States."

Those registering concerns about the revised standards, according to newspaper reports, tended to be educators, school administrators, and college professors (Farmer, June 18, 1995, p. A-8). In a seeming concession to the "education establishment," Bosher, who prior to assuming his state post had been Superintendent of Henrico County Public Schools, constituted a team to revise the social studies standards. In a further effort to placate critics, James P. Jones, chair of the State Board of Education, created an advisory committee to oversee revisions of the standards. The committee included representatives from the original four district-based writing teams as well as the Champion Schools Commission.

On June 22, 1995, the Virginia Board of Education met and approved the revised standards for every grade in mathematics, science, and language arts. Action on the social studies standards was postponed until additional changes, based on public feedback, were made. The Board divided over the adoption of a list of approved books for English and language arts, and consequently the proposed list was not adopted. Supporters of the list made it known, however, that parents had questions about many of the readings chosen by the "education establishment" (Farmer, June 23, 1995, p. A-10). In July of 1995 copies of the Standards of Learning were distributed to all school divisions in the Commonwealth with the understanding that they would begin incorporating the standards into their K–12 curricula.

Robley Jones, the President of the Virginia Education Association, expressed support for the State Board's willingness to make adjustments in the standards and his belief that teachers were ready to help students meet the standards (Farmer, June 23, 1995, p. A-1). Disagreements, though, arose between the Virginia Department of Education and members of the advisory committee on social studies regarding the total cost of implementing the new Standards of Learning. Estimates for test development and teacher training by the advisory committee ran as high as $45 million, a figure Bosher believed was highly exaggerated (Farmer, June 23, 1995, p. A-10).

CREATING HIGH-STAKES TESTS

Armed with an almost-complete set of revised standards, the Virginia Board of Education next turned its attention to the matter of measurement. While Virginia had possessed standards for several decades, it had lacked an assessment system linked directly to the standards, a system that would permit school officials and the public to determine whether individual students and schools were meeting expectations.

Having secured funding from the General Assembly in the early part of 1996, the Department of Education initiated the test development process by constituting Content Review Committees made up of teachers, curriculum specialists, and representatives of educational organizations. Working with Department personnel and representatives of Harcourt Brace, the firm that was awarded the state test development contract, the committee generated "test blueprints" and reviewed test items for field-testing. In the late spring of 1996, school divisions received notification of test content. Local superintendents again were informed of test content in November. From December 1996 through March 1997, regional meetings were conducted by Department personnel to explain the new testing program.

Field tests of the new SOL tests were given to 350,000 students in April 1997. Data from these tests were reviewed by committees of educators in order to eliminate confusing test items and items that might entail bias. A second field test was administered to 60,000 students in September 1997. Following another round of review and analysis, tests of the Standards of Learning were prepared for the first official administration in the spring of 1998. A total of 27 tests were involved, covering the core areas of mathematics, science, language arts, and social studies as well as computer technology. Tests were given to students in grades 3, 5, and 8 as well as high school students enrolled in designated courses.

Once the first tests had been given and the raw scores shared with school divisions, the Virginia Board of Education confronted the issue of passing scores

on the tests. Eight Standard Setting Committees were appointed to develop recommendations for passing scores on each test. Committees consisted of teachers,
curriculum specialists, principals, and other education officials. To oversee the
entire process and ensure its integrity, the Board created a Standard Setting Advisory Committee, chaired by former State Superintendent Bosher.

In the fall of 1998, the Board received recommendations from the Standard
Setting Committees and established passing scores for each test. Two "levels" of
passing scores were designated: "proficient" and "advanced." This process was
followed closely by parents and educators across the Commonwealth because,
while the tests were being developed and field-tested, the state also was revising
its accreditation standards for schools, the third component of the comprehensive
accountability plan. Failure to pass state tests would carry consequences for individual students and their schools.

REVISING THE STANDARDS OF ACCREDITATION

Revising the Standards of Accreditation (SOA), not surprisingly, represented the most contentious part of Virginia's accountability plan. Without the
SOA, the curriculum standards and tests lacked "high stakes." Discussion of revisions in the accreditation standards officially began in August of 1996, as the
SOL tests were being developed. Public hearings across the state were held at
this time to gather input regarding how to ensure that the SOL were implemented
successfully. Additional hearings were held between March and July of 1997,
when a draft of the revised SOA became available for public review. On September 4, 1997, the Board of Education approved the new Regulations Establishing Standards for Accrediting Public Schools in Virginia (Virginia Department of Education, September 4, 1997). Governor George Allen declared that the
new standards represented one of his administration's greatest achievements and
predicted that they would raise academic quality and enable the young people of
Virginia to thrive in a global economy (Stallsmith, September 5, 1997, p. A-1).

The new SOA raised from 21 to 22 the number of credits required to earn
a standard diploma and from 23 to 24 the number of credits to earn an advanced
diploma. The SOA also specified how many of these credits had to be "verified,"
meaning that students had passed the statewide SOL test in the subject area.
Beginning with the Class of 2004, students earning a standard diploma needed to
accumulate six verified credits. An advanced studies diploma required nine verified credits. Graduation requirements in the SOA indicated how many total credits and verified credits were needed in particular subject matter areas.

One aspect of the revised SOA that constituted a new dimension of educational accountability in the Old Dominion involved prescribed minimum pass
rates on SOL tests. Beginning with the 2006–2007 school year, every secondary
school, in order to be "fully accredited," was required to achieve pass rates of at

least 70 percent in the four core subject areas. This meant that 70% of the eligible students had to pass the state tests. Elementary schools had to achieve 70% pass rates in English/reading and mathematics and 50 percent pass rates in science and history. The only students who were exempted from calculations of pass rates were those "whose IEP or 504 Plan or LEP committee excludes them from participating in the testing program" (Virginia Department of Education, September 4, 1997, p. 25).

Running 31 pages, the SOA also included standards related to virtually every aspect of school organization, from administrative leadership to school safety. Part V, for example, dealt with the role of the principal, clearly indicating that instructional leadership was expected. Part VII addressed school and community communications. In this part appeared the fourth element of the new accountability plan, School Performance Report Cards. According to the provision, each school in the Commonwealth was required to provide parents of schoolchildren and other community members with an annual "report card" specifying the following:

- schoolwide test scores on the SOL tests

- statewide averages and division averages for the most recent 3-year period

- students with disabilities and limited-English-proficient students' participation in the SOL tests

- attendance rates

- incidents of physical violence and weapons possession (Virginia Department of Education, September 4, 1997, pp. 22–23)

Report cards for secondary schools were required to include additional data:

- number and percentage of students taking Advanced Placement courses and the number and percentage of those earning a score of 3 or better on the Advanced Placement test

- dropout rates for the current and previous 3 years

- the accreditation rating awarded to the school for the current and previous 3 years (Virginia Department of Education, September 4, 1997, p. 23)

Most aspects of the revised SOA generated relatively little controversy. Several provisions, though, were not universally well received. One Board member opposed the absolute standard of a 70% pass rate for accreditation (Stallsmith,

September 5, 1997, p. A-5). He argued for accreditation to be awarded based on a pass rate of 70 percent or better averaged over a 3-year period. The two provisions that created the greatest opposition, though, had less to do with accountability than with the political agenda of the "religious right." These provisions allowed local school divisions to decide whether or not to offer family life education and whether to hire elementary school counselors or reading specialists. The previous standards had required family life education and elementary school counselors. When the revised SOA made these provisions optional, Cheri James of the Virginia Education Association complained that the Board of Education listened more to special interest groups than the citizens who attended statewide public hearings (Stallsmith, September 5, 1997, p. A-5).

IMPLEMENTATION AND APPREHENSION

In the period immediately following the adoption of the SOL, the SOA, and the SOL tests, educators across the commonwealth busied themselves with the work of policy implementation. In-service training related to the new standards and tests was conducted. School divisions launched projects to integrate the SOL into existing curriculums. Public relations campaigns informed students and parents about the importance of doing well on the SOL tests and the consequences for individual students and schools of inadequate performance. Along with implementation, however, came a growing sense of uneasiness related to various aspects of the accountability plan.

Some of the apprehension derived from concerns that the SOL placed too much emphasis on factual knowledge and not enough on understanding and critical thinking. Teachers and students complained about having to devote too much time to pretest reviews of subject matter, some of which had been taught years before (Mathews, April 19, 1998, pp. B-1, B-10). When the first round of SOL tests was given in the spring of 1998, complaints about the design of the tests and particular test items were expressed (Berry, April 19, 1998, p. C-8).

In a letter to the *Washington Post* (May 3, 1998, p. C-8), Mark Christie, a member of the Virginia Board of Education, attempted to address the chorus of criticism and concern. He reminded educators and parents of the reasons that the Board had pressed for the accountability plan: (1) one in four graduates of Virginia public high schools must do remedial work before attempting college classes, (2) nearly one in three sixth graders in Virginia public schools fails the Literacy Passport Test, and (3) Virginia's business community expresses dissatisfaction with the reading, writing, and math skills of employees with Virginia high school diplomas. He acknowledged that "reasonable people" may disagree about particular standards, but that there was no call for rejecting the *idea* of learning standards.

The new year brought a hangover of a different sort for Virginia educators. Headlines said it all. On the front page of the *Richmond Times-Dispatch,* the headline proclaimed, "Only 2% of Va. Schools Meet New Standards." The *Washington Post* on the same day ran a front-page article with the heading, "97% Fail First Round of Key Tests in Virginia." After more than 6 months of test scoring and analysis, the verdict was in. Thirty-nine out of 1,800 public elementary and secondary schools achieved sufficient pass rates on the SOL tests to meet the new accreditation standards. Educational leaders claimed they were not caught completely off guard by the dismal results. They noted that the high school students who took the initial round of tests knew in advance that their performance would have no effect on their ability to graduate. An effort to have test scores entered on students' official high school transcripts was beaten back by parents who argued that no warning had been given prior to administering the tests.

The immediate aftermath of reports of the test scores can best be characterized as a period of reflection and determination to do better. VEA President Cheri James was quoted in the newspaper as saying, "If we look at this process as a journey, then we are at the beginning" (Stallsmith, January 9, 1999, p. A-6). Fairfax County Superintendent Daniel Domenech applauded the state's commitment to raise student performance, but warned that the General Assembly would need to provide additional resources to ensure that students received the help they needed (Stallsmith, January 9, 1999, p. A-6). State Board President Kirk Schroder voiced cautious optimism, saying that "everyone has a lot of work to do," but adding that scores were bound to improve as students and teachers became more familiar with the SOL (Mathews & Benning, January 9, 1999, p. A-6).

A RISING TIDE OF CONCERN

Throughout the winter and spring of 1999 Virginia educators continued to work on implementing the SOL and preparing students for the next round of tests. At the same time, however, anxiety and apprehension began to give way to the formalization of concern and the organization of opposition to the accountability plan. Interestingly, the fact that Virginia students posted gains on each of the 27 SOL tests administered in the spring of 1999 did not stem the criticism. While Republican Governor Jim Gilmore, who succeeded George Allen in January of 1998 and enjoyed a legislature in which his party controlled both houses, vowed to press forward with the accountability plan and stated that the improvements in test scores demonstrated that the hard work of teachers and students had paid off ("News in Brief," August 4, 1999, p. 26), a group of Virginia parents were lobbying for changes.

Parents Across Virginia United to Reform SOLS (PAVURSOLS), which claimed in the fall of 1999 to represent over 1,500 "parents and grandparents," challenged the wisdom of a "one-size-fits-all" SOL system (Parents Across Virginia United to Reform SOLS, 1999, p. 1). The grassroots group cited five primary objectives in their position paper:

1. The amendment of state law in order to prohibit the use of SOL test scores as the primary basis for promotion and retention, graduation and awarding of diplomas, and school accreditation.

2. A moratorium on the use of SOL test results for any purpose until independent assessment experts can evaluate the tests.

3. The amendment of state law to replace reliance on a single measure of student achievement with provisions calling for multiple measures.

4. A review of the Standards of Learning by a "broad-based" group of educators.

5. "The development of a system that recognizes and supports more than one successful path to high school graduation and diplomas."

In the fall of 1999, the Fairfax County Council of PTAs filed a request under the Virginia Freedom of Information Act to obtain all the questions used on the first two versions of the SOL tests (Samuels, October 9, 1999, p. B-5). The Virginia Department of Education had previously released sample test items, but no items actually used on the tests. Without seeing actual test items, no assessment could be made of their age-appropriateness or validity, claimed the head of the Fairfax County Council of PTAs. On October 18, 1999, State Superintendent of Public Instruction Paul Stapleton indicated that the Department of Education would not comply with the group's request (Benning, October 19, 1999, p. B-4). He reasoned that releasing the test items would jeopardize the security of the tests.

Demands for changes in the accountability plan heated up on the eve of the November elections for state legislators when Virginia superintendents from Region VI, which included Roanoke and Danville, held a press conference. While expressing their support for the state's efforts to raise standards and hold educators accountable, they noted a variety of concerns with the existing accountability plan (Bowman, November 2, 1999, pp. A-1, A-7). Test results should not be the sole basis for determining whether a student graduates from high school, they argued. Furthermore, tests should be administered at the end of courses, rather than four to six weeks before the end of a semester, as called for by the Department of Education. The superintendents also asked that local educators be permitted to unofficially score the SOL tests before sending them to Richmond. In this way, teachers could begin helping low-performing students immediately, rather than waiting weeks or months to receive test results. Though it was not stated, this provision also would allow teachers to review actual test items.

Kirk Schroder, president of the State Board of Education, responded that the Board was exploring ways to administer the SOL tests later in the semester so that students would have more time to cover required content (Noz, November 5, 1999, p. A-13). One possible strategy would be to computerize the tests, thereby allowing them to be given at the end of the semester without unduly delaying the reporting of test results. Schroder expressed his hope that the General Assembly would appropriate the funds needed to develop and administer computerized tests.

On the matter of not requiring students to pass SOL tests for high school graduation, Schroder was less conciliatory. He insisted that the SOL tests were essential for quality control and pointed out that students could retake the tests as often as they needed in order to pass them (Noz, November 5, 1999, p. A-13).

The *Richmond Times-Dispatch*'s front-page story covering Schroder's reactions to the Region VI superintendents suggested that Virginia superintendents were divided in their feelings about the accountability plan. When the Virginia Association of School Superintendents (VASS) published its legislative positions in December of 1999, however, it was apparent that the superintendents were united in their concerns. Among the positions on the accountability plan that were either adopted, amended, or carried over from previous years were the following (Virginia Association of School Superintendents, December 14, 1999, pp. 5–8):

- VASS opposes the concept of Standards of Learning becoming regulations.

- VASS supports the review, revision, and approval for the SOA by the General Assembly, with such legislation to include a sunset clause.

- VASS supports the use of an improvement model to determine accreditation status during and after the implementation years.

- VASS supports local scoring of SOL tests.

- The state should assume a role of support and direction rather than one of punitive enforcement in accountability and accreditation.

- The SOA requirements should not restrict or limit opportunities currently available to challenge students. Choices should remain for students such as: the arts and humanities, health and physical education, vocational education, including technical courses which serve to facilitate such programs as school-to-work transitions.

The positions advocated by the superintendents clearly reflected a desire to maintain a high degree of local control. Given the choice of centering authority for educational accountability with the State Board of Education, which was appointed by the governor, or the General Assembly, which was elected by the citizens of the Commonwealth, they preferred the latter. They also endorsed the idea that *improving* schools should qualify for accreditation, not just schools that achieved predetermined pass rates. The last position statement reflected their fear that emphasis on SOL courses and passing state tests could adversely affect students' opportunity to choose elective courses and courses in which no state tests were given.

State Superintendent of Public Instruction Paul Stapleton announced his resignation in December (Melton, December 9, 1999, p. B-7). While various reasons for his departure were hinted at, some insiders noted that he had been unwilling to silence the superintendents' opposition to various aspects of the accountability plan. State leaders may have expected Stapleton, a division superintendent prior to assuming the role of State Superintendent, to ensure that his former colleagues fell into line behind the accountability plan.

Division superintendents were not alone in their criticism of the accountability plan. In November of 1999, the individual referred to as the "father of SOL tests," University of Virginia English Professor E. D. Hirsch, complained publicly that state efforts to implement his idea of a "core" of essential learning had been "messed up" by the State Board of Education (Still, November 13, 1999, p. B-5). While stressing his continued commitment to the value of a common core of knowledge, Hirsch decried the quality of the tests designed to measure the SOL and the state's modification of his recommendations for what young children should know. The latter problem he traced to bullying by "early childhood romantics" who did not believe that first and second graders should be required to learn challenging content. Hirsch also criticized state authorities for not providing sufficient financial and technical support to train teachers and develop materials needed to implement the accountability plan.

On November 30, 1999, public hearings were held across the commonwealth to give citizens an opportunity to express their views on the accountability plan and various proposals for modifying it (Boria, December 1, 1999, p. A-1, A-16). While some speakers attacked the entire plan, others recommended ways to "fine-tune" it. Educational leaders reiterated their call to move the SOL tests to the end of the semester and to avoid basing decisions on students' educational futures solely on test scores. Kirk Schroder did not deny the need for alterations in the accountability plan, but he clearly had no sympathy for those, including Parents Across Virginia United to Reform the SOLs, who attacked the entire plan without offering alternatives.

A week after the public hearings, Schroder asked the leaders of seven state education groups to "back up their complaints about new statewide achievement tests with specific recommendations for change" (Mathews, December 7, 1999, pp. B-1, B-2). At the same time, Schroder and fellow board member Mark Christie stated that they would not "give in to demands from some parent and teacher groups that schools use student grades and teacher evaluations to determine who gets a high school diploma" (Mathews, December 7, 1999, p. B-1). A line appeared to have been drawn in the sand regarding how much change the State Board of Education would entertain. The new millennium would provide an opportunity to test that resolve.

Meanwhile the old millennium ended with Governor Gilmore proposing to allocate an additional 27 million dollars to help students pass the SOL tests (Melton, December 10, 1999, pp. B-1, B-8). The new money would be earmarked for expanding the kindergarten Early Reading Intervention Program and initiating a remedial mathematics program for seventh and eighth grades. The education budget already included $2.5 million for "independent reviewers" to help schools with low pass rates meet state Standards of Accreditation.

CAUTIOUS CONCILIATION

The new year began with a variety of efforts to make adjustments in the accountability plan. Legislation was introduced by several Northern Virginia lawmakers that would prevent SOL test results from being used as the sole basis for determining whether students graduate from high school and require the state to release copies of previous SOL tests promptly (Benning, February 3, 2000, pp. VA-1, VA-10). Board President Kirk Schroder indicated in early February that a new "basic diploma" was being considered for special education students who demonstrated "competency in reading, writing and math and show they have the skills to get a job" (Benning, February 3, 2000, p. B-2). Special education advocates felt that many young people with disabilities would be unable to earn a diploma under the existing requirements. Less than a week later, Schroder was reported to be considering a suggestion that the requirement of 70% pass rates on SOL tests be changed (Benning, February 8, 2000, pp. B-1, B-5). Responding to a report by the conservative Fairfax-based Thomas Jefferson Institute for Public Policy that argued the 70% pass rate was unrealistic for many state schools, he acknowledged that it may be prudent to link state accreditation to demonstrated improvement on state tests rather than achievement of a designated pass rate.

The developing climate of conciliation and compromise was dampened when Governor Gilmore quickly reaffirmed his support for the requirement in the SOA that public schools achieve a 70% pass rate on state tests by 2007 or lose their accreditation (Benning, February 9, 2000, p. B-3). Coming just a day after Schroder's remarks, the governor's statement appeared to constitute a firm reminder that he had no intention of allowing the basic tenets of the accountability plan to be altered.

On February 11, 2000, the House Education Committee, as if acknowledging the governor's concerns, voted 13 to 9 to carry over to the next year all eight bills dealing with multiple graduation criteria. Schroder stated that multiple criteria "are buzz words used by some people to gut the SOLs" (VASS News, February 2000, p. 2). The administration in Richmond seemed determined not to permit local school systems to employ alternatives to the SOL tests.

Several weeks later, though, Schroder was entertaining yet another possible change, albeit a relatively minor one. In a move seemingly designed to placate teachers, the School Performance Report Card would be expanded to include the results of an annual survey of teachers (Stallsmith, February 24, 2000, p. B-4). Teachers would be asked how well their schools were meeting their instructional needs, including planning time. To help those who received the report cards to understand contextual issues, Schroder and Acting State Superintendent Jo Lynne DeMary also suggested than an index be added. The index would be based on the percentage of students receiving free and reduced-price lunch, drop-out rate, and other indicators. Schroder noted, however, that the index would not affect accreditation requirements.

While legislators, the State Board of Education, and the State Department of Education had been considering proposals for modifying the accountability plan, leaders of education groups in Virginia also were busy. An unintended by-product of Schroder's December challenge to education groups to offer specific suggestions to improve the plan was to provide an impetus for coalition-building. The coalition consisted of the Virginia Education Association, the Virginia Association of School Superintendents, the Virginia Association of Elementary School principals, the Virginia Association of Secondary School principals, the Virginia Parent-Teacher Association, the Virginia School Counselors Association, and the Virginia Counselors Association.

On February 24, 2000, the President of VASS, acting on behalf of the coalition, presented a set of suggested changes in the accountability plan to the State Board of Education (Benning, March 2, 2000, pp. B-1, B-4). The proposals focused primarily on the state tests and the accreditation standards and included the following:

- Divide the SOL tests into four parts and give them quarterly.

- Allow students who do poorly on the SOL tests to retake them immediately.

- Use other tests besides the SOL tests to determine whether a student should receive a diploma (for example, a national automobile mechanics exam for a vocational education student).

- Add diploma options, such as a diploma for vocational and technical education students.

- Develop a schedule for reviewing and revising the SOL curriculum standards.

- Assess schools based not only on the SOL test scores, but also on results of other standardized tests (such as the Stanford 9, a Virginia requirement).

- Revise School Performance Report Cards to include data on students, such as the percentage of students on free and reduced-price lunch.

Schroder received the recommendations as constructive suggestions. He was quoted in the *Washington Post* as saying (Benning, March 2, 2000, p. VA-4):

Overall, I was pleased with the tone and nature of their comments. . . . They made it clear that they are not against the SOLs, standards and accountability—they are not against the assessment program. My sense is that they are looking for ways to improve the administration and the overall accountability process, and I view their proposals as being very workable.

It is important to note that Virginians were not alone in their desire to reconsider certain aspects of their state accountability plan. Sensing mounting concern nationally, U.S. Secretary of Education Richard W. Riley called for a "midcourse review" of the "standards movement" in his February 22, 2000, "State of American Education" speech (Sack, March 1, 2000, pp. 1, 32). He warned that standards should be "challenging, but realistic" and advised states not to rely on a single test to measure students' knowledge of the standards.

The spring of 2000 brought several indications that the State Board of Education was taking to heart the concerns of parents and educators. The role of the SOL Test Advisory Committee was expanded to include all aspects of the accountability plan, thus addressing a recommendation that had been made by the coalition of education groups (Swensen, March 28, 2000, p. B-1). The Accountability Advisory Committee, as the reconstituted group was known, was asked to review several of the coalition's suggestions, including the establishment of a process to allow students who performed well during the year but failed their SOL test to still receive a verified credit toward graduation.

A month later the Board indicated preliminary support for changing the requirement that all high school students pass SOL tests in order to graduate (Benning, April 29, 2000, p. B-1). Serious consideration was given to a coalition-backed provision to grant verified credit to students who failed the SOL tests, but otherwise possessed a strong academic record. Authority to decide which students would receive this concession would be vested in local school boards.

Just when relations between the State Board and educators showed signs of thawing, however, Schroder's predecessor, Michelle Easton, publicly condemned the proposed changes in the accountability plan, claiming they would kill the standards "by a thousand cuts" (Benning, May 2, 2000, p. B-1). Whether she had been prompted to speak out by the governor was unclear, but his press secretary stated that Gilmore "will not support any proposals that water down the Standards of Learning tests" (Benning, May 2, 2000, p. B-4). The press secretary went on to remind people that the proposed revisions were just that—proposals.

The Board did not vote on revisions to the accountability plan until the end of July. Meanwhile newspapers were filled with information related to educational accountability. Bowing to public pressure, the Maryland State Board of Education, for example, voted to delay by at least 2 years a requirement that high school students pass a series of state exams in order to graduate (Argetsinger, May 25, 2000, pp. B-1, B-8). June brought reports of inappropriate teacher coaching of students before tests were given (Benning, June 8, 2000, pp. B-1, B-7). A front-page article in the *Washington Post* in late June noted that large numbers of principals were retiring or being moved because of pressures related to accountability initiatives (Nakamura and Samuels, June 25, 2000, pp. A-1, A-17). A survey of parents in Northern Virginia found that parents did not trust the SOL tests, with only 17% believing that the tests accurately measured their children's achievement (Benning, June 27, 2000, p. B-2).

The Board met on June 22, 2000, and unanimously adopted standards in foreign languages. Hearings on the proposed standards previously had been held across the state. The Board also approved the development of an additional SOL test for World Geography and received public comment on the proposed revisions to the SOA.

The attention of educators and parents was riveted on Richmond on July 27 as the State Board announced its decisions regarding proposed changes in the accreditation standards. The Board agreed to "relax" new graduation rules for high school students, but it refused to back off requiring students to pass state tests in order to receive a diploma (Mathews, July 28, 2000, pp. A-1, A-4). For the first time since the SOA had been adopted 3 years earlier, the Board was willing to grant concessions. Students would be allowed to substitute a list of national and international tests for the SOL tests. The substitute tests included the Advanced Placement, SAT-II, and International Baccalaureate exams. Students entering ninth grade between 2000 and 2002 were allowed greater flexibility in choosing the individual SOL tests they must pass in order to graduate. The Board also approved a new diploma option, the Modified Standard Diploma, for students in special education. When the Board originally proposed a basic diploma for special education students, the recommendation had been modified to apply to all students. Fear that the basic diploma would be used to track low-performing students caused Board members to reconsider the move, however.

Virginia educators reacted quickly to the Board's revisions. The headline in the *Washington Post* on July 29 indicated that the accreditation standards still were regarded as "too strict" (Seymour, July 29, 2000, p. B-1). Observers noted that allowing students to substitute national and international tests for the state

SOL tests would not benefit most at-risk students, who were unlikely to be able to pass these challenging tests. Many were disappointed that the Board had declined to enact the coalition-backed proposal to allow students with strong academic records to earn verified credits, despite failing SOL tests. They hoped that the Board, having displayed a willingness to compromise on some issues, eventually would consider multiple criteria for determining academic success.

The beginning of the 2000–2001 school year brought good news and bad news for supporters of the accountability plan. On a positive note, scores improved on most of the SOL tests that had been taken the previous spring. Governor Gilmore took advantage of the opportunity to argue that the plan was working (Benning and Mathews, September 8, 2000, pp. A-1, A-15). Several days later, the *Washington Post* published the results of a survey it had conducted of 1,031 registered Virginia voters (Mathews and Benning, September 11, 2000, pp. A-1, A-12). Disputing Governor Gilmore's assessment, 51% of the respondents felt that the accountability plan was "not working." Only 24% indicated that the SOL tests should be continued "as is." The upcoming Senate election between incumbent Chuck Robb, a Democrat, and George Allen, the Republican governor responsible for the accountability plan, came to be regarded by some observers as a crucial test of voter support for the plan.

CONTINUING UNCERTAINTY

As the November election approached, education became a bigger and bigger issue for Virginia's two senate candidates. George Allen claimed that steadily improving SOL test scores vindicated his much-criticized education record. "Our children in Virginia's public schools are learning more than ever before," he proudly announced in a campaign speech at a Fairfax County elementary school that dramatically improved its test scores (O'Hanlon and Melton, September 21, 2000, p. B-1). Incumbent Chuck Robb, realizing he faced a tough challenge from Allen, countered that funding for public education during his opponent's administration suffered substantial cuts (O'Hanlon and Melton, September 21, 2000, pp. B-1, B-7). He reminded voters that education spending increased during his own term as governor (1982–1986).

October brought an escalation of campaign rhetoric, as the Robb camp attacked the Gilmore administration for using taxpayer money to run television ads promoting the Standards of Learning. While Gilmore argued the ads were a legitimate effort to inform parents and students about the success of the accountability plan, Democrats insisted that the ads were intended to promote the Allen campaign (Melton, October 6, 2000, p. A-1). As Democrats in the General Assembly threatened to sue Governor Gilmore for spending $1.2 million in state funds for political ads, Chuck Robb launched a direct attack on the SOL tests. "It's all stick and no carrot," he stated (Melton, October 10, 2000, p. B-2). He went on to decry pressure felt by teachers to "teach to the test" and heightened anxiety on the part of Virginia students and parents.

As the election drew closer, Democrats received good news and bad news. On a positive note, the state yielded to public pressure and withdrew the television ads touting the success of the accountability plan (Whitley, October 12, 2000, p. B-1). At the same time, the Virginia Department of Education released test scores for all school divisions, revealing "overall improvement" and offering Republicans an opportunity to claim that the accountability plan was working (Stallsmith, October 12, 2000, p. B-1). Virginia students posted modest gains on 21 of 27 tests, declined on three tests, and remained at the same level on three tests. The Department of Education, 1 day after publicizing test results, released the findings of a statewide survey of teachers. The survey of nearly 31,000 teachers, or about 35% of the total population of teachers, indicated that more than two thirds of the teachers felt they were getting the support and training they needed to help their students pass the SOL tests (News Release, October 12, 2000).

Two weeks later supporters of the accountability plan received more good news. Analyses of school pass rates indicated that 22% of Virginia's schools met the benchmarks for accreditation that were scheduled to take effect in 2007 (Benning, October 26, 2000, p. B-1). This figure was up from 6.5% the previous year. An additional 38% of schools achieved the newly created benchmark for satisfactory improvement, suggesting that they would soon meet the 70% pass rate. The next day Governor Gilmore announced that $1.2 million, the exact amount spent on the controversial television ads, would be made available to help the 189 schools with very low scores on SOL tests in English and mathematics (Benning, October 27, 2000, p. B-9).

On November 7, 2000, Virginians went to the polls and elected George Allen to replace Chuck Robb as junior Senator from the Old Dominion. If the election was, in part, a mandate on the state educational accountability plan, then Allen's 52% of the popular vote seemed to put to rest any doubts about the future of the SOL and state tests. Politics and certainty are rarely bedfellows, however. Within 2 weeks of the election, a new challenge to the accountability plan had been raised and from an unexpected source.

State legislators, after listening to witnesses describe the hardships caused by the SOL tests and accreditation standards, vowed to take matters into their own hands. Expressing disappointment with the failure of the State Board of Education to ease the requirement that students pass various SOL tests in order to graduate, members of the Education Committee of the House of Delegates created a special subcommittee to "explore options to the SOLs' pass-to-graduate mandate" (Associated Press, November 17, 2000, p. B-1). While Democrats led the move, Republicans also were represented. Conservative Republican delegate Jack Reid expressed a key source of concern when he was quoted as saying:

Let's say a child makes a B average in his classes but doesn't pass the SOL test. Then does he graduate? I think that's something a lot of people are concerned about and it's not something that we can just blow off. (Associated Press, November 17, 2000, p. B-3)

In a seeming effort to counter this latest criticism of the accountability plan, the State Board of Education released a report by the six-member SOL Test Advisory Committee that indicated the testing program "is technically sound, valid and reliable" (Boria, November 22, 2000, p. B-1). Made up of national experts in test design, the panel had been appointed by the Board to analyze the testing program. While the chair of the panel registered concern over the tight time schedule for determining pass-fail cutoff points, he expressed the opinion that Virginia was doing better than some states in ensuring that its tests are accurate, consistent, and free of bias (Boria, November 22, 2000, p. B-1).

The year ended with no clear indication of whether or not the principle of multiple graduation criteria would replace SOL test performance as the sole criterion recognized by the Standards of Accreditation. Five and a half years had passed since the first element of the accountability plan—revised Standards of Learning—had been approved. Virginia had implemented an ambitious program to raise student achievement and hold educators accountable for performance. Controversy and contention marked every phase of implementation. As the date when students actually would be denied graduation for failing state tests approached, the determination of critics and advocates hardened. In the balance hung the fate of thousands of students who did not perform well on standardized tests.

PASS RATES AND POLLING BOOTHS

Virginians went to the polls to elect a new Governor in November of 2001. While the economic downturn, exacerbated by the tragic events of September 11, took center stage, education issues waited in the wings. Supporters of the accountability plan had much about which to feel good. Figures released just prior to the November election indicated that the number of Virginia public schools meeting accreditation standards climbed from 2% in 1999 to 40% in 2001 (Richard, 2001). Outgoing Governor Gilmore proudly proclaimed, "Virginia is showing the nation the way to raise achievement" (Richard, 2001). State Republicans believed that education gains would help their candidate, Mark Earley, succeed Gilmore.

Earley, however, was soundly defeated by his Democratic challenger, Mark Warner, thus ending 8 years of Republican control of the Governor's Mansion and the commonwealth's education agenda. Warner's election probably had more to do with Republican in-fighting over the state budget and Governor Gilmore's pledge to rescind the car tax than with education issues, but it is noteworthy that Warner ran on a platform that promised modifications in the state's accountability plan. The new governor appeared, for example, to be more sympathetic to multiple measures of student achievement than his predecessors.

Warner's position may have been influenced by continued lobbying by the Virginia Education Coalition and Parents Across Virginia United to Reform SOLs. In August of 2001, the Virginia Education Coalition, representing the major education interest groups in the state, released its "Blueprint for Virginia Public Schools," containing seven primary goals. While embracing the idea of state curriculum standards, the report questioned the value of high-stakes tests, especially for the neediest students (Virginia Education Coalition, 2001, p. 10). Mickey VanDerwerker, cofounder of Parents Across Virginia United to Reform SOLs, challenged the value of fear as a motivator for struggling students ("Virginia's SOL Debate . . . ," 2001). By the summer of 2001 even newly elected President George W. Bush, a staunch advocate of tough accountability programs, began to soften his position on accountability. He warned lawmakers against setting unrealistically high education standards, thereby echoing a concern voiced by many critics of Virginia's plan (Fletcher and Milbank, 2001).

Other problems related to the accountability plan surfaced during the period prior to the November election. Allegations of "improprieties" in the administering of SOL tests made the headlines in June (Associated Press, 2001). A month later an article in the *Washington Post* (Seymour, July 17, 2001) reported that teachers frustrated with the heavy emphasis on state tests were switching to courses and grade levels where students were not subject to state tests or leaving teaching entirely. Continued complaints about the Standards of Learning in social studies led the Virginia Board of Education to lower the score needed to pass four state tests in social studies (Seymour, November 28, 2001, p. B-1). The most serious problem, however, concerned the continuing disparity in achievement on state tests between rich and poor school divisions (Seymour, October 17, 2001, p. B-4). As a school's poverty rate, as measured by the percentage of students receiving federally subsidized lunches, rose, so too did the likelihood that it fell short of meeting state accreditation benchmarks.

REFLECTIONS ON ACCOUNTABILITY IN VIRGINIA

Tracing the history of state-initiated efforts to promote educational accountability in Virginia prompts a number of reflections. As a case study of policy development, the creation of the so-called accountability plan challenges the theory that policy unfolds in discrete stages. As an example of the politicization of education, it is a story filled with irony and contradiction. As a chronicle of one state's efforts to raise student achievement, it offers lessons concerning the challenges of centralized approaches to educational accountability. In this concluding section, we explore each of these topics.

Incrementalism with a Twist

A traditional model of the policy process holds that policy develops in distinct stages. While the number and nature of the stages may vary, most models include agenda setting, policy formulation and legitimation, implementation, and evaluation (Sabatier, 1999, p. 6). Stage models have been criticized in recent years for creating an unrealistically linear and logical portrait of the policy process. As Sabatier (1999, p. 7) has noted with regard to stage models:

> The assumption that there is a single policy cycle focused on a major piece of legislation oversimplifies the usual process of multiple, interacting cycles involving numerous policy proposals and statutes at multiple levels of government.

Virginia's three-decade quest for educational accountability clearly cannot be captured in a single set of stages. In some ways, the process has been more illustrative of incrementalism (Lindblom, 1959; Wildavsky, 1964). In other words, policy concerning educational accountability has evolved slowly over time, beginning with the Standards of Quality in the early 1970s and continuing through the Graduation Competency Program and the initial Standards of Learning in the late 1970s and early 1980s, the Governor's Commission on Excellence in Education and the Literacy Passport Test in the mid-1980s, the World Class Education Program, Common Core of Learning, and Outcome Accountability Project in the early 1990s, and eventually the four-part accountability plan. Despite the fact that each new administration in Richmond took credit for introducing educational accountability as the antidote for inadequate student achievement, the current initiative is clearly the result of a prolonged iterative process characterized by policy refining, rejection, and revision.

It is worth noting that the original conception of educational accountability implicit in the Standards of Quality was a far cry from the current notion. The SOQ represented standards for schools, essential "inputs" that every school division was expected to provide for every student. As the years passed, the focus of state accountability efforts widened to encompass curriculum standards (Standards of Learning) and student performance on standardized tests. Educational accountability in Virginia by the late 1990s came to represent a guarantee that most students had passed state tests of curriculum standards. The state indicated its willingness to take action against schools that failed to achieve specified pass rates.

The evolution of state educational accountability policy in Virginia has not been a linear or conflict-free process. Certain administrations have given greater attention to policy adjustments than others. The Wilder administration actually reversed itself on the matter of curriculum standards, withdrawing plans for outcome-based education in the face of criticism from several quarters. The "religious right" raised questions about specific outcomes related to student values and psychological development as well as the motives behind OBE, while educators voiced concerns about erosion of local control.

The Wilder reversal suggests that pure incrementalism alone cannot capture the entire policy development process. Punctuated-equilibrium theory may come closer to the mark. This theory holds that policy evolves for the most part in increments, but that these increments are "punctuated" periodically by dramatic events (True, Jones, and Baumgartner, 1999, pp. 97–115). Ironically, the rejection of state-dictated learning outcomes by the Wilder administration set the stage for the succeeding Allen administration to reintroduce and gain approval for a revised set of state curriculum standards. To understand this curious chronicle requires an appreciation of the politicization of public education.

State House and Schoolhouse

Today, with nearly every state involved in dictating what students must learn, it is hard to imagine that there was a time in the not so distant past when most state governments avoided getting involved in curriculum decisions. While it would be inaccurate to claim that education used to be free of politics, the intensity of politicization of education clearly has increased in recent years. Politics being a realm of irony and contradiction, this process has yielded some interesting results. The coming of educational accountability to Virginia is no exception.

That Governor Allen was able to press ahead with state-dictated curriculum standards after his predecessor had failed in a similar effort is due, in no small way, to the fact that Wilder was a Democrat and Allen was a Republican. In a state like Virginia, characterized by well-organized conservatives, any proposal by a Democratic administration to introduce state learning standards, especially when the standards included affective outcomes, was bound to generate suspicion and resistance. When a primary source of Democratic support, local educators, also rallied against the Common Core of Learning because they regarded it as an intrusion on their authority, Governor Wilder knew he had no choice but to retreat. Governor Allen, on the other hand, was the darling of Virginia conservatives. He could not be accused of trying to push through a measure that would lead schools to address controversial matters related to values and psychological development or to take actions that might erode local control and expand the state's role in education.

The irony, of course, is that Allen and his successor, Jim Gilmore, both Republicans, pushed through a set of measures that did more than any previous

Democratic administration had done to erode local control of education and expand the state's role in determining what students must learn and how schools must operate. If state-dictated curriculum standards, state-initiated standardized tests, state-determined pass scores for the tests, and state-enforced accreditation standards for schools are not clear indications of centralized control and "big government," it is hard to imagine what are.

In a further touch of irony, Governor Allen had made a point of attacking "unfunded mandates" by the state, arguing that state government had no business passing laws and regulations that involved financial consequences for localities without also allocating funds to offset these consequences. Allen's second State Superintendent of Public Instruction, Richard LaPointe, insisted that the accountability plan was "fiscally neutral" and that school divisions could meet the proposed standards "with the same teachers, you just have to reconfigure them" (*VASS News*, May 1997, p. 5). Virginia's accountability plan, however, was regarded by many superintendents as a largely unfunded mandate (*VASS News*, May 1997, p. 5). They argued that the success of the accountability plan was contingent on smaller class sizes, more teachers, new curriculum materials and textbooks, better training and staff development for teachers, remediation programs, and summer schools. Funds to support these improvements were not forthcoming during the Allen administration. The Gilmore administration, however, did offer limited state support for staff development and some remediation programs aimed at helping students pass the SOL tests.

Lessons on State Accountability Initiatives

The final chapter on Virginia's accountability plan remains to be written, but as of 2001, when every public school student in grades K–10 was subject to consequences for failing state tests, several lessons have been learned about the state's efforts to raise student achievement.

The first lesson is that universal support for high stakes tests as the basis for determining who graduates from high school does not exist, at least not in Virginia. A substantial number of parents and educators have serious reservations about placing too much emphasis on standardized test performance alone. It is interesting, in this regard, to speculate on the reasons why some politicians persist in their reliance on test performance as the sole basis for accountability. Do they wish to send a message that teachers' grades and judgments about student performance cannot be trusted? Do they believe that standardized multiple choice tests are the best way to measure student learning? Do they prefer accountability-by-testing because it is cheaper than other educational improvement strategies, such as raising teacher salaries and reducing class size?

The second lesson is that there are risks to "building the plane while flying it." Proponents of the accountability plan seemed to be willing to make adjustments as long as educators did not question the overall purpose and framework of the initiative. Educators, however, found it difficult to separate the bigger issues from the details. Details, such as the timing of state tests and provisions for students who failed the tests, directly affected the lives of students and teachers. Perhaps these details could have been anticipated and addressed more effectively if the planning process had taken more time or been less politicized. One thing is clear. To those required to implement state policy and those whose futures are affected by it, the "idea" of accountability cannot be decoupled from the way it is implemented and enforced.

The third lesson relates to criticism of the accountability plan. Once criticism began to surface, it took on a life of its own, independent of actual events. Critics of the accountability plan, for example, failed to acknowledge improvements in test scores for the second and third administrations of the state SOL tests. It would seem that, once an issue becomes highly politicized, opponents and probably proponents as well will minimize or ignore any data that contravenes their basic position.

The final lesson concerns the spillover effect of a major policy initiative such as Virginia's accountability plan. Once the plan became formalized and educators realized that Richmond was serious about implementing it, the plan became a reference point for virtually every educational debate and funding measure. If local educators wanted to open school before Labor Day, it was in order to provide students with more learning time before taking the state tests. If local educators wanted to air condition schools, it was in order to create comfortable summer school environments for students who needed additional preparation for the state SOL tests. While invoking the accountability plan to justify local requests is politically prudent, it clearly increases confusion regarding the actual impetuses for these requests.

REFERENCES

Argetsinger, A. (2000, May 25). "Md. delays requiring exams for graduation." *Washington Post*, pp. B-1, B-8.

Associated Press. (2000, November 17). "Panel to ponder required SOLs." *Daily Progress*, pp. B-1, B-3.

Associated Press. (2001, June 8). SOLs criticized after alleged improprieties. *Daily Progress*, pp. B-1, B-2.

Baker, D. P. (1986, March 27). Baliles asks education commission for bold ideas. *Washington Post*, p. B-7.

Baker, D. P. (1986, November 8). Baliles backs test to enter high school: Shift in teacher education also supported. *Washington Post*, p. C-1.

Benning, V. (2000, February 3). Bills aim to soften testing program. *Washington Post*, pp. VA-1, VA-10.

Benning, V. (1999, January 14). Doubts arise on low scores. *Washington Post*, pp. VA-1, VA-9.

Benning, V. (2000, February 9). Gilmore rejects easing of school accreditation rules. *Washington Post*, p. B-3.

Benning, V. (2000, February 3). New diploma proposed for special-ed in Va. *Washington Post*, p. B-2.

Benning, V. (2000, May 2). Proposed concessions on Va. tests draw fire. *Washington Post*, pp. B-1, B-4.

Benning, V. (2000, March 2). SOL exam revisions are likely. *Washington Post*, pp. VA-1, VA-4.

Benning, V. (2000, October 27). SOL funds to pay for tutoring. *Washington Post*, p. B-9.

Benning, V. (2000, April 29). Va. board endorses concession on SOLs. *Washington Post*, pp. B-1, B-7.

Benning, V. (2000, February 8). Va. may ease exam penalties. *Washington Post*, pp. B-1, B-5.

Benning, V. (2000, June 27). Va. parents don't trust exam, poll says. *Washington Post*, p. B-2.

Benning, V. (2000, October 26). Va. schools improve sharply on tests. *Washington Post*, pp. B-1, B-4.

Benning, V. (1999, October 19). Virginia refuses to reveal test questions. *Washington Post*, p. B-4.

Benning, V., & Mathews, J. (2000, September 8). Statewide scores up on most Va. tests. *Washington Post*, pp. A-1, A-15.

Berry, D. (1998, April 19). Suspect standards for student achievement. *Washington Post*, p. C-8.

Boria, R. R. (1999, December 1). Comments: SOLs raise concern, little support. *Richmond Times-Dispatch*, pp. A-1, A-16.

Boria, R. R. (2000, November 22). Panel: SOLs pass the test. *Richmond Times-Dispatch*, pp. B-1, B-5.

Bowman, R. (1999, November 2). School chiefs seek changes in SOL tests. *Richmond Times-Dispatch*, pp. A-1, A-7.

Bradley, P. (1991, September 26). Reform schools: Wilder, education panel initiatives announced. *Richmond Times Dispatch*, p. A-17.

Christie, M. (1998, May 3). Why Virginia needs school standards. *Washington Post*, p. C-8.

Farmer, R. (1995, June 18). Revision battle lines formed. *Richmond Times-Dispatch*, pp. A-1, A-8.

Farmer, R. (1995, June 23). State board votes higher standards. *Richmond Times-Dispatch*, pp. A-1, A-10.

Fletcher, M. A., & Milbank, D. (2001, August 2). Bush urges realistic education standards. *Washington Post*, p. A-2.

Glass, J. (1995, April 28). Virginia pupils' reading skills drop: Tougher standards needed, education board chief says. *Roanoke Times & World News*, p. B-1.

Governor's commission on excellence in education. (1986). Excellence in education: A plan for Virginia's future. Richmond: Author.

Harris, J. F. (1990, September 27). Year-round schooling urged in Virginia: Area educators say move is necessary. *Washington Post*, p. A-1.

Harris, J. F. (1993, September 16). Wilder abandons curriculum change: Conservatives, local boards objected to plan. *Washington Post*, p. B-1.

Harris, J. F. (1993, September 18). Outcome-based education dies: Wilder proposal restricts power of school boards. *Daily Press*, pp. C-1, C-2.

Isikoff, M. (1983, July 30). Tougher standards: Virginia to overhaul schools. *Washington Post*, p. A-1.

Jenkins, K. (1989, September 12). Education and crime Virginia campaign topics: Wilder, Coleman stump in Northern Virginia. *Washington Post*, p. B-5.

Klein, G. (1990, September 16). Education goals: Gains, but nothing comes easily. *Richmond Times Dispatch*, p. A-10.

Lindblom, C. (1959). The science of muddling through. *Public Administration Review, 19,* 79–88.

Mathews, J. (1999, December 7). School officials solicit specifics on changing Va. standards. *Washington Post*, pp. B-1, B-2.

Mathews, J. (2000, July 28). Va. easing rules on testing. *Washington Post*, pp. A-1, A-4.

Mathews, J. (1998, April 19). Va. teachers, students set to put exams to the test. *Washington Post*, pp. B-1, B-10.

Mathews, J., & Benning, V. (1999, January 9). 97 percent of schools in Va. fail new exams. *Washington Post*, pp. A-1, A-6.

Mathews, J., & Benning, V. (2000, September 11). Va. poll gives SOLs vote of no confidence. *Washington Post*, pp. A-1, A-12.

Melton, R. H. (1999, December 10). Gilmore proposes more SOL spending. *Washington Post*, pp. B-1, B-8.

Melton, R. H. (2000, October 10). Robb calls SOL tests obstacle to learning. *Washington Post*, p. B-2.

Melton, R. H. (2000, October 6). SOL TV ad costs Va. $1.2 million. *Washington Post*, pp. A-1, A-11.

Melton, R. H. (1999, December 9). Virginia school chief to resign. *Washington Post*, p. B-7.

Melton, R. H. (1988, February 22). Key committees back basics of Baliles budget; panels vote to fund sex education plan. *Washington Post*, p. D-1.

Morse, G. C. (2000, October 2). A foe of his former self. *Washington Post*, p. A-25.

Nakamura, D., & Samuels, C. (2000, June 25). In school, changes at the top. *Washington Post*, pp. A-1, A-17.

News in Brief. (1999, August 4). *Education Week*, 26.

News Release. (2000, October 12). Survey details teacher views on SOL implementation. Virginia Department of Education.

Noz, K. (1999, November 5). Local chiefs divided on SOLs. *Richmond Times-Dispatch*, pp. A-1, A-13.

O'Hanlon, A., & Melton, R. H. (2000, September 21). Allen claims credit for education gains. *Washington Post*, pp. B-1, B-7.

Parents across Virginia united to reform SOLs. (1999). Working for reasonable standards and meaningful curriculum. Web site: http://personal, cfw.com/~dday/vasols. htrr.

Richard, A. (2001, October 24). More Va. schools hit mark on exams used for ratings. *Education Week*, p. 26.

Ruberry, W. (1990, May 3). Public schools bring home 4th bad grade. *Richmond Times Dispatch*, pp. A-1, A-12.

Sabatier, P. A. (1999). The need for better theories. In P. A. Sabatier (Ed.), *Theories of the policy process* (pp. 3–18). Boulder, CO: Westview Press.

Sack, J. L. (2000, March 1). Riley urges 'review' of standards. *Education Week*, pp. 1, 32.

Samuels, C. A. (1999, October 9). PTA group demands a look at state tests. *Washington Post*, p. B-5.

Seymour, L. (2000, July 29). Educators say Va. tests still too strict. *Washington Post*, pp. B-1, B-4.

Seymour, L. (2001, July 17). SOL tests create new dropouts. *Washington Post*, pp. A-1, A-8.

Seymour, L. (2001, October 17). Schools making headway on SOL. *Washington Post*, pp. B-1, B-4.

Seymour, L. (2001, November 28). Va. lowers the bar for some SOL Tests. *Washington Post*, pp. B-1, B-8.

Stallsmith, P. (1999, January 9). Only 2% of Va. schools meet new standards. *Richmond Times-Dispatch*, pp. A-1, A-6.

Stallsmith, P. (1997, September 5). New school standards pass. *Richmond Times-Dispatch*, pp. A-1, A-5.

Stallsmith, P. (2000, October 12). SOL trend: 'Overall improvement.' *Richmond Times-Dispatch*, p. B-1.

Stallsmith, P. (2000, February 24). Teacher survey considered. *Richmond Times-Dispatch*, p. B-4.

Still, K. (1999, November 13). Father of SOL tests sounds off at education forum. *The Daily Progress*, p. B-5.

Swensen, E. (2000, March 28). School groups pleased with board response. *The Daily Progress*, pp. B-1, B-3.

True, J. L., Jones, B. D., & Baumgartner, F. R. (1999). Punctuated-equilibrium theory: Explaining stability and change in American policymaking. In P. A. Sabatier (Ed.). *Theories of the Policy Process* (pp. 97–116). Boulder, CO: Westview Press.

Tyack, D. B., & Cuban, L. (1995). *Tinkering toward utopia*. Cambridge, MA: Harvard University Press.

UPI. (1990, May 3). Dyke says program problem comes before financial one. *Richmond Times Dispatch*, p. B-5.

VASS News. (2000, February), 1–2.

VASS News. (1997, May), 5.

Virginia Association of School Superintendents. (1999). *2000 legislative positions*. Charlottesville, VA: Author.

Virginia Department of Education. (1997, September 4). *Regulations establishing standards for accrediting public schools in Virginia*. Richmond: Author.

Virginia Department of Education. (1994). *Superintendent's annual report for Virginia: 1993–94*. Richmond: Author.

Virginia Department of Education. (1981). Superintendent's annual report for Virginia: 1979–1980. Richmond: Author.

Virginia Education Coalition. (2001). Blueprint for Virginia public schools.

Virginia's SOL debate reveals bitter division. (2001, July 31). *Washington Post*, p. A-9.

Virginia's world class education flop. (1993, September 17). *Washington Times*, p. A-22.

Walker, R. (1991, September 18). School coalition tries to force Virginia's hand. *Richmond Times Dispatch*, pp. A-1, A-8.

Whitley, T. (2000, October 12). Lottery pulls ad on SOL. *Richmond Times-Dispatch*, pp. B-1, B-3.

Wildavsky, A. (1964). *The politics of the budgetary process*. Boston: Little, Brown.

Chapter Three

INITIAL RESPONSES OF VIRGINIA HIGH SCHOOLS TO THE ACCOUNTABILITY PLAN

Daniel L. Duke
AND
Pamela D. Tucker

This chapter presents the findings of a study of the initial efforts of 16 Virginia high schools to respond to the challenges posed by the state's new accountability plan. Responses were identified in four areas: local policies, practices, programs, and personnel. The study also examined perceptions of the accountability plan's initial consequences for students and educators in the commonwealth. The implications of the study's findings for school leadership are addressed at the close of the chapter.

A word of caution is necessary before going further. The study on which this chapter is based was conducted in the fall of 1999 and winter of 2000. During this time and, indeed, throughout the following year, changes in various aspects of the accountability measures continued to be made (see chapter 2). In other words, the accountability plan is an evolving set of policies. For this reason, we stress that our focus is the "initial" responses of selected Virginia high schools. Trying to respond conscientiously to state mandates that keep being adjusted and reinterpreted is something like hitting a moving target from a moving vehicle. The context is always changing, necessitating constant reassessment and redesign of local responses.

WHY INVESTIGATE LOCAL RESPONSES DURING EARLY IMPLEMENTATION?

Some may argue that it makes more sense to wait until all aspects of the accountability plan have been clarified and agreed on before investigating how high schools are responding. Such an argument overlooks the fact that state policies may continue to evolve for years. In just the few years since Virginia embarked on its present course, conflict has arisen over particular standards, particular tests and test items, cut-off scores on the tests, which students must be included in test-score reporting, graduation requirements, differentiated diplomas, parental access to test questions, consequences for not passing the tests, consequences for schools with high failing rates, and resources to help low-performing schools. Local educators cannot afford to delay their responses until every issue has been resolved. The first group of students to be subject to the new graduation requirements will finish high school in 2004.

Meanwhile it is important to understand how different high schools, the schools most affected by the accountability plan, are beginning to respond. Such information can help state and local policy-makers consider the impact of various accountability measures and the extent to which variations in responses characterize different high schools. Variations, where they exist, may help explain why some high schools fare better than others on state tests. The identification of unintended consequences also may inform the process of policy revision and school improvement.

THE DESIGN OF THE STUDY

The focus of the study is the high school, not individual students, classrooms, or school systems. Put differently, we sought to determine how high schools as organizations were being affected by the various elements of the accountability plan, how they were responding to the plan, and the implications of these responses for the role of high school principal. To gather data, we decided to rely on the individual most likely to have a comprehensive understanding of all aspects of the high school—the principal. In many cases, we also were able to interview other staff members, including assistant principals and guidance counselors. In every case, however, an extensive interview was conducted with the high school principal. We also reviewed various documents, including each school's state "report card."

The questions asked of every interviewee were developed during several pilot studies conducted by University of Virginia graduate students in education. These individuals examined their own high schools for changes in policy, practice, programs, and personnel that had resulted directly from the SOL, SOA, state tests, and School Performance Report Cards. We took these accounts and generated a master list of, and classification system for, local school responses. Questions then were developed to match each general type of response in the classification system. In addition, a brief survey of the principal's perceptions of the impact of state accountability measures was created. Copies of the survey and classification system can be found in Appendix A.

The strategy for selecting high schools for the study reflected our belief that responses might be influenced by two factors—how well a high school's students performed on the first administration of the SOL tests in 1998 and the financial resources available to the high school. High schools were identified that were in the top quartile of Virginia high schools for passing rates in the four core areas (English, math, social studies, science) and the bottom quartile, as a result of the first administration of the SOL tests for high school students. High schools in the top quartile were labeled "low-need" schools because they had a relatively low need to make major changes in their policies, practices, programs, and personnel, at least based on student performance. High schools in the bottom quartile were labeled "high-need" schools because they had a relatively high need to make changes, based on student performance.

High schools also were identified based on the per-pupil allocation of their school division as of 1998. High schools in the top quartile of school divisions, based on per pupil allocation, were labeled "high-ability" schools, meaning they had a relatively high ability to fund responses to the accountability plan. High schools in the bottom quartile of school divisions were labeled "low ability" schools because they were relatively poor and therefore less able to fund responses to the accountability plan.

Based on these two dimensions—need to respond and ability to respond, four types of high schools were identified: low-need/high-ability, low-need/low-ability, high-need/low-ability, and high-need/high-ability schools. The high schools facing the greatest challenge from the accountability plan appeared to be the high-need/low-ability schools—the ones with relatively poor student performance on state tests and relatively low levels of financial resources. The high schools with the most advantageous position seemed to be the low-need/high-ability schools—those with relatively high student passing rates and relatively high levels of financial resources.

Table 3.1 indicates the number of Virginia high schools that were identified, as of the fall of 1999, for each of the four categories. From each category, a

**Table 3.1. Distribution of Virginia High Schools by
Student Performance on SOL Tests and Per-Pupil Spending (1999)**

| | | Ability to Respond (Per-Pupil Spending) | |
		High (Top Quartile)	Low (Bottom Quartile)
Need to Respond (Student Test Performance)	High (Top Quartile)	8	5
	Low (Bottom Quartile)	15	5

purposive sample of four high schools was selected, yielding a total sample of 16 high schools. Schools were chosen to represent different parts of the state and sizes of school division.

HEEDING THE CALL FOR REFORM

A review of the data from the 16 high schools indicates that every school made some effort to respond to Virginia's accountability plan. In many respects, the responses were similar across most of the high schools. In other cases, responses varied considerably from one school to another. In this section, we shall identify some of the responses that were similar. These included increased curriculum coordination and focus, adjustments to mathematics course offerings, greater teacher collaboration, changes in instructional planning, changes in instructional practice, changes in classroom assessment, development of special programs, and increased quality control. Table 3.2 summarizes the responses on which there was the greatest agreement.

Increased Curriculum Coordination and Focus

The Foreword to the *Standards of Learning for Virginia Public Schools: Secondary Courses* states that the standards were adopted "to emphasize the importance of instruction in four core subjects—English, mathematics, science, and history and social science." The Virginia Department of Education developed "blueprints" to guide local educators in their efforts to ensure that all secondary students were exposed to the Standards of Learning. By the fall of 1999, 4 years after the SOL were approved, each of the 16 high schools in the study had examined and revised one or more areas of the curriculum covered by the SOL.

In five cases, the entire district undertook a comprehensive effort to align core courses with the SOL. In other instances, schools focused on particular courses or disciplines. Four high schools stressed the importance of "horizontal articulation," initiating planning designed to ensure that all teachers of the same subject covered the same basic objectives. In three high schools, changes in textbooks in selected courses resulted from curriculum coordination efforts. Another high school opted to target one area of the curriculum for improvement each year. The net result of these responses, in the judgment of most principals, has been to focus teachers' energy squarely on the SOL.

Changes in Mathematics

Mathematics was the subject area that experienced the most change as a result of the accountability plan. Relatively low passing rates in subjects like Algebra I and Geometry probably accounted for this focus on the mathematics curriculum, but it is worth noting that passing rates typically were even lower in history and social studies. While several high schools in our sample made adjustments in history and social studies, these changes tended to be in course sequencing and were not nearly as extensive as those in mathematics. Every one of the 16 high schools in the study made at least one adjustment or change related to the mathematics curriculum.

Algebra was the target for many of the changes, most of which represented variations in the time allocated for instruction. Six high schools divided Algebra I into Part 1 and Part 2 to enable lower-achieving students a greater opportunity to master the subject before taking the state test. Another high school gave students an option to complete Algebra I in one, two, or three semesters. Two high schools with four-by-four block schedules decided to offer core mathematics courses like Algebra I twice a year so that students who did not do well the first time could retake the course during the same school year. Another high school with a four-by-four block schedule opted to require all students to take Algebra I during both fall and spring semesters, effectively doubling their exposure to the challenging subject. Yet another high school blocked Introduction to Algebra and Algebra I, thereby giving "slower" students more time to prepare for the state test on Algebra I.

Three high schools eliminated lower track mathematics courses such as Consumer Math, and another high school reduced the ability levels of mathematics courses from three to two. One high school altered the sequence of mathematics courses so that students could take Algebra II immediately after Algebra I, instead of taking Geometry.

Other kinds of adjustments to the mathematics curriculum were reported. One high school took the initiative to request that algebra concepts be introduced to students during middle school. Graphing calculators were fully incorporated into the mathematics curriculum in three schools. Eight high schools acquired special software to enable students to prepare for state tests on their own. Another high school adopted a new Algebra I textbook that was better aligned to the SOL.

As a possible result of the high level of curricular attention to mathematics, it was the area that reflected the greatest average growth from 1998 to 1999 across the 16 high schools. The average growth in the percentage passing rate for mathematics was 12.07 as compared to increases of 5.44 in science, 5.0 in English, and 1.86 in history. While the relatively large improvement in mathematics cannot be traced to any one particular modification or strategy, the increased efforts to improve math instruction seem to have been beneficial.

More Teacher Collaboration

One of the most constructive responses to the accountability plan involved efforts by high school faculty members to work together more collaboratively. Eleven of the 16 high school principals reported increased levels of joint planning among teachers, especially in high schools where achievement was lowest.

Table 3.2. Perceived Impact of Educational Reforms Summary of All Respondents (N = 16)

	Strongly Agree 1	Agree 2	3	Disagree 4	Strongly Disagree 5	No Response 0
Staff Morale—Since the advent of state reforms . . .						
The stress level among teachers has increased.	8	6	1	0	0	1
Teachers are spending more time talking with each other about teaching, learning, and curriculum.	7	5	3	1	0	0
Teachers are engaged in more collaborative planning.	5	6	2	3	0	0
Teachers feel that everything they do must focus on preparing students for state tests.	7	5	2	0	0	2
Committee work for staff members has increased.	3	10	2	1	0	0
School administrators are under greater pressure.	7	8	1	0	0	0
Counselors spend less time counseling students because of increased paperwork and duties associated with testing and record keeping.	7	4	1	2	2	0
Staffing—Since the advent of state reforms . . .						
The most capable teachers have been assigned to teach the grade levels and/or courses in which students must take SOL tests.	1	8	4	3	0	0

(continued on next page)

Table 3.2 (*continued*)

	Strongly Agree 1	Agree 2	3	Disagree 4	Strongly Disagree 5	No Response 0
Instruction—Since the advent of state reforms . . .						
Field trips have been eliminated or curtailed.	1	11	2	2	0	0
Teachers must move too quickly through the curriculum in order to cover all of the SOLs before the state tests.	4	9	1	2	0	0
The recall of facts is being emphasized too much in subjects where students must take state tests.	1	9	3	3	0	0
Teachers have become more strict when students request to leave class for legitimate reasons (guidance, clinic, rest room).	1	11	3	1	0	0
Teachers are spending more time helping individual students.	3	6	6	1	0	0
Teachers are making more of an effort to differentiate instruction in order to "reach" all students.	1	13	1	1	0	0
Teachers stress conventional assessment, rather than performance assessment, in order to prepare students for SOL tests.	1	9	4	2	0	0
Students—Since the advent of state reforms . . .						
Students who are the furthest behind in their learning are receiving more assistance and attention.	0	9	5	1	0	1
Students who take longer to learn are having more trouble keeping pace with their classmates.	4	9	3	0	0	0

Planning was not limited to within-department cooperation, but included efforts by teachers of non-SOL courses to work with teachers of core subjects to reinforce the state standards. Also, regular and special education teachers were reported to be working more closely together in three schools where the accountability plan had resulted in greater mainstreaming. Teachers also engaged in regular reviews of student progress and team-based assistance programs for students experiencing difficulties on state tests. Teachers in several high schools were reported to regularly share ideas for covering the SOL. Collaboration, of course, can come at a price. Principals in 13 high schools indicated that committee work for teachers and administrators had increased significantly. It is also unclear to what extent teachers have felt compelled to cooperate.

Changes in Instructional Planning

Teachers were reported to be changing their approach to instructional planning in many of the high schools. For example, pacing guides keyed to the SOL were used to set daily instructional objectives in seven high schools. In several schools, progress in covering course objectives was closely monitored by peers, department heads, or administrators. Three high schools employed a standard lesson format that called for the identification of SOL objectives for every lesson. Principals in eight high schools indicated that they expected teachers to tie their instructional planning directly to state curriculum guidelines. In schools where several teachers taught the same courses, instructional planning often was undertaken collaboratively in order to ensure that, regardless of the teacher, students were exposed to the same content.

Changes in Instructional Practice

Principals in all 16 high schools indicated that changes had occurred in instructional practice as a result of the accountability plan. In 14 high schools, for example, teachers were making a greater effort to differentiate instruction. Nine principals reported that teachers spent more time working with individual students. These changes were necessitated, in part, by the elimination of special courses for lower ability students and the decision to mainstream more special education students. Teachers had to accommodate a wider range of abilities in many classes, but they also recognized the need to assist all students in achieving at higher levels. Possibly as a result, teachers in 13 schools were concerned about moving too quickly through the curriculum for some students. If they did not push the pace of instruction, though, they felt they could not cover all of the SOL objectives before the state tests were given; so they continued to move the class along but worked with individual students to the extent possible.

Another change in instructional practice concerned reteaching and review. Teachers in three high schools conducted more reviews in order to keep students "fresh" on SOL material before they took state tests. Principals in three other high schools reported that teachers devoted more time to reteaching material that was not learned well than they had done prior to the accountability plan. Various computer software packages were used to review material, monitor progress, and simulate SOL tests.

As instruction has come to be dominated by the SOL, teachers have expressed a variety of concerns. In 10 high schools, principals indicated that there was too much focus on facts and simple recall of knowledge. Teachers spent less time on more stimulating learning activities and the development of higher order thinking skills. Four high schools reported a lack of sufficient time for students to deal with reflection and analysis. In 1 high school, non-English teachers no longer had time to teach writing skills because of the emphasis on content. In 3 high schools, teachers were reported to resent being unable to teach subjects of personal interest any longer, while in 5 other high schools they were afraid to try anything new.

In order to give more attention to the SOL, traditional enrichment activities have been cut back. Twelve high schools curtailed or eliminated field trips. Students attended fewer assemblies in 2 high schools, and teachers in 12 schools reported that all instructional time had to be geared to specific SOL.

Changes in Classroom Assessment

As a result of the accountability plan teachers in many of the high schools changed some of their assessment practices. In 11 high schools, for example, teachers were reported to be using the formats for state tests—multiple choice questions and writing prompts—as the basis for in-class tests. In the case of algebra teachers in one high school, however, giving students multiple-choice algebra tests posed a problem because they felt students should have to solve problems rather than guess at multiple choice answers. Teachers in three high schools routinely pretested students at the beginning of a course or a new unit on SOL objectives. This practice enabled them to isolate areas where students might require additional assistance. In one high school, teachers of SOL subjects made a special effort throughout the year to simulate conditions during the state tests.

More Special Programs

The accountability plan has spawned a variety of programs to assist students in passing state tests. A total of 36 new programs were introduced in 13 of the high schools in the study. Three high schools offered no new programs. New programs encompassed tutoring during school, after-school assistance, and summer programs.

To help students during regular school hours, arrangements were made in two high schools to have teachers tutor students on the SOL during their non-teaching duty periods. Two other high schools with block schedules required students who failed one or more state tests to use their unscheduled block (every other day) to get assistance. Another school created a special activity period for students who needed extra help preparing for state tests. Special personnel were hired by two high schools to tutor students. One high school retained a "math coach" to help students prepare for the Algebra I test, while the other high school hired a teacher aide to come to school from 10:00 A.M. to 6:00 P.M. every day to tutor students. Two high schools created special computer labs to enable students to work on software aligned with the SOL.

After-school assistance was available in several forms. Tutoring was provided after school at six high schools, but only three of them offered students transportation home on late activity buses. One high school opened its special computer lab after school so students could review for the state tests. Another high school purchased laptop computers so students could take them home and work on SOL-aligned software.

Summer school was the focus of assistance for five high schools. One high school got school board approval to require summer school for students who failed one or more state tests. Voluntary summer programs were provided by three high schools for students who failed state tests. The last high school offered students who were weak in Algebra a special "head start" program just before the beginning of fall semester.

Other special programs were targeted to build parent and student awareness of the accountability plan and support student success in the regular school program. Four high schools developed special campaigns to inform parents of the importance of the SOL and state tests. One high school initiated programs to cut down on tardiness and absenteeism so that students would attend class more often and therefore be better prepared to take the state tests. The same high school also scheduled a pep rally before state tests to encourage students to do their best. Finally, two high schools created ninth-grade teams to facilitate the coordination of academic work across the four core areas of the SOL.

More Quality Control

It is not surprising that demands for increased accountability at the state level would result in greater local efforts to monitor teaching and learning. Interviews indicated that superintendents, principals, department chairs, teachers, and counselors were playing new roles regarding quality control. Counselors in 11 high schools, for example, had become so busy administering state tests and monitoring student progress on the SOL that they were reported to be doing less counseling.

Much of the responsibility for quality control has fallen on the shoulders of building principals. Even the language in the Standards of Accreditation specified that principals must take the lead in promoting greater student achievement. It is therefore not surprising that 15 principals admitted to increased levels of personal stress. In four high schools, principals reported taking the lead in curriculum alignment efforts. Three principals indicated that they personally reviewed reports from teachers on student progress on specific subtests of state SOL tests. One principal said that he had to spend a great deal of time convincing teachers that they needed to cover more material than just the SOL.

Most of the 16 high schools have made changes in grading policies and assessment practices as a result of the accountability plan. Sometimes the changes were prompted by divisionwide action, while in other cases they resulted from school-site decisions. Policy changes included the introduction of incentives, such as exemption from taking final exams, to encourage students to do well on SOL tests. In several cases, principals reported that these changes generated complaints from parents, who feared that failure to pass SOL tests might prevent their children from getting credit for courses that they completed.

Teachers are clearly on the front-lines of the accountability plan. If students are not meeting the SOL, teachers are the first to know. Three high schools required teachers to meet on a regular basis to review student progress on the SOL. In one case, teachers were provided with a common planning period to facilitate these reviews. Other high schools left the responsibility of monitoring student progress up to individual teachers. Four of these high schools implemented special spreadsheets and information management systems to assist teachers in this process. One high school delegated responsibility for quality control to a schoolwide testing committee. Another high school required teachers to send home interim report cards indicating how every student was progressing on SOL objectives.

Several high schools took special steps to help students do their best on state tests. One high school, for example, required state tests to be given during the first 2 hours of the school day, when students presumably were most alert. Another high school required students taking state tests to be proctored by the teachers who had taught them the subject being tested. One of the study's most significant findings was that nine high schools reported assigning their most capable teachers to teach courses in which students took state SOL tests. Five principals reported raising class sizes in non-SOL courses so that teachers of SOL courses could work with fewer students.

VARIATIONS IN RESPONSES TO THE ACCOUNTABILITY PLAN

While our interviews revealed similarities in responses across the 16 high schools, they also indicated variations. One way to capture a sense of these differences is to describe briefly how 2 high schools[1] responded to the challenge of Virginia's accountability plan.

Fillmore High School

Located in a poor, rural county, Fillmore High School serves close to 800 students with a staff of 59 teachers and five teaching assistants. The school division of which Fillmore is a part spends less per pupil than the vast majority of Virginia's school systems. Teacher salaries are among the lowest in Virginia. When statewide SOL tests were first administered in 1998, Fillmore students failed to achieve a 70% passing rate in any subject. The same was true for the second year of state tests, but passing rates improved in every subject except English. Still, the highest passing rate for any subject was barely 50%.

When asked how Fillmore had been affected by the accountability plan, the principal said that the overall reaction of teachers was one of frustration. They no longer felt that they could teach what they wanted to teach or what students found to be enjoyable. Instead, the pressure was on to spend every available minute preparing students to take the state tests. "Teachers now teach what is tested, not what they love," reported the principal. Staff morale has plummeted and the stress level on teachers and administrators was very high.

The central office for the school division provided the Fillmore faculty with specific feedback on student performance for each subtest of the state tests with the expectation that each academic department would identify the strengths and weaknesses of its program. During the summer of 1999, the division brought together teams of teachers in the core curriculum areas to "unpack" the SOL, develop pacing guides, and identify strategies that might be effective in areas where student performance was low. Action plans with specific goals for improving test scores were developed by each team.

Unlike many high schools, Fillmore has yet to implement any special programs to assist students who do not pass state tests. The principal wanted to initiate a tutoring program either in the mornings before school or in the late afternoons, but he was unable to find teachers willing to work extended hours for $13 an hour (the amount of money made available by the state through a special grant). A second problem concerned the fact that the school division had no funds to provide students with transportation if they decided to come to school early or stay late for help. A few teachers stayed after school to assist students, but they did so of their own accord and for no reimbursement.

Fillmore made several adjustments to its curriculum offerings in response to the accountability plan. Algebra I, for example, was divided into Part 1 and Part 2. Since Fillmore operated on a four-by-four block schedule, the decision was made to repeat Algebra I, Part 1, during second semester for students who were struggling. Of the 16 students who initially were placed in Algebra I, Part 1, because they needed extra time to master the SOL, only 4 students passed the course. The teacher indicated that there was little way that these students, with fourth- and fifth-grade math skills, could hope to pass Algebra I, no matter how much extra time they were given.

The Fillmore faculty has begun to reconsider the four-by-four block schedule currently in place because they do not believe that students can concentrate on learning new material for a 90-minute stretch. To break up the block of time, part of each class is spent on practice, seatwork, and homework. As a result, students are not covering all the material they need to cover for the state tests. It may be better, the principal reasons, to return to a schedule where students take each subject for 45 minutes a day, 180 days a year.

To induce students to try harder on the state tests, Fillmore has introduced an incentive policy. Students who pass an SOL test and have an A average in class are exempted from taking the final exam. For students who pass the SOL test, but have an average less than an A, 25 points are added to their grade on the final exam. Any student who passes the SOL test but fails the course is given a final passing grade of 70. Students who pass a course but fail the SOL test are expected to take a remedial course before they retake the SOL test. Refusal to take this course can result in a variety of sanctions, including loss of the privilege to drive to school. The incentive program depends, however, on the ability of the test developer to return test results in a timely manner. According to Fillmore's principal, this has been a problem.

Fillmore has tried to raise parental awareness on the importance of the SOL tests. A special team of teachers and parents sponsored an evening meeting for all parents to apprise them of aspects of the accountability plan. Only 15 parents showed up.

When asked how he would use any additional funds to boost student performance on state tests, the principal was quick to say that he would hire at least one more teacher in each core area in order to reduce class sizes, especially in the lower ability classes. He also would hire tutors to provide individual instruction for selected students during one "block" a day.

Coolidge High

In physical appearance, size, location, funding level, and student performance Coolidge High School and Fillmore High School could not be more different. A gleaming new facility in an affluent suburb, Coolidge's student body dwarfs Filllmore's. Per pupil allocation in Coolidge's division is one of the highest in Virginia. When Coolidge students took the first series of state tests in 1998, they reached passing rates of 70% or better in 6 out of 11 tests. In 1999, 70% or better passing rates were achieved in every subject except U.S. History. Passing rates in Algebra I and Algebra II jumped 26% and 30%, respectively.

When the first round of state test results appeared in the newspaper, Coolidge parents phoned and faxed both the principal and the PTA president to register their concern. Anger was expressed, not so much with the school as with the state for requiring that students be tested in order to graduate. Parents supported Coolidge's commitment to teach students "thinking skills." They worried that the SOL would lead to an overemphasis on factual knowledge and memorization.

Knowing that they could not risk a second year of lower-than-expected passing rates, the Coolidge faculty and administration rolled up their sleeves and took a hard look at course offerings. Courses that did not support the academic program—such as Gourmet Cooking and Technical Drawing—were dropped. New courses were added, including "Latin for Reluctant Learners," a foreign language course especially designed for students with learning disabilities. Because a large number of students needed more time to master Algebra I, Introduction to Algebra was expanded. Coolidge students were given the option of completing Algebra I in one, two, or three semesters. By readjusting the schedule, Algebra I was blocked with Introduction to Algebra, allowing students to get a "double dose," if necessary. Students who were relatively weak in mathematics also were expected to attend a two-week math program offered just before the beginning of fall semester. This program was designed to give them a "running start" on Algebra I.

Coolidge already had a full-time reading teacher to help students who struggled to comprehend challenging material. The principal reasoned that poor reading skills often accounted for low test results. She also acknowledged transferring her strongest teachers to courses in which state SOL tests were given. These moves occasionally produced tension, as some teachers wanted no part of the pressure that accompanied SOL courses. Teachers who were assigned to SOL courses expressed a reluctance to take on student teachers and teacher interns because they feared the consequences of inadequate instruction.

To maintain quality control, the principal has required interim report cards to be sent home for every student. As a result, parents get direct feedback every four-and-a-half weeks regarding their child's progress. In another bold move, the principal insisted that every teacher whose grades consisted of more than 20% D's and F's must submit an improvement plan specifying how students will be helped to raise their grades.

The principal's predecessor allowed Advanced Placement courses to have relatively low enrollments. As a consequence, class sizes swelled in other courses. Coolidge's current principal has reversed this policy. In addition, all SOL courses were capped at 28 students, while non-SOL courses were allowed to enroll up to 33 students.

A cadre of Coolidge teachers were sent for staff development instruction on standards-based classrooms. They returned to Coolidge and offered training to their colleagues during duty-free periods. Providing staff development during the school day, rather than after school when teachers were exhausted, proved to be a hit with the faculty.

Improved passing rates on state tests at Coolidge has come at a cost. The principal and her administrative team noted that the workload for teachers, particularly those teaching SOL courses, has increased dramatically. Teachers complained that they rushed through course content in order to cover all SOL objectives before state tests were administered. Some students, they admitted, simply could not keep up. Last year the principal said that every learning-disabled student who took the Algebra I test failed it. Teachers also were upset that Coolidge raised passing rates last spring in 10 out of 11 subjects, yet received a "warning" from the state because the passing rate in one subject fell by two percentage points!

Asked how she would use additional resources to respond to the accountability plan, Coolidge's principal, like Fillmore's, focused on hiring more teachers. Besides lowering class sizes, she would obtain a second reading teacher and expand the "extended" Algebra I program.

Varied Responses

The profiles of Fillmore and Coolidge High Schools suggest some of the differences, as well as the similarities, that have characterized the responses of Virginia's high schools to the accountability plan. The main areas where differences were noted in our study concerned special programs and curriculum initiatives.

High schools with better-than-average resources and higher-than-average passing rates initiated only 4 new programs, while the other three categories of high school averaged 11 new programs. It did not appear that resources were tied directly to program initiation, however. High schools with better-than-average resources accounted for 17 new programs, while high schools with lower-than-average resources accounted for 19 new programs.

Resources, however, may have played a role when it came to curriculum changes. High schools with better-than-average resources were reported to have initiated 17 course changes, while high schools with lower-than-average resources initiated only 11 course changes. It should be noted that course changes typically did not entail hiring additional faculty.

Interestingly, the greatest impetus to program creation seemed to be student performance on the first round of state tests. High schools with lower-than-average passing rates initiated 23 new programs, while high schools with higher-than-average passing rates initiated only 13 new programs. The same pattern, though, was not found for curriculum changes. High schools with lower-than-average passing rates accounted for 11 curriculum changes, as opposed to 17 curriculum changes for high schools with higher-than-average passing rates. In part, this finding may be attributed to the fact that high schools with higher-than-average passing rates on state tests were more likely to (1) eliminate lower ability courses like consumer math and (2) reduce the number of electives available to students.

We do not know enough at this point to indicate exactly how resources affect a high school's ability to respond to Virginia's accountability plan. Based on our study of 16 high schools in the Commonwealth, we are inclined to believe, however, that it is not only the amount of resources available, but how they are used, that makes a difference. For example, one high school with lower-than-average passing rates and lower-than-average resources initiated six new programs to help students pass state tests, while another high school in the same category failed to initiate any new programs. Differential responses of this kind are likely to be a function of the quality of school leadership.

We found no evidence to suggest that there is a magical way to raise passing rates on SOL tests without resources. Whether the resources represent reallocations or new funds, they are a key to high schools' responses to Virginia's accountability plan. Resources are needed to run after-school and summer programs and provide transportation so that all students in need of assistance can take advantage of these programs. Resources are needed to acquire SOL-aligned software, computers, and new textbooks. Resources are needed for staff development and reimbursement for work on curriculum development. Resources are needed to hire specialists, reduce class sizes in SOL courses, and attract and retain talented teachers capable of preparing students to pass state tests. Seeing that resources are available for these purposes is one of the chief responsibilities of school principals.

THE PROMISE OF ACCOUNTABILITY

While it is far too early to assess the ultimate impact of Virginia's accountability plan, it is possible at this point to detect some very encouraging developments.

Perhaps the most promising finding from our study is the fact that almost every school raised its passing rates on state tests from 1998 to 1999. When we compared the aggregated passing rates for English, mathematics, history, and science in 1998 and 1999, we found that 7 high schools raised their passing rates in all four areas, and 8 high schools raised their passing rates in three out of four areas. Only one high school's passing rates dropped, and in this case they dropped in three areas. The average gain in passing rates for our sample of schools in the four core subject areas was a total of 26 points. Gains were not equal across subject areas, however. The highest average gains in passing rates for the 16 high schools were made in mathematics (12.07) and the lowest gains were made in history (1.86).

When teachers and administrators work together to raise student achievement, and the results justify their efforts, subsequent feelings of efficacy and pride can generate improved school climate and increased community support for public education. There were indications in a number of schools that teachers were increasingly willing to "own " lack of student improvement as well as take some credit for student progress. The true test, of course, will come when student performance on state tests actually "counts" toward graduation and school accreditation.

A second promising development, related to the first, is the heightened level of cooperation among teachers and administrators. Practically every high school was reported to have engaged teachers within and across departments in collaborative efforts, including aligning curricula with SOL objectives, creating pacing guides, monitoring student progress, and generating plans of assistance for struggling students. Principals in several high schools stated that teachers were communicating about substantive issues in ways they never had communicated before. Ideas for teaching various SOL objectives were being shared, and some teachers of non-SOL courses had expressed a willingness to do whatever they could to reinforce SOL instruction.

For the past two decades, principals in the United States have been encouraged to function as instructional leaders, and over the same time period many principals, particularly at the high school level, have argued that they were too busy handling school management issues to focus on curriculum, instruction, and assessment. The accountability plan seems to have created the impetus for Virginia high school principals to concentrate on being instructional leaders. Most of the principals that we interviewed cited a variety of examples of how they had begun to work closely with department heads and teachers on ways to improve course offerings, align curriculum, upgrade the quality of teaching, and track student progress on SOL objectives. Most of the principals personally reviewed all state test and subtest results and helped pinpoint areas of weakness in SOL courses.

The development of special programs to assist students in passing state SOL tests has been another constructive response to the accountability plan. Most of the high schools that we studied offered students tutorial help during or after school. Some also provided special personnel, incentives, and summer programs. Most of the 16 high schools had created, or were in the process of creating, information management systems to allow student progress on SOL objectives to be tracked more easily. Many schools had invested in educational software to help students review for state tests.

THE PROBLEMS OF ACCOUNTABILITY

Reform is never easy. When the scale of reform is unprecedented, as in the case of Virginia's accountability plan, the challenge of change can be truly daunting. Based on our study of 16 high schools, we believe that seven problems must be addressed effectively before the accountability plan can be said to rest on solid ground. These include the following:

1. Standardization of course content

2. Reduced choice

3. Standardization of instructional practice

4. Erosion of school climate

5.   Centralization of authority

6.   Complexity of school organization

7.   Triaging of students

Standardization of Course Content

In theory, the state of Virginia has done nothing to limit what can be taught in SOL courses. It simply has developed objectives to ensure that certain minimum expectations will be met. The problem is that, in practice, minimums sometimes become maximums. Knowing that they will be judged on the basis of how their students perform on state SOL tests, teachers are inclined to concentrate on covering the SOL objectives. The SOL objectives, however, represent only a portion of the material that students need to know if they subsequently are to tackle advanced work. Teachers of honors and advanced courses fear that if students focus exclusively on the basic knowledge represented by the SOL objectives, they will be poorly prepared to handle such challenging courses as Calculus, Advanced Placement Chemistry, and Advanced Placement European History.

These concerns represent an irony. In their desire to raise standards, state officials actually could lower the level of academic performance, particularly for higher achieving students. Concern over this issue may lead some school divisions to track more able students into special programs. In other cases, where advanced tracks are unavailable, parents may opt to withdraw their children and place them in nonpublic schools. If the price of raising standards for some students is to suppress performance for more able students, the price may be judged to be too high by some observers.

Reduced Choice

In an effort to reallocate resources to strengthen instruction in SOL courses, high schools have begun to eliminate electives and lower-track courses that do not lead to graduation credits. Principals in half the high schools we studied believed that enrollment in vocational programs had been adversely affected by the accountability plan.

It is too early to tell what effect diminished choice will have on students. Obviously some "Mickey Mouse" courses should be purged from high school offerings, but other courses may meet the needs and interests of particular groups of students. It is interesting to note that some high schools, feeling the need to offer certain students less academically rigorous courses, have turned to non-SOL courses like Physics and developed special offerings geared to non-college-preparatory programs. Perhaps high schools also will be compelled to offer vocational and technical courses on site, rather than busing students to special vocational-technical schools, in order to save time and allow students a greater opportunity to complete SOL courses.

The time may have come to reexamine the entire course of study for students who are not going to college immediately after graduating from high school. Is it necessary for every student, for instance, to complete Algebra II? Who is to say that some students would not be better served by taking Computer Graphics or Automotive Mechanics? Equating equity with the completion of core courses that realistically may only benefit a small number of students may not be prudent educational policy.

Standardization of Instructional Practice

A number of indications were found that teachers were moving toward common instructional practices. Pacing guides, lesson plan templates, emphasis on factual knowledge, and adoption of SOL-test formats for classroom assessment reflected an acknowledgment by teachers that preparing students to pass state tests had become their primary mission.

Standardization of instruction, of course, is not automatically a problem. One benefit of standardization is that it allows teachers to cover a lot of content in a relatively brief period of time. "Coverage" of content, however, is not the only purpose of instruction. Teachers hope that students will understand what they are studying and why it is important. Content, presumably, should not be learned simply because it may appear on a state test. It takes time for teachers to explain to students why content is important and help them to understand what it means. Many teachers feel so pressed to cover the SOL objectives before state tests are given that they are reluctant to take time to promote understanding. The most they can hope for is that students will memorize the information necessary to pass the tests.

One reason why teachers feel rushed is that they have less time to cover course content. State tests are administered approximately 4 to 6 weeks before the end of school. This means that teachers have about 20 to 30 fewer days to cover key material. Many teachers admit that the school year effectively concludes with the state tests.

In the rush to cover essential content, students who are slower to learn are frequently being left behind, according to the principals we interviewed. Evidence of this disturbing development can be found in the high schools that have added an extra semester of Algebra I to help struggling students. Unfortunately, schools cannot add an extra semester to every SOL course. Concern for slower students has led to the proliferation of special remediation programs in an effort to provide assistance to students outside of class because there is so little time available in class for help.

Erosion of School Climate

The accountability plan predictably has increased the pressure on teachers and administrators for "results." The eventual consequences for failure to teach the SOL effectively include loss of school accreditation and failure of individual students to earn a diploma. Most principals acknowledged that this pressure has translated into greater stress on all staff members. In some cases, teachers have opted to retire early or transfer out of SOL courses.

While high schools always have had to contend with the perception that certain courses are more important than other courses, the accountability plan has legitimized this perception. No one disputes the fact that SOL courses are now the most important courses in the high school curriculum. Student graduation depends on earning verified credits in seven SOL courses. This requires passing the course itself and the end-of-course SOL test.

Teachers of non-SOL courses have been marginalized in ways they never were traditionally. To the credit of some, they are exploring ways that they can reinforce SOL objectives in their courses, but it is a "stretch" in the case of many electives. Principals openly admit to moving their strongest teachers to SOL courses, and why not? Too much is riding on student performance to staff these courses with mediocre teachers. School climate, however, is unlikely to be enhanced when a clear distinction is made between the courses and teachers who "count" and those that do not.

The fear is that teachers who feel marginalized will begin to detach emotionally from the school. Since many of these teachers work with some of the neediest students in high school, the impact of such psychological withdrawal could be great. One of the important challenges facing high school principals in Virginia is to find ways to ensure that teachers of non-SOL courses continue to feel valuable and valued.

Centralization of Authority

Like standardization, centralization of authority is not necessarily a problem. It only becomes a problem when people who have gotten used to exercising local control and professional judgment believe that they have lost a measure of autonomy. In Virginia, local control long has been a key concept guiding educational policy. In recent years, both state policy makers and local superintendents also have pressed for site-based management in the belief that educational decisions should be made as close to the "front lines" as possible. The accountability plan is perceived by many of the principals we interviewed as a reversal of this commitment.

With so much riding on student performance on state tests, it is understandable, of course, why educational decision making is becoming centralized. School officials cannot afford variations in policies, programs, and practices across schools or classrooms. Students must be assured that they will receive comparable instruction no matter which school they attend. Centralization, however, comes at a cost.

When educators feel that all the important decisions will be made in Richmond or at the central office, they may be less inclined to regard themselves as professionals and educational leaders. What's more, there is little incentive to innovate or develop unique solutions to local problems. Many Virginia educators feel that they have been asked to take on more responsibilities at the same time that much of their authority has been diminished.

Complexity of School Organization

Running a high school has always been fraught with complexity, but there are indications that the level of complexity has increased substantially in the wake of the accountability plan. The combined impact of School Performance Report Cards that allow the public to compare the performance of individual schools on multiple criteria and Standards of Accreditation that hold all schools to common expectations has left local educators with no place to hide.

To respond to these developments, principals and teachers have had to initiate a variety of quality control measures, including information management systems and regular reviews of student progress. The proliferation of special programs, ranging from after-school tutorials to summer schools for students who fail state tests, has required additional planning and coordination. Parents must be informed about the consequences if their children do not pass state tests. Teacher evaluation takes on new importance when each teacher's passing rates on state tests can be compared.

Adding to the complexity of school organization is the increased politicization of schooling in Virginia. Many school boards in the commonwealth are now elected, rather than appointed. This recent development means that prospective board members can run on a platform that aims to correct problems at schools perceived to be underperforming on state tests. To contend with their new "visibility," principals must become adept at public relations, lobbying the central office for additional resources, and defending their schools in public.

Increased organizational complexity comes at a time when it is increasingly difficult to find teachers and, especially, high school administrators. Policy makers will have won a pyrrhic victory if they succeed in institutionalizing the accountability plan, but are unable to staff high schools, particularly those with a track record of low student performance. Such staffing problems are likely to exacerbate existing achievement disparities between schools.

Triaging of Students

Will high schools start to operate like triage units in battlefield hospitals? In other words, will educators begin to allocate their time and energy based on judgments of which students are most likely to benefit from their help? Imagine a high school with a passing rate in Algebra I of 67%. The state requires a passing rate of 70%. Should math teachers focus their assistance on students who do not have a chance of passing the state test in Algebra I or on students who, with a few more right answers, could pass the test?

This latter group has come to be known as "bubble students." They are on the "bubble," close to passing the state test. Our interviews revealed that some high schools are concentrating their special programs on these students in the hopes of achieving the necessary 70% passing rate. What, then, becomes of the students with little hope of passing the state tests? It is ironic, but entirely possible, that these students—the ones who are furthest behind—are more likely to receive systematic help in higher performing high schools than lower performing schools. A high school that already has achieved a 70% passing rate has little to lose by assisting its neediest students, but a high school that has yet to reach a 70% passing rate might feel compelled to focus on achieving that benchmark—which could mean triaging students.

Also lost in the triaging process is the group of students who easily pass the SOL tests and are functioning at the upper ends of the achievement spectrum, those students who are hungry for a richer and more demanding curriculum. In some schools, students who are passing the tests are forgotten, and instructional effort is directed to those who are not. While this makes sense from a pragmatic point of view, it compromises the educational benefits of our strongest students. As was reported earlier, there is concern among some educators that stronger students are not receiving the full breadth of instruction necessary to prepare them for higher-level course work because of a narrow curricular focus on the SOL. Triaging therefore has the potential to harm both the weakest and the strongest students.

It is too early to speculate on the long-term consequences of triaging. One possibility is that students who are furthest behind will drop out. Another is that they will transfer to GED programs at 16 (Virginia recently lowered the legal age at which students could take the GED test). Triaging also could lead to more students seeking eligibility for special education services and placement in alternative schools, or private schools not subject to the accountability plan.

TIME TO REASSESS SCHOOL LEADERSHIP?

Leadership experts long have recognized the relationship between what leaders do and the context in which they do it (Northouse, 1997; Yukl, 1989). It is reasonable, therefore, to ask whether changes in the context of public education occasioned by new accountability initiatives have created a need for new forms of school leadership.

The present study did not find high school principals undertaking things they had never done before. Highly effective principals have always encouraged teachers to collaborate on curriculum development and alignment. They have always championed the cause of struggling students and seen that assistance programs were in place. There is nothing new about principals insisting that the primary focus of attention should be student achievement.

It would be a mistake, however, to conclude that yesterday's models of school leadership will fit today's schools. With the era of accountability, at least in Virginia, have come several changes of such significance that a new model of school leadership is necessitated. Foremost among these changes is the ability of virtually anyone to judge whether what principals do makes a difference in student achievement on state tests. In the past, the public had little access to data that allowed them to make such judgments. Now they have School Performance Report Cards for every school. Data are available not only for the current year, but for previous years. Each principal's efforts can be compared with the efforts of predecessors and principals in other schools. Initiatives undertaken simply to cover one's backside or to foster the illusion of responsiveness now can easily be detected.

As principals gain a sense of which of their endeavors contribute the most to improved student achievement, they should begin to prioritize their efforts in ways they might not have done previously. Evidence of more judicious use of time by principals emerged from the present study. Many principals noted that they spent more time working with teachers to understand where students were having difficulties on state tests and what could be done about it. Principals also reported having to reallocate resources in various ways to facilitate instructional improvement. They reduced class size in courses where students were required to take state SOL tests and allowed class size in other courses to climb. They also eliminated nonessential electives and created programs during school hours as well as after school and in the summer so that students could receive additional help in preparing for state tests.

In the past, much has been written about the need for school leaders to provide a sense of direction for their schools. Principals were exhorted to develop a vision or mission statement to guide teachers and other staff members. Direction was needed to combat the ambiguity to which most organizations are heir (McCaskey, 1982, pp. 4–6). To some extent, Virginia's accountability plan has eliminated ambiguity regarding what schools are expected to accomplish. It is clear now that high schools must achieve designated passing rates in specific courses or else they will not be accredited. Having been relieved of the need to provide a sense of direction, principals presumably can focus more of their energy on ensuring that teachers, students, and parents are *committed* to the direction established by the state.

Many of the principals who were interviewed provided examples of how they were winning commitment to improved performance on state tests. Meetings with parents were scheduled so that the importance of the new state tests could be explained. Similar meetings were held with students, and incentives were created to induce them to exert their best efforts to pass the tests. Teacher commitment was won in various ways, including reassignment of the most capable teachers to courses in which students took state tests, frequent faculty meetings that focused on the content of state tests and student performance, and special staff development activities.

Principals constitute a primary source of troubleshooting (Duke, 1987). In other words, they are expected to anticipate problems before problems arise or mushroom out of control. Virginia's accountability plan has occasioned the need for such troubleshooting. As the preceding section suggested, the accountability plan has the potential to create problems as well as benefits. School principals are in the best position of any individual to monitor problems and see that they are addressed in a timely manner. Seeing that problems are addressed does not mean, however, that principals always must be the problem solvers.

Adjusting to the demands of the new culture of accountability requires the expertise and leadership of other individuals besides principals. The present study found evidence that principals were looking to department chairs, counselors, and veteran teachers to undertake curriculum alignment, analyze student performance on state tests, develop common lesson formats, and design programs to assist students in passing state tests. These findings confirm Leithwood's (2001) acknowledgment that the new era of accountability will demand an increase in *distributed* leadership—leadership at all levels of the school.

APPENDIX 3.1
SURVEY OF PERCEIVED IMPACT OF EDUCATIONAL REFORMS

The state of Virginia has initiated a broad-based set of reforms, including Standards of Learning, Standards of Accreditation, statewide high-stakes tests, and school performance report cards. We are interested in your judgment concerning the intended, and unintended, consequences of these reforms—over and above their impact on student test scores. We appreciate your willingness to complete this survey.

Daniel L. Duke, Pamela D. Tucker, and Dan Butin
Thomas Jefferson Center for Educational Design
at the University of Virginia

1. Background Information

1.1   NAME OF SCHOOL:

1.2   NAME OF SCHOOL DISTRICT:

1.3   GRADE-LEVEL OF SCHOOL:

1.4   PERSON COMPLETING THE SURVEY AND TITLE:

1.5   DATE:

For each of the following items, please circle the number that best represents your judgment of the impact of state education reforms in Virginia on your school.

2. Staff Morale

Since the fall of 1998, as a result of Virginia's
education reforms . . .

2.1	Staff morale has improved.	1	2	3	4	5
2.2	The stress level among a majority of teachers has increased.	1	2	3	4	5
2.3	Teachers have resigned or retired early (citing the state reforms as their primary reason).	1	2	3	4	5
2.4	Teachers are spending more time talking with each other about teaching, learning, and curriculum.	1	2	3	4	5
2.5	Teachers are engaged in more collaborative planning.	1	2	3	4	5
2.6	Teachers feel that everything they do must focus on preparing students for state tests.	1	2	3	4	5

2.7   Teachers are afraid to try anything
      unrelated to the Standards of Learning in
      their classes.   1   2   3   4   5
2.8   Committee work for staff members has
      increased.   1   2   3   4   5
2.9   School administrators are under greater
      pressure.   1   2   3   4   5
2.10 Some teachers must teach more students
      as a result of the lowering of class size in
      SOL courses.   1   2   3   4   5
2.11 Counselors spend less time counseling
      students because of increased paperwork
      and duties associated with testing and
      record keeping.   1   2   3   4   5

3. Staffing

Since the fall of 1998, as a result of Virginia's
education reforms . . .

3.1   The most capable teachers have been
      assigned to teach the grade-levels and/or
      courses in which students must take SOL
      tests.   1   2   3   4   5
3.2   Teachers have requested to be transferred
      out of grades or courses where SOL testing
      is done.   1   2   3   4   5
3.3   Vocational education enrollments are
      declining because students must meet more
      academic requirements.   1   2   3   4   5

4. Instruction

Since the fall of 1998, as a result of Virginia's
education reforms . . .

4.1   Teachers must move too quickly through
      the curriculum in order to cover all of the
      SOL before the state tests.   1   2   3   4   5
4.2   Course content covered after the state
      tests are given is not taken very seriously
      by teachers.   1   2   3   4   5
4.3   The recall of facts is being emphasized too
      much in subjects where students must take
      state tests.   1   2   3   4   5
4.4   Teachers have become more strict when
      students request to leave class for
      legitimate reasons (guidance, clinic, rest
      room)   1   2   3   4   5

4.5   Teachers of subjects other than
      English/language arts are not teaching
      writing as much because of the need to
      focus on factual content.   1   2   3   4   5
4.6   Teachers are spending more time helping
      individual students.   1   2   3   4   5
4.7   Teachers are making more of an effort to
      differentiate instruction in order to "reach"
      all students.   1   2   3   4   5
4.8   Teachers stress conventional assessment,
      rather than performance assessment, in
      order to prepare students for SOL tests. 1   2   3   4   5
4.9   Teachers of some advanced courses are
      afraid that overemphasis on SOL will
      cause students to be inadequately prepared
      for advanced work.   1   2   3   4   5

5. Students

Since the fall of 1998, as a result of Virginia's
education reforms . . .

5.1   Students who are the furthest behind in
      their learning are receiving more
      assistance and attention.   1   2   3   4   5
5.2   Students who take longer to learn are
      having more trouble keeping pace with
      their classmates.   1   2   3   4   5
5.3   Students who are close to passing SOL
      tests receive more attention from teachers
      than students who are not close to passing
      SOL tests.   1   2   3   4   5

6. Other

Since the fall of 1998, as a result of Virginia's
education reforms . . .

6.1   School resources have been taken from
      areas that are not involved with testing for
      the SOL and shifted to areas where
      students take SOL tests.   1   2   3   4   5

7. Greatest Impact of State Reforms

In your opinion, what has been the biggest impact of Virginia's education
reforms (SOL, statewide tests, etc.) on your school?

NOTE

1. The names of both high schools have been changed.

REFERENCES

Duke, D. L. (1987). *School leadership and instructional improvement*. NY: Random House.
Leithwood, K. (2001). "School leadership and educational accountability: Toward a distributed perspective." In T. J. Kowalski (Ed.), *21st century challenges for school administrators* (11–25). Lanham, MD: Scarecrow Press.
McCaskey, M. B. (1982). *The executive challenge*. Marshfield, MA: Pitman.
Northouse, P. G. (1997). *Leadership: Theory and practice*. Thousand Oaks, CA: Sage.
Yukl, G. A. (1989). *Leadership in organizations*, 2nd ed. Englewood Cliffs, NY: Prentice-Hall.

Chapter Four

THE PRINCIPALSHIP: RENEWED CALL FOR INSTRUCTIONAL LEADERSHIP

Pamela D. Tucker

Accountability has become an unquestioned assumption of current educational policy with standards, assessment programs, and reform efforts as the typical response from a majority of the states. The popular press and academic articles attest to the pervasiveness of these circumstances nationwide. Standards and the associated testing regimens are the tools of accountability that are thrust on teachers and principals who are then judged by their results. According to *Education Week* (Olson, 2000), "The push for standards-based reform—and the pressure on schools to deliver in terms of academic performance—have raised the demands and pressures on principals and brought an unprecedented level of public scrutiny to their job performance" (p.16). Admittedly, as asserted by Richard Riley, Secretary of the U.S. Department of Education, the principal's role is pivotal in school improvement efforts.

> [The principalship is] a position that is absolutely critical to educational change and improvement. A good principal can create a climate that can foster excellence in teaching and learning, while an ineffective one can quickly thwart the progress of the most dedicated reformers. (as cited in ERS, 2000, p. 1)

What does it mean to be a "good principal"? What are the skills required to "foster excellence in teaching and learning"? The demand for better or redefined leadership has focused on the instructional aspects of the principal's role. According to Gerald Tirozzi, Executive Director of the National Association of Secondary School Principals, principals today are expected "to provide the instructional acumen, curriculum support, professional development opportunities, data-driven decision making, and visionary perspective to mold a faculty of teachers into a unified force to advance academic achievement for all students" (Tirozzi, 2000, p. 68).

Some observers (National Policy Board for Educational Administration, 2002; Olson, 2000) have viewed this as "new thinking" about school leadership and have noted, "A dominant belief in policy circles, driven in large part by the academic-standards movement, is that principals, instead of being building managers, should become leaders of instruction—dynamic, inspirational educators focused almost exclusively on raising student achievement" (Olson, p. 1). Calls for instructional leadership ironically date back at least 20 years and can hardly be considered "new thinking." In 1981, Lipham noted that:

> The improvement of teaching and learning is the foremost function of the principal. The single most important factor in determining the success or failure of a school is the ability of the principal to lead the staff in planning, implementing, and evaluating improvements in the school's curricular, co-curricular, and extracurricular programs. (pp. 12–13)

The instructional role of the principal has been acknowledged for years but seemingly has been overlooked by some observers because of the other myriad job responsibilities that consume the long hours each day for the principal.

The recognition of the principal as an instructional leader is derived from the effective schools research in the 1970s and 1980s (Edmonds, 1979; Frederickson, & Edmonds, 1979), which substantiated the importance of principals' contributions to instructional effectiveness. Research (Hallinger & Heck, 1998; Leithwood & Jantzi, 1999) has continued to support this premise, but there is a new urgency and emphasis on instructional leadership due to the current context of accountability. As noted by Marc Tucker of the National Center on Education and the Economy, "The success of the entire standards-based agenda depends upon having effective leadership at the school level" (Olson, 2000, p. 15). This leadership is squarely focused on instructional challenges.

THE VIRGINIA EXPERIENCE

Virginia's policy response has included the typical accountability features, and responsibility for implementation has been laid squarely at the principal's doorstep. The Virginia Standards of Accreditation state:

> As the instructional leader, the principal . . . shall . . . seek to ensure that successful attainment of the knowledge and skills required for students by the Standards of Learning tests. (8 VAC 20–131–210B.5)

Principals are mandated to be instructional leaders in Virginia with the explicit task of ensuring student success on the standards-based tests.

In addition, principals are now evaluated based on "student academic progress." Legislation that was passed subsequent to the accountability reform package, entitled the "Educational Accountability and Quality Enhancement Act of 1999," requires the annual evaluation of teachers, principals, assistant principals, central office administrators, and superintendents based, in part, on measures of student learning. It is assumed that the General Assembly intended to spread responsibility for student learning across the whole spectrum of educators with this legislation; however, in reality, the test results are reported by individual schools. Therefore, principals remain the most visible persons responsible or accountable for student achievement. The collective effect of these different policies is a renewed call for instructional leadership on the part of Virginia's principals and unprecedented pressure to produce results.

INSTRUCTIONAL LEADERSHIP

While the current high-stakes accountability environment may be uncomfortable and even stressful for the principal, research (Cotton, 2000) supports the importance of leadership in improving schools. The centrality and importance of the principal's role to the effectiveness of instructional programs in schools is often traced to the work of Ron Edmonds and others on effective schools (Smith & Andrews, 1989). This body of research (e.g., Brookover et al., 1982; Edmonds, 1979; Frederickson & Edmonds, 1979) suggested that effective schools had principals who were strong instructional leaders. By the mid-1980s, "instructional leadership became the new educational standard for principals" (Hallinger, 1992, p. 37). Subsequent studies have continued to support this premise (Cawelti, 1999; Guskey, 1988; Skrla, Scheurich, & Johnson, 2000). A recent review of the research on instructional leadership spanning the years of 1980–1995 by Hallinger and Heck (1998) found that "the general pattern of results drawn from this review supports the belief that principals exercise a measurable, though indirect effect on school effectiveness and student achievement" (p. 186).

During this same period of time, there had been an abundance of literature focused on identifying the specific characteristics and behaviors of principals who were instructional leaders (Murphy, 1992). An important contribution to this effort was the work of Hallinger (1984), who described a comprehensive set of 10 behaviors that were critical to instructional leadership and included framing school goals, high visibility, supervising and evaluating instruction, coordinating the curriculum, and monitoring student progress. More recent research by Sheppard (1996) has supported the relationship between the behaviors identified by Hallinger and teacher commitment, professional involvement, and innovativeness. Smith and Andrews (1989) took a different approach and stressed the importance of the principal as (1) resource provider, (2) instructional resource, (3) communicator, and (4) visible presence. In some of the most recent work in this area, Blase and Blase (1999) identified the two major themes of reflection and growth as fundamental to instructional leadership with 11 associated behaviors.

For the purposes of this study of Virginia principals, Duke's framework of instructional leadership (1987) was used. Duke's work drew on the research base provided by many of the authors discussed above and focused on situational competence. According to Duke, "no single set of behaviors characterizes all successful instructional leaders" (p. 81) and that success is context-specific, or "situational," depending on a variety of factors including the particular skills of the principal, resources, student needs, available personnel, and political demands. Krug (1992) concurred that principal effectiveness is based on the ability to understand the meaning of contextual variables and respond thoughtfully to them.

The seven research-based domains of instructional leadership identified by Duke (1987) are: (1) teacher supervision and development, (2) teacher evaluation, (3) instructional management and support, (4) resource management, (5) quality control, (6) coordination, and (7) troubleshooting (p. 81). They are not discrete functions in practice but interrelated and dynamic, and can be fulfilled in a variety of ways depending on both the managerial skills and leadership qualities of the principal. The managerial skills of a principal often determine "what" and "when" certain actions are taken, but personal qualities associated with leadership shape "how" something is said or implemented. This perspective is what Sheppard (1996) considers "a broad view" of instructional leadership that "entails all leadership activities that affect student learning" (p. 326).

DESCRIPTION OF THE STUDY

The material for this discussion was drawn from a larger investigation that focused on how high schools as organizations were affected by the reform efforts taking place in Virginia during the 1999–2000 school year. In the larger study reported in chapter 3, 16 high school principals were surveyed and interviewed about a range of topics including staff morale, instruction, staffing, and students. The principals were selected to represent a range of different school environments, those with high and low expenditures per student and those with high and low passing rates on the Standards of Learning (SOL) tests. For the following discussion, the author used Duke's framework for instructional leadership (1987) to organize and interpret the principals' involvement in instructional activities. Of particular interest were those efforts by principals that have emerged or taken on greater importance as a result of the accountability climate in Virginia.

FINDINGS

Principals reported that there was no question their role was changing as a result of the reform initiative in Virginia. Fifteen out of 16 principals reported more pressure and more work because the Standards of Accreditation placed the responsibility for student achievement directly on their shoulders and published schoolwide testing results that reflected their performance as the school administrator. One principal quipped, "I feel like I have a bull's-eye on my back because I'm the target for every new idea that anyone suggests." Principals reported being more involved in general supervisory work with teachers and believed their supervision was more likely to focus on curriculum, instruction and assessment. The specific nature of their work is detailed below.

Supervision and Evaluation

This area of instructional leadership for the principal is focused on the elements of supervision and evaluation systems with particular attention to the quality and substance of performance data used in evaluation, the availability of assistance for teachers, and the skills of the evaluator.

Most principals reported spending more time supervising teachers, but they also noted that the purpose and focus of supervision and evaluation had changed as a result of the reform initiative. Observations and teacher conferences are now used to monitor the implementation of the SOL and to assess results on the state assessments. An overriding concern is the pacing and content of instruction. Principals have attempted to support teachers by providing substantial professional development to address these challenges.

A majority of the principals (12 out of 16) said that "teachers are spending more time talking with each other about teaching, learning, and curriculum." They reported more informal peer assistance around specific problem areas in the curriculum, discussion of pacing issues, introduction of new concepts, and new instructional activities to support the SOL. These were perceived as positive developments by principals, and they encouraged them by scheduling common planning periods and dedicating time for this purpose as a form of professional development. Some principals were content to play a supportive role in this process while others were more actively involved providing resource and curriculum information for teachers. Principals with many new teachers felt a heightened sense of obligation to provide them with copies of the curriculum, pacing guides, and instructional materials.

A notable change in the supervisory landscape was a clearer understanding of who was not teaching the prescribed curriculum as measured by the Standards of Learning assessments. In some cases, whole departments had relatively low passing rates, while in other cases specific teachers had low passing rates. With assessment data over a two-year time span, patterns were emerging that were troubling to principals. Conversations with the principals suggested that they were becoming impatient with teachers who had low passing rates. They had begun to apply pressure on these teachers to improve or transfer to non-SOL courses.

Staff Development

This area concerns the development of groups of individuals, including their learning and growing together toward common goals. Duke (1987) suggested that staff development could be thought of as a means to "nurture a spirit of community and common interest" (p. 162). The SOL certainly have created a common goal, but not necessarily the "spirit of community" envisioned by Duke. While most schools have mobilized behind a common goal of full accreditation,[1] the external nature of the goal has made it difficult to develop a sense of ownership by principals and teachers alike. However, with each passing year, there has been greater resignation that the standards are here to stay and must be addressed. Most principals reported an acceptance of the SOL by 1999–2000, when the interviews were conducted, and a readiness to begin the necessary work to help students pass the state assessments.

Consistent with the focus on the state standards, professional development efforts at the local, regional, and state levels have been targeted at the SOL. Paid summer workdays, professional leave days, and time before and after school have been dedicated to workshops run by local teachers, consultants, and/or staff members from the Governor's Best Practice Centers. Teachers and principals are attending state-level conferences where teachers share effective instructional strategies for improving SOL test scores. Attending teachers often are asked by principals to share ideas and materials with colleagues in their local school systems.

Staff development has been more piecemeal and lacking in an overarching plan than Duke (1987) recommends, but it nonetheless has been relevant and easily accessible for most teachers. In many schools, principals have worked with department heads and instructional support personnel from the central office to coordinate curriculum work focused on alignment, implementation, and assessment; but in smaller schools, principals have served this function and have hired teachers to do some of the curriculum work during the summers.

Instructional Management and Support

This function encompasses the "development of school policies and procedures for dealing with predictable or recurring instructional matters" and "efforts to establish and maintain school climates conducive to teacher and student growth" (Duke, 1987, p. 182).

Statewide policies delineated in the Standards of Accreditation have superseded many school-level policies regarding academic standards, particularly for high schools, because students must pass certain courses and the associated SOL assessments to receive verified credits for graduation. The SOL, however, have spawned the review, revision and development of other types of policies at the local level. Principals reported specific interest in policies regarding attendance and grading. Another area in which principals have rethought past practice is the grouping of students and the number of students assigned to high- and low-ability classes. Some principals are adopting a more flexible approach to regrouping after the first semester, if students need more time in a particular subject, like Algebra. Principals also are putting more students in higher-level courses and fewer students in lower level courses.

To support a productive school climate, principals are trying to reduce the stress felt by both teachers and students. In many schools, principals have empowered teachers by involving them in the development of strategies to increase passing rates. Test data are being shared with departments, and work sessions are focused on data analysis and interpretation. Department chairs are assuming greater responsibility thus distributing leadership across more individuals within schools (Spillane, Halverson, & Diamond, 2001). Principals are sponsoring informational meetings for students and parents to help them understand the importance of the SOL and garner their support. Some schools are having pep rallies to encourage students to attend school and do their best on tests.

Resource Management

Resource management refers to how school leaders make use of resources including personnel, time, and learning materials. Because needs typically exceed resources, principals must work with teachers to set priorities and judge the benefits of various types of investments. They must leverage limited resources to facilitate student success.

The reform initiative has had a definite impact on the recruitment and selection of personnel. During initial interviews with prospective teachers, many principals reported that they discussed the standards-based environment at length to determine their willingness to work with a prescribed curriculum and their understanding of expectations for student achievement. Determining the level of commitment was just as important for the hiring of noncore teachers as those in core subject areas because noncore area teachers were expected to indirectly support the SOL in as many ways as possible.

There have also been changes in the assignment of personnel. More than half of the principals reported assigning more capable teachers to teach courses in which students must take SOL tests. Many principals have hired additional staff (teachers, teacher aides, and tutors) to provide intensive assistance in English and math for weaker students. In terms of personnel changes, a few principals reported retirements that were a direct result of the SOL. The impact was perceived as a knowledge drain in some cases and a positive development in others because some teachers were unwilling to adjust to the new expectations. A half-dozen principals, all in rural areas, noted high turnover rates that exacerbated the challenge to improve student achievement on the SOL assessments.

Principals have reexamined the use of time as another instructional resource. Schoolwide events such as assemblies have been scrutinized carefully for instructional relevance and have been scaled back. The scheduling of core courses has taken on greater importance with more flexible arrangements for repeating courses being introduced. Principals are encouraging teachers to use common planning times and workdays to do joint planning. Time is no longer simply scheduled, but it is leveraged for maximum benefit to students and faculty.

Principals have become more involved in the selection and purchase of learning materials. With access to more testing information, there has been a greater recognition of the mismatch between existing textbooks and skill levels of students, so that alternative instructional materials are being used, particularly in English and math. Principals have become a conduit for new SOL-aligned materials that are being developed by the Virginia Department of Education and commercial groups. Working in collaboration with their faculty, principals are spending time obtaining state materials and committing instructional funds to the purchase of supplemental materials. They are actively encouraging the exchange of materials and ideas among teachers.

Quality Control

It is the principal's primary responsibility to ensure that all students receive quality instruction. Quality control refers to such strategies as setting clear instructional goals, assessing the attainment of these goals, and developing processes to focus on continual school improvement.

The reform initiative in Virginia has emphasized quality control with the high-stakes testing program and its direct link to school accreditation. The school principal's role is to monitor progress toward the SOL goals and address school improvement efforts. Some principals have taken a direct hand in supervising the curriculum pacing of teachers and the assessment programs for students through classroom visits, reviews of lesson plans, and the requirement of quarterly reports. In larger schools, principals have worked with department chairs to set goals, monitor pacing, and develop improvement strategies. One principal organized an administrative retreat to analyze schoolwide test data and develop school-level goals for improvement.

In some school divisions, the initiative for monitoring the quality of instruction is a divisionwide effort with support from central office while in others, monitoring efforts have been left to the discretion of the principal. A few principals reported that the superintendent dictated SOL-related target goals, but most reported school-based development of instructional goals. Principals are working with department chairs and individual teachers to set target goals based on test data.

Monitoring of curriculum, instruction, and assessment has demanded that principals become more adept at using complex information management systems to track student performance and analyze test results. Data analysis is necessary to set goals, evaluate gains, and modify instructional strategies or programs to address problems. More than ever, principals are required to understand how to connect test scores diagnostically to programs, teaching strategies, and curricula. While departments and department chairs have taken on much of the data analysis function, principals continue to have a role in reviewing and making sense of test scores.

For example, principals have scrutinized subject areas with low passing rates. During the first two years of testing (1997–1998 and 1998–1999), mathematics was a primary focus of attention because of low passing rates in Algebra

I. As a result, a variety of strategies were used to restructure how this course was offered. The result was a 12-point mean gain in the percent passing all math course assessments for the 16 high schools in the study.[2]

Coordination and Troubleshooting

"Coordination and troubleshooting encompass a variety of activities that cut across all the preceding areas . . . including efforts designed to stimulate cooperation" (Duke, 1997, p. 236) and minimize possible threats to an organization and its goals. Unfortunately, the accountability initiative has generated a host of potential problems for principals, loss of accreditation being the most immediate. They are concerned about increased stress on students and teachers; negative impacts on the curriculum; and the possible lack of support by their community during the improvement process. Yet, it is in this climate of uncertainty that they must work to maintain productive working relationships to achieve their goals. In fact, the coordination of resource management, curriculum, assessment, and the improvement process may be the greatest challenge for principals in this current context.

Coordination and troubleshooting typically are achieved through planning, group meetings, collaborative decision-making, and problem solving. Principals reported committing more time to all these activities. Principals are trying to foster schoolwide understanding of the challenges posed by the new accreditation standards and to engender cooperation within and across subject areas to develop responsive and coordinated efforts to address the demands. Better strategies for sharing information and mechanisms for identifying and responding to student problems are being developed. As a result of the pressure, there is more committee work being done to discuss the curriculum, instructional strategies, and materials, as well as the needs of individual students.

Given the magnitude of the coordination required by these various activities, principals have leaned heavily on their department heads and assistant principals to assist with the curriculum work and test data analysis for improvement purposes. Personnel from central office, where available, have provided assistance. In addition, principals are relying on guidance counselors to coordinate the testing program and identify individual student needs.

Based on the experiences of 16 high school principals, instructional leadership activities are becoming more mainstream in the wake of Virginia's accountability initiative. While all the management functions of running a safe and well-organized school continue to form the foundation of the high school principalship, instructional leadership has taken on an immediacy and centrality that did not characterize the role in the past. Not surprisingly, when principals were asked how should leadership preparation programs be changed, three-fourths recommended greater emphasis on teaching and learning. They wanted better preparation for data analysis, student assessment, curriculum design, professional development, and the instructional improvement process. Accountability has placed a premium on the skills and knowledge associated with instructional leadership and what is described as the changing role of the principal (National Policy Board for Educational Administration, 2002).

PROFILES OF TWO REMARKABLE INSTRUCTIONAL LEADERS

To better understand the underlying beliefs that guide instructional leaders in an age of accountability, follow-up visits were made to 2 of the 16 schools that had particularly dynamic, energetic principals. These leaders were selected based wholly on the powerful impression they had made during the first round of interviews. They both possessed a vehement commitment to making their schools better places for students to learn. Their schools could not have been more different; one was small (343 students) and rural, the other was large (2,100 students) and suburban. The rural school struggled to reach the 70% passing mark in all subject areas and the suburban one had just achieved "full accreditation" for the 1999–2000 school year, with passing rates far above the 70% required minimum. The two principals, however, shared a common drive to make their schools excel.

Joan Miller

Joan Miller is a pseudonym for an articulate, dynamic female principal with 20 years of administrative experience, 8 years of which were at a suburban high school (SHS). She is part of the fabric of the community in which she lives, and as a result, she feels a deep loyalty, especially to "her students" who number over 2,000. Not only does Joan live in the community, but 65% of her teachers also live in the area, giving them a tremendous sense of responsibility for their "successes" and their "mistakes." Being part of the community demands accountability, according to Joan, and she spends 12 to14 hours a day making SHS a vital, energetic place for teenagers. "That's the philosophy we agreed on in our mission, we are not going to put ourselves first, we are going to put kids first."

She believes that the SOL have done some good in that they have standardized the curriculum and prioritized the objectives for schools. While she doesn't agree with the priorities that have been established, she recognizes the need to meet these goals for the well-being of her students and the school. Her broader-based goals are captured in her annual school plan, which addresses all aspects of school life, including visual arts, physical education, daily comportment, and community involvement. The annual plan is illustrative of her "organic approach" to integrating the views and expectations of all constituencies in everything she does. The faculty, parents, and students collectively developed the annual plan. It contains both the beliefs and understandings that drive the processes and the concrete goals that must be met. Within the document are poignant statements from students about what they want from their school, such as,

> I want to respect you [the teacher] and what you do. Teachers are amazing people but I also need respect. It's a mutual thing. (School Plan, p. 4)

and hard-nosed indicators of achievement such as,

> The percent of students passing at the proficient and/or advanced levels on the SOL tests in Geometry will increase to the 80% level. (School Plan, p. 7)

While the goals in the annual plan follow the traditional subject area groupings for a high school, the actual academic program is organized into schools of study such as the "School of the Humanities" and the "School of International Studies," each with a sequence of courses that goes beyond the basic state requirements.

Clubs and sports are also a major part of life at SHS (there are 81 possibilities) and a majority of students participate in one or more activities. The principal views her school as a "human ecosystem," where everyone is growing and developing on a continuous basis. Her role is to develop a rich environment of options for individual expression and fulfillment during and after school hours. This requires an environment of challenge and risk-taking that she tries to encourage and model constantly for students and faculty alike. For example, she taught the rumba during a recent student government event and she dresses up in costumes for all the holidays and special events like homecoming.

Group meetings are very important for sustaining SHS's culture and the overall program that exists at SHS. These include department meetings, instructional planning team meetings, the faculty advisory council, the student council, the human relations council, and so on. One of the meetings that Joan values most is her monthly principal's cabinet, consisting of about 30 students representing the broad spectrum of the student body. The cabinet meetings are honest, confidential discussions of what's *really* going on in the school. Joan credits the students with informing her about serious situations that need attention, from teacher misconduct to threatened suicide.

While Joan is very committed to "her students," she also supports her faculty and attends to their needs in various ways, from offering yoga and health classes to sponsoring biannual faculty parties. Teachers are empowered to make curriculum decisions and recommendations for hiring new teachers. And Joan *always* hires the teachers recommended by her faculty. An indicator of her faculty's dedication is the school's high teacher attendance rate; Joan reports that it is the highest in the county. She aggressively pursues corporate sponsorships to raise extra money for requested equipment and materials. Even though she recognizes that she demands a lot from teachers in terms of meeting individual students' needs and keeping in touch with parents, her experience has been that success is rewarding. Once teachers see the positive results of their collective efforts, there is usually a greater investment in the school. Teacher turnover at SHS, with over 150 faculty members, is in the single digits. There is a waiting list of teachers who want to transfer to SHS.

An important element in SHS's academic success, according to Joan, has been the introduction of vertical teaming, involving one department per year, over her eight years as principal. Each teacher has been required to teach both a low- and a high-level course, such as pre-Algebra and Trigonometry, thereby ensuring that all teachers appreciate the vertical sequencing of skills and knowledge of each discipline. The teams for each course are expected to develop a common set of exams for each quarter, midterm, and final. This process forced teams to discuss and agree on what was important to teach. The vertical teaming work predated the SOL and serves as the foundation for the current curriculum at SHS. While the SHS curriculum has been aligned with the SOL, there is a sense of ownership in the curriculum that is more reflective of teachers' curricular priorities.

SHS's success, not only its full state accreditation, but the positive climate within the school, is the result of many factors: a well-defined and broad-based curriculum, dedicated teachers, a student-responsive administration, well-developed feedback mechanisms, and strong and stable leadership over an 8-year period.

Keith Robinson

Keith Robinson is a pseudonym for a committed, energetic male principal with 6 years of administrative experience, 3 years of which he served as principal of a small, rural high school enrolling 343 students (RHS). After 3 years of hard work, the faculty believes it can create a model small, rural high school, and that is Keith's ultimate goal. He firmly believes that good teaching is the key to creating a model high school and that the SOL scores will take care of themselves with excellence in the classroom. After addressing discipline during his first year and introducing new programs during his second, he is now focusing on supervision and evaluation of faculty during his third year.

As a testament to this commitment, he pointed out a calendar on the wall that detailed his classroom observations and those of his assistant principal throughout the fall semester. He plans to visit all teachers at least once in the fall and then to begin more focused work with newer and less proficient teachers in a second round of observations in January. With more skilled teachers, he encourages self-evaluation and self-reflection on their work. He does not schedule his observations in advance because he prefers to see a typical lesson, rather than the best possible lesson. During follow-up conferences, he talks in detail with teachers about the relationship between what he has seen in class and the curriculum guide notebooks in which teachers are asked to keep units of study, student activities, assessments, and rubrics. His primary concern is assessment and the reteaching of poorly learned material. Keith emphasizes this aspect of teaching based on research by Benjamin Bloom that found one could enhance student learning substantially with a systematic cycle of teaching, testing, and reteaching.

With no formal department heads or instructional support from central office, Keith is directly responsible for the development of curriculum. He works with an advisory team of subject area representatives that assists him with staff development and new program initiatives. During his first 2 years as principal, the advisory team and the assistant principal helped Keith to revise and reorganize a number of the courses and course sequences. With the assistance of a few teachers, they developed a specialized ninth-grade English class with a heavy emphasis on reading and writing for a high-risk group of students that, because of its success, is now part of the required program for all ninth graders. In a major overhaul of social studies, the entire course sequence was realigned with the SOL. In response to low math achievement, Keith and the team have set up a math lab with computerized instruction using the Cortez program. In conjunction with the skill building done in the math lab, small breakout sessions are held with students to provide intensive math instruction in identified areas of weakness.

New additions to the overall program include the introduction of a whole course in character education for all ninth graders and the senior project. Keith spearheaded both of these programs and wrote most of the curriculum material for them. The senior project was a concept that appealed to Keith as a capstone experience for his graduating seniors to give them a sense that they had accomplished something more than the completion of courses and passing scores on tests. It reflected a different type of accountability, culminating in a final paper and presentation of findings before a panel of teachers and community members.

Keith argues that his school's small size, 343 students and 33 faculty members, has allowed him a great deal of flexibility in introducing new programs, especially individualized ones like the senior project. It also has meant limited resources, both human and financial. In addition, during 1999–2000, he had one third of his faculty depart because of retirements and higher salaries offered elsewhere. This made it difficult to build momentum with his initiatives because so many teachers had to start from scratch that year. In the most recent year, 2000–2001, he was able to retain key math teachers and there was a more positive atmosphere. All teachers meet by subject area on a weekly basis and continue to refine the curriculum, materials, and assessments. Keith believes his teachers are some of the hardest working people he knows.

RHS is a school that lacks the tangible resources of Suburban High School but is rich in the freshness of ideas and energy of a young, dedicated administrative team. Keith and his advisory team share a vision for the school that includes the SOL but goes beyond them in terms of developing students who are good citizens and who can integrate their knowledge (e.g., senior project). While proud of the double-digit improvement on many SOL assessments during the previous year, the primary goal is to make RHS a model rural high school. Keith possesses a clear idea of what this entails: a well-developed curriculum, opportunities for students to apply what they learn, character education, and dedicated, quality teachers.

There are striking similarities between these two principals.

1. Both teach on a regular basis. Joan and all of her administrators teach as guest lecturers in different classes. One year, Joan taught a unit on DNA in AP Biology, and another year she taught *Macbeth* for 2 weeks in English 10. Keith teaches a character education class for every ninth grader using a curriculum he wrote for the class. His assistant principal also teaches.

2. Both principals take teacher quality seriously and devote a substantial amount of time to classroom observation. In addition, Joan interviews students in each teacher's class to get the student perspective. Joan and Keith reward high-quality teaching but also remove unsatisfactory teachers. Joan reported removing three teachers during the previous year, and Keith released four teachers.

3. Both principals stress the continuous assessment of student achievement and use of assessment data to enhance instruction, regroup students, and provide additional assistance. They do not use SOL assessments as their sole source of feedback on student learning.

4. Both principals demonstrate the value they place on teaching by the time they commit to it and in the ways they support their teachers. They clearly recognize teaching and learning as the main business of the school and have defined missions for their schools that are broader than the state-defined curriculum.

5. Though the state tests are not an exclusive focus, both schools had double-digit improvements in passing rates by students from 1998 to 1999 to 1999 to 2000 on the SOL assessments.

CONCLUSIONS

True instructional leadership has been an aspiration of principals for years, but the demands of the job have made it a difficult goal to realize. Time-consuming responsibilities have distorted the job such that "the management tasks become the main goal, and instructional improvement is worked in wherever there is time" (Drake & Roe, 1994, p. 187). In studies dating back 20 years, principals have expressed a preference for spending more time in the areas of program development, supervision, professional development, and planning, but analyses of daily activities have shown consistently that the time dedicated to these functions is limited (Duke, 1987; Lipham, 1981: National Association of Secondary School Principals, 2001). Unfortunately, "the reality of the principal as instructional leader continues to lag well behind the rhetoric" (Hallinger, 1992, p. 45).

In our interviews of Virginia high school principals, however, we found that they were heavily engaged in many areas of curriculum, instruction, and assessment. Working with department heads and teachers, they have made substantial modifications in the sequence and content of courses, realigned curriculum, visited classrooms, and analyzed test data to drive instructional improvements. Virginia's accountability initiative has introduced an external challenge for schools and educators that has pushed principals to work together and with teachers to reexamine existing curricula, find available resources, develop new materials, and redefine their role in terms of instruction. Principals are beginning to see instructional issues as central to their work as effective principals.

The pressure for greater accountability has precipitated a shift in the traditional priorities of principals. The avowed preferences of principals to engage in instructional functions are now in greater alignment with the externally validated expectations for increased student achievement. The existing complacency in Virginia was shaken by the dismal results of SOL testing in the early years. The schools that initially managed to achieve high passing rates were located in wealthy communities. The black-white achievement gap was substantial in many schools (see chapter 7 for further discussion). The public disclosure of test performance and the push for accreditation have created a sense of urgency that Kotter (1996) argues is necessary for change to occur. The external performance feedback offered by the SOL assessment results has jarred educators' sensibilities and demanded attention.

In addition to the substantial pressure that principals are feeling, some conditions in the educational community have changed in fundamental ways to support and reward an instructional focus in schools. With the reforms since 1995, there has been enhanced goal clarity about student achievement, technical assistance from the Virginia Department of Education for schools, additional funding to support remedial efforts in schools, policy changes at the state and local level to support instruction, and redefined role expectations for principals. A focus on student learning has become codified in the Interstate School Leaders Licensure Consortium (ISLLC) Standards that have been used to revise the licensure requirements for principals in Virginia and other states. Furthermore, the ability to enhance student learning is a required component of evaluation for Virginia teachers, principals, and superintendents. Principals now have a public mandate to make instruction their number one priority, and instructional leadership skills are beginning to be valued and respected as essential prerequisites for success in school leadership roles.

Of course, other more routine tasks and their associated time demands have not disappeared. Attempting to juggle managerial and instructional responsibilities has increased the strain and tension of the job for individual principals (Steinberg, 2000). Conditions in Virginia undoubtedly have created a sense of urgency and pressure to change, but the increasing stress reported by principals suggests that the counterbalancing support for change has not been commensurate with the demands. As described in the two principal profiles, some principals have garnered the necessary resources and employed distributed leadership models (Elmore, 1991) to inspire and engage whole schools in the instructional development process, but others are still struggling to change their traditional practices and gain support. Principals need assistance and guidance to acquire the skills and expertise necessary for true instructional leadership. Helping principals to deal with the managerial aspects of the job while shifting their focus to instruction has become a vital educational challenge (Pierce, 2000). Support for the primacy of instructional leadership must be commensurate with the pressure for accountability if schools are to meet heightened learning expectations for all students. Leadership in an age of accountability requires not only pressure to achieve high academic standards and systemic conditions to support an instructional focus but assistance for individual principals to orchestrate such an effort at the school level. Based on our interviews, we have a long way to go in balancing the pressure and support equation for principals.

NOTES

1. Only one school had not made the SOL a major focus of its staff development, and this school had achieved full accreditation.

2. During the same time period, gains in the percent passing for the 16 high schools in the study were 5 points in English, 2 points in history courses, and 5 points in science courses.

REFERENCES

Blase, J., & Blase, J. (1999). Principals' instructional leadership and teacher development: Teachers' perspectives. *Educational Administration Quarterly, 35*, 349 378.

Brookover, W. L., Beamer, L., Esthin, H., Hathaway, D., Lezotte, L., Miller, S., Passalacqua, J., & Tornetsky, L. (1982). *Creating effective schools*. Holmes Beach, FL: Learning Publications.

Cawelti, G. (Ed.). (1999). *Handbook of research on improving student achievement*. Arlington, VA: Educational Research Service.

Cotton, K. (2000). *The schooling practices that matter most*. Alexandria, VA: Association for Supervision and Curriculum Development.

Drake, T. L., & Roe, W. H. (1994). *The principalship,* 4th ed. New York: Macmillan College Publishing Company.

Duke, D. L. (1987). *School leadership and instructional improvement*. New York: Random House.

Edmonds, R. (1979). Effective schools for the urban poor. *Educational Leadership, 22*, 22–23.

Educational Research Service. (2000). *The principal, keystone of a high-achieving school: Attracting and keeping the leaders we need*. Arlington, VA: Author.

Elmore, R. (1999, September). *Leadership of large-scale improvement in American education*. Paper prepared for the Albert Shanker Institute.

Frederickson, J. R., & Edmonds, R. R. (1979). Identification of instructionally effective and ineffective schools. Paper presented at the annual meeting of the American Educational Research Association, San Francisco, California.

Guskey, T. R. (1988). Teacher efficacy, self-concept, and attitudes toward the implementation of instructional innovation. *Teaching and Teacher Education, 4*(1), 63–69.

Hallinger, P. (1984). *Principal instructional management rating scale.* New York: Leading Development Associates.

Hallinger, P. (1992). The evolving role of American principals: From managerial to instructional to transformational leaders. *Journal of Educational Administration, 30*(3), 35–48.

Hallinger, P., & Heck, R. H. (1998). Exploring the principal's contribution to school effectiveness: 1980–1995. *School Effectiveness and School Improvement, 9*(2), 157–1991.

Kotter, J. P. (1996). *Leading change.* Boston, MA: Harvard Business School Press.

Krug, S. E. (1992). Instructional leadership: A constructivist perspective. *Educational Administration Quarterly, 28*(3), 430–443.

Leithwood, K., & Jantzi, D. (1999, April). The effects of transformational leadership on organizational conditions and student engagement with school. Paper presented at the annual meeting of the American Educational Research Association, Montreal, Canada.

Lipham, J. M. (1981). *Effective principal, effective school.* Reston, VA: National Association of Secondary School Principals.

Murphy, J. (1992). *The landscape of leadership preparation: Reframing the education of school administrators.* Newbury Park, CA: Corwin Press.

National Association of Secondary School Principals. (2001). *Priorities and barriers in high school leadership: A survey of principals.* Reston, VA: Author.

National Policy Board for Educational Administration. (2002). *Instructions to implement standards for advanced programs in educational leadership for principals, superintendents, curriculum directors, and supervisors.* Arlington, VA: Author.

Olson, L. (2000). New thinking on what makes a leader. *Education Week, XIX*(18), 1, 14–15.

Pierce, M. (2000). Portrait of the 'super principal.' *Harvard Education Letter.* [Online]. Available: www.edletter.org/current/principal.shtml

Sheppard, B. (1996). Exploring the transformational nature of instructional leadership. *Alberta Journal of Education Research, 42*(4), 325–344.

Skrla, L., Scheurich, J. J., & Johnson, J. F. (2000). *Equity-driven achievement-focused school districts: A report on systemic school success in four Texas school districts serving diverse student populations.* Austin, TX: The Charles A. Dana Center, The University of Texas at Austin.

Smith, W. F., & Andrews, R. L. (1989). *Instructional leadership: How principals make a difference.* Alexandria, VA: Association for Supervision and Curriculum Development.

Spillane, J. P., Halverson, R., & Diamond, J. B. (2001). Investigating school leadership practice: A distributed perspective. *Educational Researcher, 30*(3), 23–28.

Steinberg, J. (2000, September 3). Nation's schools struggling to find enough principals. *New York Times*, pp. 1, 18.

Tirozzi, G. N. (2000). School reform's missing imperative. *Education Week, XIX*(25), 68, 44.

Chapter Five

A STUDY OF SUCCESSFUL TEACHERS PREPARING HIGH SCHOOL STUDENTS FOR THE STANDARDS OF LEARNING TESTS IN VIRGINIA

MARGARET GROGAN
AND
PAMELA B. ROLAND

BACKGROUND

This chapter reports on a study of nine high school teachers and their principals in Virginia's Region 5, located in the west-central part of the state. The Governor's Best Practice Center[1] (Center) in Region 5[2] commissioned the study in the school year 1999/2000 to try to find out what successful teachers and their principals were doing to prepare students to pass the Standards of Learning (SOL)[3] tests. Despite some gains in test scores over the 3-year administration of the tests, student passing rates were still very low. Only 6.6 percent of Virginia's schools met the criteria for full accreditation in 1999 (Virginia Department of Education, News Release, 10/25/00). Many educators and community members were concerned about how to increase test scores, particularly since the first group for whom these tests would determine graduation were to enter the ninth grade in Fall 2000. Administrators at the Center designed the study in the hope that researchers would be able to identify replicable classroom strategies that successful teachers were using and key principal responses that were supporting teachers' efforts. The research questions were: What are high school teachers whose students score above average on the SOL tests doing to prepare students for these tests? and What are their principals doing to facilitate the preparation of students to succeed on the SOL tests? The chapter is organized in five sections. This first section briefly explains the context for the study. The second section outlines the design and methodology of the study. The findings are reported in the third section, and the fourth section widens the aperture a little to discuss the findings in relation to some relevant literature. Finally, some implications for leadership in an age of accountability are discussed.

DESIGN AND METHODOLOGY

Center administrators approached high school principals in a variety of different high schools across the region. They sought schools with high numbers of students eligible for free and reduced lunch and schools with low numbers of such students. They also wanted to study urban, suburban, and rural schools. The region includes no cities with a population over 70,000, however. An attempt was also made to observe classrooms with diverse students. Few high schools in the study enrolled more than 5% to 10% minority students, but one of the schools in the study had a significant number of different ethnic groups and a strong ESL program. Principals chose the nine teachers based on their success rate. They were teachers who had achieved passing rates of 80% or better on at least the latest one or two administrations of the test. It was also required that teachers were teaching either students grouped heterogeneously or at least two groups of students of different ability levels. Three biology teachers, three algebra teachers, and three English teachers agreed to participate in this qualitative study. Seven high schools from five school districts were represented.

The two researchers together interviewed all nine teachers and all seven principals. Two of the principals had two teachers participating in the study. The interviews lasted from 60 to 70 minutes and all were taped and transcribed. In addition, both researchers observed all teachers in their classrooms for four periods each. The periods ranged from 45 minutes to 90 minutes. The English periods were all 45 minutes and the biology and algebra periods were all 90 minutes. In total, the researchers spent 45 hours in the classrooms. The choice of subjects was based on an attempt to understand what teachers were doing in end-of-course tests where students had experienced much difficulty (Algebra I), some difficulty (Biology), and little difficulty (English). As a rule, these three end-of-course tests are also typically taken at different high school grade levels: Algebra I in 9th grade, Biology in 10th grade, and English in 11th grade. Thus, researchers hoped to see a range of classroom experiences shaped by factors such as the maturity level of the students and the contrasting demands of different disciplines. The data were analyzed both within disciplines and across disciplines.

No attempt was made to seek a diverse teacher sample. Principals simply were asked for names without regard to age, gender or ethnicity. All but one of the recommended teachers agreed to participate in the study. One female biology teacher declined on the grounds that she did not wish to be singled out in this way. Several others commented on a similar fear in the interviews. In the end, eight of the nine teachers studied were female and all were Caucasian. Their ages ranged from mid-20s to early 50s, and their experience with teaching ranged from about 3 years to over 20. Interestingly, several of the teachers in the study had not been teaching school for their entire careers. A few had taught at the community-college level or college level and one had been a research scientist. Of those that had taught continuously, some had taken time off to raise families.

Similarly, no attempt was made to consider the age, gender, or ethnicity of the principals. They were approached as representatives of high schools with specific characteristics. Five of the principals were white males and two were white females. Their experience as principal in each school ranged from 2 years to 14 years. The average length of service as principal in each school was 6.7 years. Four of the seven principals had been principal in the same school when the SOL tests were first introduced in 1997. Of the three that were brought in to be principal after the first administration of the tests, two were experienced principals and one was a novice.

Qualitative methods were used in this study to capture the nature of teachers teaching in the classroom. Both observations of and interviews with the teachers were important in this regard. As researchers, we were able to discuss what we had seen in the classroom with the teachers. We were able to ask them why they did what they did. We were also able to confirm or disconfirm what teachers were telling us about themselves and their strategies by watching them teach on several different occasions. Our visits to classrooms were several days and sometimes weeks apart. We conducted semistructured interviews (Patton, 1990) with both principals and teachers (protocols are included as an appendix). We were in the field during one school year (1999/2000). Our first interviews and observations took place in late September and early October just as students were being introduced to the important concepts and procedures that they would need to know to be able to perform well on the multiple-choice end-of-course tests. We concluded our study in May, having been with students and their teachers for both last-minute reviews and posttest discussions.

Our analysis of the data was ongoing throughout the year. Using the "constant comparative method" (Strauss, 1987), we coded and recoded data. We reflected on initial categories in the light of new data in an iterative process that consistently interrogated findings. Data from observations and interviews were scrutinized and compared. Principal interviews were analyzed in light of what the teachers had reported and vice versa. We kept categories fluid as we discussed what we were finding on each occasion. Since both researchers were present at all interviews and observations, much of the data analysis emerged in debriefing sessions during travel to and from sites. Logs were kept and disagreements between researchers were recorded.

FINDINGS

This section is divided into two parts. The first part, Replicable Strategies and Approaches, deals with the first research question: What are high school teachers whose students score above average on the SOL tests doing to prepare students for these tests? The second part, Principal Support, addresses the second research question: What are their principals doing to facilitate the preparation of students to succeed on the SOL tests?

Replicable Strategies and Approaches

It became clear during the course of this study that teachers considered test preparation to be synonymous with teaching. In most of the classrooms, teachers had displayed the relevant SOL for every lesson. Because the SOL tests included higher order thinking tasks as well as factual ones, teachers explained that they were preparing students to pass the tests in every lesson. This did not translate into a constant drilling of students, however. Teachers were far more concerned with teaching concepts and procedures than with rote memorization tasks. Many of the teachers continued assessing students in a variety of different ways, including short answer tests, essay tests, laboratory reports, oral presentations, and project work. They also gave students practice with multiple-choice tests similar to the SOL tests. Teachers either created their own tests or used commercially available ones, although the publisher had not released past Virginia SOL tests to the public at that time.

We observed very few lessons where the teacher and students were not engaged in a discussion of SOL or SOL tests. While some of this was surely for the benefit of the researchers or passing administrators, some of the routines had obviously become ingrained. Teachers' lesson plans were organized around the SOL, and artifacts displayed in the rooms were closely associated with the SOL. Teachers were very knowledgeable both of the content of the SOL and of how they were to be assessed.

Very few differences were observed in the teaching strategies or specific methods of test preparation among the teachers studied. While it was true that we found fewer examples of discussion in the algebra classes than in the other classes, most of the teachers used a mix of direct instruction and small group activities. Algebra teachers tended to individualize instruction after whole-group direct instruction. Biology teachers used labs to illustrate material covered in lectures. Structured whole-group discussion was observed most often in English classes; although two of the biology teachers also invited discussion and comment frequently. We also saw few modifications of teaching strategies for students in lower ability classes. In one honors biology class, students were doing more demanding research work outside the classroom than their regular biology classmates. In a regular English class, the teacher created more notes on the chalkboard than she did for her honors class. Another regular English class was moving through the same literature at a slower pace than the honors class was. However, many of the classes we observed were heterogeneous with stronger students and weaker ones grouped together to work on the same challenging material. Because the preparation for the tests demanded coverage of the material, students in these classes were constantly encouraged to meet with the teacher on an individual

basis. We saw very little variability in class size. With the exception of one honors English class of 7, all the classes we observed had between 18 and 23 students.

All the teachers believed they were good at helping students pass these
tests. Preparing students for end-of-course tests was just "business as usual." One
English teacher commented that "actually I didn't do a whole lot. Don't tell my
friends about this. I really didn't, I really didn't change much" (TS, 3). Others
talked about changing their pacing, rearranging content matter, paying more
attention to what was being tested or giving different homework assignments.
"My homework assignments changed. Instead of repeating the technical writing
again, I pulled out our ecology homeworks. Like when we were doing photo-
synthesis, I said, 'Now do the energy pyramid, do the food chain'" (WP, 5). They
approached the task of preparation as a problem to solve for which they had lots
of data. In consultation with other department members, teachers reported pour-
ing over test results, scrutinizing Blueprints,[4] and making sure curricula were
aligned. "I know I try to emphasize the SOLs, I try to teach to the test, but that's
O.K. because what the SOLs apply to are things they need to know. That's fine.
We just needed to know . . . what those SOLs were" (KN, 17).

In summary, a profile of the successful teacher emerged (see Figure 5.1).
The profile includes: having deep knowledge of content and love of teaching;
maintaining good relationships with students; making themselves available to students for extra help; managing and organizing the classroom effectively; planning
carefully for instruction; demonstrating a wide range of instructional skills and
strategies; maintaining a professional stance and high expectations for all students; and maintaining professional pride in their own development as teachers.

Principal Support

Six of the seven principals in this study had a positive attitude toward the
SOL tests. Only one principal was adamantly against the tests.

> You know [the tests] have pitted one faculty member against another . . . and peo-
> ple are taking early retirement that might not have taken it . . . we got to watch out
> here, because not only are we losing some good people, . . . when young people
> hear the teachers they look up to and respect say, "Don't go into [teaching]," you
> know. That's killing us. It's terrible. It's terrible. (VG, 12)

All of the principals, however, regretted losing some of their teachers to
early retirement. The added stress and tension of preparing students for the tests
certainly seemed to take its toll on all the high school faculties we studied. Principals not only expressed fears for teachers but also fears that some of their students would eventually be penalized by the tests. The biggest concern was that
when students have to earn verified credits[5] to graduate, dropout rates could
increase. At present, there is no alternative diploma available for students who do
not get at least six verified credits. Many principals are concerned about students'

Figure 5.1. Profile of a Successful Teacher

TEACHER OBSERVATION THEMES

A. Content mastery and passion for teaching

All English 11, Algebra I, and Biology teachers . . .

1. demonstrated deep knowledge of content;
2. liked the subject matter they teach;
3. connected the material to student experiences and lives.

B. Relationship with students

All English 11, Algebra I, and Biology teachers . . .

1. used student names frequently throughout the lessons;
2. expressed interest in and concern about students passing the SOL tests;
3. established warm, friendly relationships with students, which included personal attention, laughter, humor;
4. highly valued student input.

C. Availability

All English 11, Algebra I, and Biology teachers . . .

1. created opportunities for additional and individual help for students outside of class time.

D. Classroom organization and management

All English 11, Algebra I, and Biology teachers . . .

1. maintained a good pace throughout the lesson;
2. established and used routines so students knew what to expect (opening of class warm-ups, work available for early completers, homework assignments, etc.);
3. minimized off-task behaviors and other distractions;
4. monitored student progress frequently by proximity.

E. Instructional Practice

All English 11, Algebra I, and Biology teachers . . .

1. paid particular attention to aligning lesson elements to SOL objectives and goals;
2. used SOL practice tests and materials regularly;

(continued on next page)

Figure 5.1 *(continued)*

3. maintained clear focus on daily objectives;
4. provided evidence of careful, thoughtful planning and preparation for each class;
5. adjusted teacher-made tests to simulate SOL format and structure;
6. designed and used age and level appropriate activities that engaged student interest and participation.

Algebra I teachers . . .

1. reduced the complexity of problem solving to a series of simple steps or procedures, which were used consistently in the lessons.

English 11 teachers . . .

1. integrated their approach to writing, language, and literature.

Biology teachers . . .

1. selected and used a text that is aligned with SOL curriculum;
2. made frequent use of labs to enrich the understanding of the curriculum.

F. Instructional skills and strategies

All English 11, Algebra I, and Biology teachers . . .

1. encouraged higher-level thinking skills
2. engaged students quickly at the beginning of class (warm-ups, quizzes, homework reviews, etc.);
3. created and provided additional study or review sheets, as needed;
4. used technical vocabulary and terminology to facilitate explanation and student understanding of content;
5. monitored student performance by questioning and observation;
6. varied activities within the class time;
7. made appropriate use of praise and feedback;
8. gave practice tests often and systematically.

Algebra 1 teachers . . .

1. devoted time regularly during class period to one-on-one instruction.

(continued on next page)

Figure 5.1 *(continued)*

Biology teachers . . .

1. used audiovisual materials appropriately to deepen understanding of content;
2. led focused discussion group with students on subject matter.

English 11 teachers . . .

1. used audiovisual materials appropriately to deepen understanding of content;
2. led focused discussion group with students on subject matter.

G. Professional Stance

1. All teachers demonstrated a professional manner and articulated their various teaching decisions and choices clearly and with a rationale that reflected their understanding of the teaching and learning process.
2. All teachers maintained high expectations for their students both academically and behaviorally while adjusting instructional practices based on the ability of the students.

INTERVIEW THEMES
(further insights gained or confirmed through teacher interviews)

1. Teachers demonstrated positive professional attitudes about fulfilling their duties even if they did not like the test or felt the Blueprints were not aligned with the tests. These teachers did not communicate their frustrations to students. It is notable that the Biology teachers expressed fewer concerns and frustration with the test and the practices associated with it.
2. Teachers reported engaging in collegial networks and activities (aligning the curriculum, developing a syllabus, sharing teaching material and tests with colleagues or department members) that strengthened their capacity to better prepare students for SOL tests.
3. Teachers availed themselves of opportunities to deepen their knowledge of content through professional development activities as well as through district provided staff development.
4. Teachers have internalized the desire to have students do well on the SOL tests. It has become a source of pride that motivates teachers to continue to improve their classroom practices.

ability to pass Algebra I; although, for several years, students must pass the English end-of-course tests but will be able to choose any four others in which to earn verified credits. Only after 2007 will students be required to pass two English end-of-course tests, two science tests, Algebra I, and one history or social studies test. All but one of the principals in this study took the position that there is time to align human and material resources in order to give students the best opportunity to pass the tests.

The principals reported going through stages of accepting the tests over the past 3 years. When the tests were first introduced, few educators took them seriously. Few of the students took them seriously. Most believed that they were a passing fad and that there would be political wrangling over the proposed sanctions for schools not meeting the benchmarks for some time. As with other reforms imposed externally, principals and teachers in schools felt no ownership of the movement. Principals reported having very limited information early on. Although the SOL had been in place for decades, because there were no standardized assessments, principals did not have a clear idea of what was expected to be taught.

Once the State decided to release test data by district and by building, most of the principals in this study realized the implications and began mobilizing teachers. Principals' motives for turning the SOL tests into a priority for their buildings varied. In some cases, there was the element of competing with other high schools in the district. Comments ranged from "We don't want to be the bottom of the pit" (SF, 15), to ". . . in reality what we want to be is the top school in [this] county. . . . I mean we have the top students in the county, there's no reason for us not to be the top county school" (LT, 18). In other cases, there was a sense of moral obligation. "As I tell my parents and as I tell my students, . . . being fully accredited still means that up to 30% of children will fail . . . that's not acceptable. . . . That's wrong. 70% isn't good enough" (CE, 15).

Themes emerging from the principal interviews are summarized in Figure 5.2. At the time these principals were interviewed, they were fully engaged in supporting teachers and students in the endeavor to pass the SOL tests. Even the principal whose attitude toward the tests was negative expressed most of the same sentiments as his fellow principals. Principals used their administrative skills and power to: ensure that the SOL tests were taken seriously; facilitate curriculum realignment and appropriate schedule changes; offer incentives for students to pass the tests; involve all teachers in the endeavor; draw on district and department leadership and resources; establish and maintain encouraging and caring relations with students; establish and maintain encouraging and caring relations with teachers; make appropriate personnel changes; provide instructional leadership; facilitate staff development; embrace the reform initiative; and ensure that their students were competitive with students in other schools and districts.

Figure 5.2. High School Principals' Responses to the Effects of the SOL Tests and Steps Taken to Prepare Students for Success

A. Going to lengths to ensure that the SOL tests were taken seriously.

1. Principals were sensitive to the impact of testing on students.
2. Principals used administrative skills to ensure that students and teachers could concentrate on the tests.
3. Principals eliminated distractions and created environments for students to do their best—for example, converting part of a school into a test center, rescheduling fruit sales from testing time to another time of the year.

B. Facilitating curriculum realignment, schedule changes, and choice of subjects.

1. Principals created more time for students to have access to the curriculum before they were tested, for example, Algebra, Part 1 and Part 2 were offered as separate courses. Geography was taken for the verified credit in Social Studies and two credits were given for Geography and History taught together. Instead of Chemistry, Environmental Science was offered as an extra science credit, and American History was team-taught with English in 11th grade also for two credits.
2. Principals provided focused time with teachers on curriculum issues.
3. Principals guided students to make good choices about what subjects to take.
4. Principals encouraged some 9th-grade students to delay testing until they had more experience with the material.
5. Principals created remedial teams in 9th grade to strengthen reading skills and content matter.

C. Offering incentives for passing SOL tests.

1. Most principals offered exam exemptions for passing SOL tests and one school offered the possibility for students to raise their semester grade one letter grade if they passed the SOL test.

D. Getting non-SOL teachers involved.

1. Principals' efforts to get all teachers involved with SOL tests ranged from informal conversations with the whole faculty to staff development days specifically designed to involve all teachers— for example, some schools circulated vocabulary lists and

(continued on next page)

Figure 5.2 *(continued)*

concepts for history to all teachers encouraging them to see where they might teach SOL material even in nontested courses; some paired departments to see how vocational areas could match core areas; some required all teachers, SOL and non-SOL, to submit curriculum maps to show how they were teaching the SOL.

2. Principals created a schoolwide community of concern for student success.

E. Acknowledging importance of and facilitating departmental and countywide collegiality.

1. Principals made departmental collegiality a high priority and facilitated meeting time for teachers to share ideas, information, and resources.
2. Principals fostered teacher communication about instructional issues and support at both building level and across the district.
3. Principals shared data with departments and held expectations that analysis of data would take place at a department level and by individual teachers.
4. Principals relied on department structures to make sense of the data and suggest appropriate changes.
5. By studying SOL test results, principals raised awareness within departments across county schools of essential articulation between middle school and high school.
6. Principals acknowledged central office leadership as indispensable to bring teachers together across the district for dissemination of resources, providing guidance and direction for good practice.
7. Principals acknowledged central office leadership as important in creating an instructional community, improving strategies and deepening the commitment to districtwide SOL success.
8. Some principals gained district support at the building level, funding additional personnel helping to implement the testing.

F. Caring about student success.

1. Principals had high expectations for student success.
2. Principals' goals were for 100% pass rates—70% was not good enough.
3. Principals cared about those students who were struggling and were prepared to build support systems to facilitate the process.

(continued on next page)

Figure 5.2 *(continued)*

4. Principals formed relationships with students creating a community of learners.
5. Principals had a deep sense of pride in student success.
6. Principals believed that success was possible, and believed that teachers would rise to the occasion and put in extra effort.

G. Caring about teachers and providing needed support.

1. Principals showed increased sensitivity to teachers' needs, listened to teachers' concerns about preparing students to take the SOL, and offered support and encouragement.
2. Principals were appreciative of the extra effort teachers were putting in, for example, cutting down on the number of preparations, offering opportunities for staff development.
3. Principals offered their own time to teachers for instructional guidance, going over lesson plans, offering suggestions for working with low achievers, particularly protecting and supporting first-year teachers.
4. Principals encouraged teacher leadership and ownership of school reforms targeted at success for all students, for example, encouraging teacher presentations at faculty meetings, teachers deciding on goals for the school improvement process.
5. Principals' attitudes generated teacher enthusiasm for success.

H. Making personnel changes/decisions.

1. Principals had frank discussions with teachers about SOL test results to help teachers analyze what their strengths and weaknesses were.
2. Principals removed unsuccessful teachers from courses with SOL tests, either accepting teachers' offers of retirement (reluctantly) or assigning them to teach courses without end-of-course tests.
3. Principals assigned better teachers to classes with weaker students.
4. Principals allowed teachers to team-teach, and allowed flexible scheduling to accommodate teachers' requests.
5. Some principals were successful in getting districts to fund an extra position or half-time position to help with remediation, test administration, or data analysis.

(continued on next page)

Figure 5.2 *(continued)*

I. Providing instructional leadership.

1. Principals focused on instructional leadership, going over details of curriculum alignment and pacing guides with teachers early in the semester.
2. Principals asked to see SOL objectives displayed in the classrooms.
3. Principals spent time in and out of classrooms frequently conversing with teachers about instructional issues.
4. Principals encouraged teachers to identify their own strengths and weaknesses and to work up a plan to address them.
5. Principals encouraged teachers to develop connections with students, to get to know them, and to comment on how they were doing in extracurricular activities.
6. Principals were aware that their most important service to teachers was to let them teach.

J. Providing staff development.

1. Principals facilitated staff development opportunities for teachers to become more proficient at preparing students for the SOL tests.
2. Principals disseminated information and communicated with central office about teacher needs for staff development.
3. Principals worked with teachers on testing and test preparation.
4. Principals found time for teachers to meet in departments for concentrated planning on SOL test preparation.

K. Finding meaning in the SOL, SOL tests.

1. Most principals expressed positive attitudes about the reform initiative.
2. Most saw SOL tests as challenges to work toward.
3. Most principals saw the responsibility to prepare students to pass the tests as a moral endeavor.
4. Principals saw the big picture and had patience that there would be growth over time, in teachers' capacity to help students and in students' capacity to be successful on the tests.

L. Perceiving competition between schools/districts.

1. Some principals were motivated to see improvement in test scores because of a competitive environment either within the district or between districts.

DISCUSSION

The purpose of the study was to find out what successful teachers and schools involved in the Virginia accountability plan were doing. The major limitation of the study is that we did not observe teachers whose students were failing. It is entirely possible that those teachers could have said the same and done the same things that the teachers in this study said and did. Such a prospect is unlikely, however, based on research both on embracing reform and on effective schools. One of the major findings of the study is that both the teachers and principals were thoroughly engaged in the reform. They were knowledgeable about the plan, accepting of the need to align curricula and teaching practices, and immersed in data. The teachers had a very good grasp of what they needed to do to be successful. Many of the themes we found in the teachers' work and in their stories resonate with instructional practices currently advocated in the literature.

For instance, in Cotton's (1999) synthesis of the effective schooling research, in almost every classroom category, as Cotton defines them, there is the same emphasis that we found in this study. Consistent with this study are such assertions as:

1.1.1. Teachers Emphasize the Importance of Learning [by] (d) Model[ing] enthusiasm for learning; [teachers] communicate through their words and actions that learning is fun. (p. 6)

and,

2.1.2. Teachers Make Efficient Use of Learning Time [by] (c) Set[ting] and maintain[ing] a brisk pace for instruction that remains consistent with thorough learning. [Teachers] introduce new objectives quickly, and provide clear start and stop cues to pace lessons according to specific time targets. (p. 21)

and,

4.1.3. Teachers Interact with Students in Positive, Caring Ways [by] (e) Shar[ing] anecdotes and incidents from their experience as appropriate to build rapport and understanding with students. (p. 46)

Over and over again, we saw teachers who demonstrated these competencies. The effective schools research emphasizes the high expectations for students that we found, the student incentives and rewards that we heard about, and the kinds of instructional support for high-needs students that were in place in most of the settings we studied. Therefore, the success the teachers were having can quite likely be attributed to their practices in the classroom, their disposition toward teaching, and their acceptance of the reform agenda. In addition, the effective schools research upholds the kind of instructional leadership we found among the principals in the study. Principals' attention to instructional improvement and professional development is highly valued (Cotton, pp. 36–39).

However, while there are also other assertions that fit with the findings of this study, the effective schools research includes some that we did not find. For example, with one exception in each case, we saw little emphasis on integration of curriculum or on activities to increase sensitivity to multicultural issues. And while we saw evidence of a variety of different assessments, clearly the focus was on making sure students had enough exposure to the kind of multiple choice items they would face on the SOL tests. Some teachers, however, did reserve more innovative assessment methods for the period after students had taken the end-of-course tests.

Unlike the kind of reform that requires a great deal of change in the way teachers teach and in the way they assess students, this reform reinforces the methods and teaching strategies with which teachers are most familiar. In studying the efforts of high schools to develop and implement authentic learning and assessment in line with the philosophy of the Coalition of Essential Schools, Prestine and McGreal (1997) make the point that "it is the level of change in classroom practices, the core technology of schools, that has consistently remained the most impervious to reform efforts" (p. 371). Teachers in this study had little difficulty adapting their classroom practices to fit the requirements of the SOL tests. By and large, we saw many examples of the "routine and comfortable, if dull and passive, pattern of the traditional secondary classroom" (p. 385). Students were more engaged than is sometimes the case because teachers and others in the school community took the end-of-course tests very seriously and communicated the need and desirability for students to pass the tests. Therefore, there were high expectations for increased student and teacher work responsibilities. We certainly detected an energy that saved the lessons from being completely "dull and passive." There were only limited opportunities, however, for students to construct their own learning (Brooks & Brooks, 1993). We did observe "hands-on" activities in laboratory sessions, of course, and also in one or two algebra lessons where students were learning about exponential equations. But the press of time to cover the material made teachers reluctant "to allow student responses to drive lessons, shift instructional strategies, and alter content" (p. 105). Fortunately, at least in English and biology, teachers encouraged class discussion, one of the strategies most likely to engage students with content to be learned (Yair, 2000).

One of the main criticisms of the SOL tests, as with many other state-mandated standardized tests, is that they rely on rote memorization and low-level thinking skills (McNeil, 2000). This can explain why teachers do not necessarily have to alter their fundamental classroom practices. In this study, though, we observed very few instances of "intensive test-practice drills, [to] 'raise scores'" (p. 732, quotation marks in the original). Good teachers have always gone beyond the basics and interested students in the ideas behind "the facts." And, some of the teachers in this study argued that the SOL tests do require higher level thinking skills. The Algebra I Test is certainly based on current NCTM standards, and the Biology End-of-Course Test, for instance, encourages students to interpret information, and to use data to make

predictions. As one of the teachers explained, "The Biology SOL test is about pro-
cessing [information] and very little of it is rote memorization. They give you a dia-
gram, can you interpret it? They give you data tables . . ." (WP, 3). Therefore, students who have had little or no exposure to at least the application of important
principles in each of the disciplines will not likely be successful.

There are certainly factors other than instructional practices contributing to
the success that these teachers and schools have enjoyed. The notion of local
capacity was developed some time ago to help understand the implementation of
educational reform (Elmore & Fuhrman, 1994; McLaughlin, 1987). Local capacity refers to the level of competence a school district develops to carry out reform
efforts. A district acquires competence by devoting human and material resources
to gathering knowledge and expertise about the reform. While the present study
did not focus on district efforts, per se, it was clear from all the interviews that
teachers and principals were not undertaking reform alone. There was strong evidence of crucial central office support. Dissemination of up-to-date information,
access to relevant curriculum materials and resource guides, participation in curriculum alignment activities and workshops, and offers of advice and encouragement from supervisors of curriculum were cited often as reasons teachers had
been successful. There was less emphasis in these districts on simply following
the rules and more on providing necessary resources for implementing the policy.
Most important, perhaps, is that the teachers we studied wanted their students to
be successful test takers. Spillane and Thompson (1997), argue that

> whether and what teachers learn depends on more than the availability of a rich
> learning environment within the district. Teachers' knowledge, beliefs, and experi-
> ences will also influence how and what they learn from the opportunities mobilized
> by district leaders. (p. 186)

This means that local capacity is created when district efforts are met by
teachers' engagement. What counts most is teachers' receptivity to reform. Not
all teachers in our study liked every aspect of the high-stakes testing, but all
acknowledged that students would suffer if they (the teachers) were not fully
informed and "on-board." Teachers were motivated to make the most of the
resources available to them. It is interesting to note that not all disciplines were
equally well supported by district personnel, a finding that leads us to suggest
that local capacity also depends on the beliefs and knowledge of individual
supervisors and department chairs.

To explain further the power of local capacity, Spillane and Thompson
(1997) use the concepts of human capital, social capital, and financial resources.
Human capital is the "commitment, disposition, and knowledge of the local
reformer" (p. 191) that is necessary to realize the reform. Teachers, principals,
and (according to anecdotes shared in our study) selected members of the central
office staff, demonstrated that drive. These educators took pride in contributing

to the success of their local school division. The external threat of sanctions imposed by the State Department of Education for schools that do not reach the desired benchmarks does not have the same motivating power.

We also detected the kind of social capital necessary to implement the policies. "Social capital concerns the relations among individuals in a group or organization" (Spillane & Thompson, quoting Coleman, 1988, p. 193). As a resource, social capital includes, on the one hand, the connections a school or school district has to external sources of knowledge. Most districts in this study drew on outside opportunities for teacher professional development in both instructional methods and content knowledge. Throughout Virginia, organizations such as universities and Best Practice Centers have been actively involved in the reform effort, providing relevant training for teachers and administrators. On the other hand, social capital also refers to the "norms and habits of trust and collaboration among local educators within the district" (p. 193). With few exceptions, departmental collaboration was much in evidence in this study. Teachers reported sharing materials, ideas, and new information with their departmental peers. Department chairs assumed leadership in sharing data and convening meetings to address departmental concerns. Departmental forces were responsible for changes in schoolwide scheduling, for example. A sense of camaraderie developed around the challenge of increasing aggregate test scores. Teachers felt they were part of a team rather than isolated. They also spoke of opportunities to discuss instructional issues with faculties from other schools in the district. Both principals and teachers cited evidence of more instructionally focused discussions both within and outside the building.

The time devoted to instruction leads to the third concept of local capacity: financial resources allocated to staffing, time, and materials. As noted at the outset of this chapter, what the principals in this study had most in common was the belief that the reform would require time to be implemented. Instead of expecting immediate results, they manifested patience and a long-range perspective. For some, this meant taking as many end-of-course tests out of the ninth grade as possible. For others, it meant forming ninth-grade teams, assigning groups of students to a cadre of teachers who would teach study skills and remedial reading as well as content. In some buildings, it also meant creating interdisciplinary courses such as American Studies, a combination of American History and English, that would give teachers more time to teach the required material in both end-of-course tests. Teachers were given opportunities to find ways to adapt their curricula to match the tests. Manipulating block schedules and cutting down on the number of preparations that teachers had to teach were other ways of using time effectively. Some districts also funded a full- or half-time position at the building level to help with test coordination and data analysis and to free up principals' time.

Students' chances of successfully passing SOL tests in high school appear to be greatly facilitated by teachers with the kind of knowledge and dispositions we encountered in this study. Their chances are also enhanced by the extent to which they are served by a district with enough local capacity to realize the reforms. Whether students are going to be better educated if they pass the SOL tests is not a question we addressed in this study. But it must be put on the table. The potential for many students to receive a better education exists. Anecdotes in this study reinforce the notion that, for many years, teachers taught what they wanted to teach. A principal told of a "biology teacher who taught a wonderful unit on birds" for most of the semester, neglecting the rest of the syllabus. She is no longer teaching. And we heard stories of teachers who never got past the Civil War in American History. Therefore, the worth of having a curriculum that is taught and tested statewide cannot be underestimated, especially if good teaching remains the goal.

Leadership throughout the organization certainly plays a role in ensuring that teachers' efforts are supported and enhanced under the accountability reform in Virginia. This study reinforces Duke's (1996) idea that the changing conditions signal a need for new approaches to leadership. Principals in this study marveled over how stimulating it was to spend time on instructional issues with teachers. Both teachers and principals spoke of the energy they derived from being mutually engaged in determining the best strategies for student success. What we found is the kind of leadership that "mobilizes the forces." But it was not necessarily top-down. Teachers took initiative and asserted themselves so that they were better prepared to do their jobs. They made known their needs and took advantage of opportunities to grow professionally. Ideas for more effective scheduling and student grouping emerged from department leaders. Central office administrators spent little time monitoring building compliance with directives, and much time providing appropriate resources to support teachers' and principals' hard work.

If we were to characterize this kind of leadership, it would certainly involve elements of the collaborative, distributed approaches found in the literature. But it retained a strong traditional focus as well. We interviewed principals whose strengths were developed during a different era—prior to high-stakes testing—when teachers closed their doors and the public knew little about student achievement. Principal leadership under those conditions was less concerned with the delivery of instruction and more concerned with maintaining order and efficiency. In the early stages of Virginia's accountability reform, the principals and teachers in this study were shifting to a new sense of what it would take to help students grow academically. They had not abandoned all of their previous beliefs and behaviors, but they had moved on and embraced new ways of doing things. Above all, the new levels of external and internal scrutiny of educators' work that the accountability reform has introduced have created a complex set of circumstances within which to teach and lead. Whatever will emerge as the reform matures, this study suggests, at the very least, that leadership in an age of accountability will be associated with instructional expertise and data-driven decision making. We hope that this combination proves as good for all Virginia students as it did for the students in Region V.

APPENDIX 5.1
A STUDY OF HIGH SCHOOL TEACHERS' PRINCIPALS' SOL TEST PREPARATION

SAMPLE INTERVIEW QUESTIONS

Teachers

1. How long have you been teaching this subject and level?
2. How many times have you prepared students for the SOL test in this subject?
3. How have you prepared your students for the SOL test?
4. What did you do the first time your students took the test?
5. How did you modify your strategies after you received the test results?
6. Have you made any other changes since then?
7. What support structures from the district or school have you received?
8. Have you received any professional development opportunities that have helped you?
9. Why do you think you are successful in helping more than 80% of your students to pass the test?
10. What else could we have asked you about SOL test preparation?

Principals

1. How long have you been principal at this school?
2. What were your impressions of the SOL tests preparation the first time you encountered it?
3. Why do you think some teachers are more successful than others in helping students pass the tests?
4. After the first set of test results came out, did you make any changes in the school to facilitate test preparation?
5. How have the faculty responded to the test preparation?
6. What have you done to support any requests they might have made?
7. What do the parents think of this school's test preparation?
8. Have you noticed any changes in the students' or teachers' attitudes over the course of administering the SOL tests?
9. What support do you receive from the district or state to facilitate test preparation?
10. What else could we have asked you about SOL test preparation?

NOTES

1. Virginia has eight Governor's Best Practice Centers spread throughout the state. The purpose of the centers, created in 1998, is to assist public schools in raising the levels of student achievement and meeting state accreditation standards.

2. There are eight Regions in Virginia. Region 5 has 21 school districts, including 34 high schools. Sixteen of the districts have only 1 high school and 5 of the districts have several high schools.

3. High-stakes tests developed by Harcourt Brace to assess the Virginia Standards of Learning since 1997.

4. A guide developed by the State Department of Education in consultation with the test manufacturer to inform teachers of how the SOL Standards will be assessed.

5. A verified credit is credit earned by passing the course in school and also the end-of-course test.

REFERENCES

Brooks, J., & Brooks, M. (1993). *The case for constructivist classrooms*. Alexandria, VA: ASCD.

Cotton, K. (1999). *Research you can use to improve results*. Alexandria, VA: Association for Supervision and Curriculum Development.

Duke, D. L. (1996). Perception, prescription, and the future of school leadership. In K. Leithwood et al., *International Handbook of Educational Leadership and Administration*. Dordrecht, the Netherlands: Kluwer.

Elmore, R., & Fuhrman, S (1994). Governing curriculum: Changing patterns in policy, politics, and practice. In R. Elmore & S. Fuhrman (Eds.), *The governance of curriculum: 1994 yearbook of the Association for Supervision and Curriculum Development*. Alexandria, VA: ASCD.

Loveless, T. (1998). Uneasy allies: The evolving relationship of school and state. *Educational Evaluations and Policy Analysis, 20*(1), 1–8.

McLaughlin, M. (1987). Learning from experience: Lessons from policy implementation. *Educational Evaluation and Policy Analysis, 9*(2), 171–178.

McNeil, L. (2000). Creating new inequalities, Contradictions of reform. *Phi Delta Kappan*, 729–734.

Patton, M. (1990). *Qualitative evaluation and research methods*. Newbury Park, CA: Sage.

Prestine, N., & McGreal, T. (1997). Fragile changes, sturdy lives: Implementing authentic assessment in schools. *Educational Administration Quarterly, 33*(3), 371–400.

Spillane, J., & Thompson, C. (1997). Reconstructing conceptions of local capacity: The local education agency's capacity for ambitious instructional reform. *Educational Evaluation and Policy Analysis, 19*(2), 185–203.

Strauss, A. (1987). *Qualitative analysis for social scientists*. Cambridge: Cambridge University Press.

Virginia Department of Education News Release (October, 2000). Available: http://141.104.22.210/VDOE/NewHome/pressreleases/oct2500.html.

Yair, G. (2000). Not just about time: Instructional practices and productive time in school. *Educational Administration Quarterly, 36*(4), 485–512.

Chapter Six

THE IMPACT OF VIRGINIA'S ACCOUNTABILITY PLAN ON HIGH SCHOOL ENGLISH DEPARTMENTS

DANIEL L. DUKE
DAN W. BUTIN
AND
AMY SOFKA

Efforts by states to promote educational accountability can be studied from various perspectives, including school division, individual school, class, teacher, and student. One vantage point that receives relatively little attention is that of the academic department and the department head. Few of the recent calls for educational reform have addressed the academic department or its possible role in school improvement (Siskin, 1991, p. 136). It is difficult to imagine significant reform of the high school, however, without attending to the nature and function of the academic department. Furthermore, department chairs are well positioned to play a key leadership role in the improvement of curriculum, instruction, and accountability.

The purpose of the study reported in this chapter was to determine how Virginia's accountability plan is affecting high school English departments. We also wanted to find out how English departments are responding to revised Standards of Learning (SOL) in English and new state tests for high school students in writing, reading, literature, and research. At the high school level, students are tested in world history (up to 1000 A.D. and post–1000 A.D.), U.S. History, Algebra I, geometry, Algebra II, earth science, biology, and chemistry, as well as English. The new state Standards of Accreditation (SOA) require that 70% of the students in each high school pass each state test in order for the school to be fully accredited. For Virginia as a whole in 1998, 71.13% of the students who took the first round of tests in high school English passed. Pass rates for the state in other disciplines were considerably lower—41.33% for mathematics, 62.83% for science, and 41.61% for history.

Data for the present study were collected in the spring of 1999, during which Virginia students took the new state tests for the second time. The mean pass rate on the English tests for Virginia's 291 high schools was 67.82%, with a median pass rate of 68.21% and a standard deviation of 11.53. These figures are reasonably close to those for the high schools that responded to our survey. Surveys were sent to all 291 high schools and received from 130, for a 45% response rate. The mean pass rate for the 130 responding high schools was 69.08%, with a median pass rate of 68.65% and a standard deviation of 10.66. We believe, therefore, that the high schools in our study are fairly representative, at least in terms of student performance in English, of high schools in Virginia.

The chapter begins with a description of the methodology used in conducting the study. This section is followed by descriptive data regarding English department chairs' views of the accountability plan's impact and their departments' responses to it. In the analysis section that follows, we investigate possible relationships between the responses of English departments and several independent variables, including school size and level of funding. The chapter concludes with a discussion of the implications of our findings for the reform of high schools and the study of accountability initiatives.

METHODOLOGY

The purpose of our study was to determine how high school English departments were being affected by and responding to a comprehensive set of state accountability initiatives. We decided that the individual best able to address these matters was the English department chair. Chairs are in a unique position to assess the impact of accountability measures on members of their departments and to exercise leadership in curriculum development, instructional improvement, and the analysis of student test results.

To facilitate data collection, we designed a four-part survey to be mailed to every high school English department chair in Virginia. The first part of the survey asked for general information on the high school and the number of full-time English teachers. Part II of the survey consisted of 31 Likert-scale items representing possible impacts of the accountability plan on teachers and students. Items were based on findings from the study in chapter 4 and a review of the literature on accountability initiatives. Part III called for chairs to indicate how their school and department was responding to the state accountability plan. A checklist with 47 possible responses, based again on findings from the study in chapter 4, was developed to facilitate data collection. The final section of the survey invited chairs to respond to three open-ended questions concerning their judgment of the single greatest impact of Virginia's accountability plan in general, the greatest impact of the plan on their department, and alternatives to state tests for raising student achievement in English.

After pilot-testing the survey with several English department chairs and fine-tuning certain items, a copy of the survey and a stamped, self-addressed envelope were sent to the English Department chair of every Virginia high school. A total of 291 surveys were mailed. Alternative schools and vocational-technical schools were excluded. As indicated earlier, 130 surveys were returned, for a response rate of 45%. While not as high as we had hoped, the profile of responding schools, in terms of performance on the state tests in English, resembled that for all public high schools.

The mean size for the 130 responding schools was 1,048 students, with a standard deviation of 649. The average English department consisted of 10.3 full-time English teachers, with a standard deviation of 6.1. The mean per pupil allocation for the 130 high schools, based on state data from 1999, was $5,969, with a standard deviation of $941.

The Likert-scale items are presented in Table 6.1 along with the means and standard deviations for each item. The plan for quantitative data analysis involved using SPSS to run Pearson correlations to determine whether any of the 31 items were correlated with the pass rate on the state English tests, drop-out rate, school size, number of full-time English teachers, and per pupil allocation. In addition, we planned to group responding high schools based on their pass rate and funding level and run ANOVAs. The four groups were as follows:

1.   High schools with high pass rates and high per-pupil allocation

2.   High schools with high pass rates and low per-pupil allocation

3.   High schools with low pass rates and high per-pupil allocation

4.   High schools with low pass rates and low per-pupil allocation

Responses to the three open-ended questions were content-analyzed for common characteristics, and these common characteristics then were condensed, based on emergent themes. Findings from these responses supplement the data from Sections II and III of the survey.

PERCEIVED IMPACT OF THE ACCOUNTABILITY PLAN

Table 6.1 contains descriptive statistics for the 31 Likert-scale items on the survey of English department chairs. These items represent perceptions of the impact of Virginia's accountability plan on high school English teachers, instruction in English, and students taking courses in English.

Items 1, 2, 3, 7, 9, 13, 14, 15, 25, 26, and 28 were considered to be examples of negative impacts. The data suggest that staff morale has not improved as a result of accountability measures and that stress levels have increased. This finding is supplemented by the fact that over half of the respondents mentioned in an open-ended question that increased stress levels were the biggest impact of the SOL on their departments. Many chairs wrote that pressure from their

Table 6.1. English Department Chairs' Perceptions
of Virginia's Accountability Plan*

	N	Mean	Std. Dev.
1. Staff morale in the English Department has improved.	129	4.1395	.8267
2. The stress level of teachers has increased.	129	1.5271	.8757
3. Teachers have retired early citing the state reforms as their reason.	127	3.2205	1.1947
4. Teachers are spending more time talking with each other about teaching.	130	2.6077	1.1446
5. English teachers are engaged in more collaborative planning.	130	2.9154	1.1414
6. Teachers spend instructional time on preparing students for state tests.	129	2.3411	1.1284
7. Teachers are afraid to try anything unrelated to the standards of learning in their classes.	130	2.5308	1.1825
8. Committee work for English Department faculty has increased.	129	1.9302	1.0246
9. Teachers must teach more students as a result of the lowering of class size in SOL courses.	126	3.2619	1.1878
10. The most capable teachers have been assigned to teach courses involving SOL tests.	129	3.3411	1.1004
11. Teachers have requested to be transferred out of grades or courses where SOL testing is done.	130	3.6308	1.0649
12. English class sizes have been reduced.	130	4.2000	.8573
13. Teachers must move too quickly through the curriculum in order to cover all of the SOLs before state tests.	130	1.9769	.9105
14. Course content covered after the state tests are given is not taken very seriously by teachers.	130	3.8385	1.0177
15. Teachers are less likely to allow students to leave class for legitimate reasons.	130	3.0692	1.0652
16. Teachers are spending more class time helping individual students.	130	3.1231	1.0040
17. Teachers make more of an effort to differentiate instruction in order to teach all students.	130	2.8308	.9972
18. Teachers stress conventional assessment, rather than performance assessment, in order to prepare students for SOL tests.	130	2.5308	.9976
19. Teachers are spending more time teaching writing.	129	2.6744	1.0168
20. Teachers are spending more time teaching American literature.	128	3.0547	.9664

(continued on next page)

Table 6.1. *(continued)*

	N	Mean	Std. Dev.
21. Teachers are spending more time teaching British literature.	130	3.5000	.9000
22. Teachers are spending more time teaching reading.	130	2.5154	.9337
23. Teachers are spending more time teaching oral language skills.	128	3.3984	.9828
24. Teachers are spending more time teaching research skills.	128	2.6953	.9603
25. Teachers of some advanced courses are afraid that overemphasis on SOL will cause students to be inadequately prepared for advanced work.	130	2.3462	1.1595
26. Teachers feel that they must spend too much time on factual knowledge and not enough time on reasoning, analysis, and higher order skills.	129	2.3101	1.2171
27. Students who are further behind in English are receiving more assistance and attention.	130	3.000	1.0997
28. Students who take longer to learn are having more trouble keeping pace with their classmates.	130	1.9769	.8578
29. Students who are close to passing English SOL tests receive more attention from teachers than students who are not close to passing SOL tests.	130	3.4231	.9714
30. Most students understand what a standard of learning means.	130	2.2538	1.0588
31. Some students are encouraged to delay taking the English SOL tests.	127	4.1890	.8885

* 1 = strongly agree, 5 = strongly disagree.

communities and administrators added to the stress level of teachers. One chair noted that "many [teachers] mention increased stress levels caused by negative media coverage, despite our students' excellent scores. Being held accountable for forces beyond their direct control also reduces the joy [of teaching]."

Opinion was divided across the 130 English departments regarding whether or not teachers were retiring in the face of statewide accountability pressures or were afraid to venture beyond the prescribed Standards of Learning in their instructional objectives. Department chairs in general did not believe that some teachers were forced to teach larger classes in order to lower class size in SOL courses. Teachers were perceived to be moving too quickly through the curriculum in order to cover all of the Standards of Learning before state tests were given, but department chairs were split over whether or not course content was being neglected by teachers after state tests were given. Teachers were not preventing students from leaving class for legitimate reasons in order to increase instructional time. There was some feeling that higher-level skills and content were not being covered adequately in order for teachers to focus more on covering the Standards of Learning. Teachers of advanced courses consequently were worried that students would come to them inadequately prepared. Department chairs felt that rushing to cover all of the Standards of Learning before state tests were given was adversely affecting the achievement of students who took longer to learn.

Items 4, 5, 6, 12, 16, 17, 27, and 30 represented positive consequences of the accountability plan. Department chairs were split regarding whether or not teachers were spending more time talking with each other about teaching and undertaking more collaborative planning. In their open-ended responses, several chairs noted that the standards had forced teachers to come together to make sure material was being sequentially and thoroughly covered. One wrote that the impact had been "teamwork among grade-level teachers; standardized exams; shift of emphasis from sports to academics; students seem more serious about education; teachers who spend too much time on a unit can no longer do so." Other chairs, however, mentioned increased competition. One stated that they saw "some indications of increased rivalry between teachers within a school and other schools because of the emphasis on publication of whose students were passing the SOL [tests]."

Chairs tended to feel that teachers were spending instructional time preparing students for state tests. Opinion was divided, though, concerning whether or not teachers were devoting more time to helping individual students, making more of an effort to differentiate instruction, and giving students who were furthest behind more assistance and attention. Department chairs tended to believe that most students understood what a standard of learning meant.

Items 8, 10, 11, 18, 19–24, and 31 were somewhat ambiguous, in that they could be interpreted as either negative or positive consequences of the accountability plan, depending on the circumstances. Department chairs believed in general that committee work had increased in their area. They were split concerning whether or not the most capable teachers were being assigned to teach courses that involved SOL tests and whether teachers were requesting to be transferred out of these courses. It was felt by many respondents that the accountability plan compelled teachers to emphasize conventional assessment rather than performance assessment. It is interesting that many chairs, in their open-ended responses, did not express hostility for the state initiatives. Rather, they agreed with the standards in theory, but not with the implementation of testing that was characterized as "unfair." Some chairs wrote statements such as: "Give teachers control of testing." One noted that "some students don't take the tests seriously and some students will never pass them."

As for content emphasis in English courses, there was a slight tendency to believe that teachers were spending more time on writing, reading comprehension, and research skills. Opinion was divided regarding whether or not American literature and oral language skills was receiving more emphasis. There was a slight tendency to believe that teachers were spending less time on British literature. Department chairs disagreed that some students were encouraged to delay taking the SOL tests in order to improve their chances of passing them.

RESPONSES TO THE ACCOUNTABILITY PLAN

Department chairs were asked to indicate what efforts were being made by their school and department to respond to the challenge of the state accountability plan. A list of 47 possible responses, based on data gathered in the study reported in chapter 4, were included on the survey. Table 6.2 presents the percentage of the 130 respondents who indicated that their school or department had adopted each of the responses.

The first eight items relate to the school schedule and calendar. While some English department chairs reported different adjustments to the daily schedule, no specific adjustment characterizes high schools' response to state accountability initiatives. It is worth noting, though, that over 23% of the respondents indicated that their high school had adopted some form of block schedule. Block schedules make it possible for teachers to work with students for longer periods of time each day and enable students to earn more credits in a year. It is also easier for students in a four-by-four block to repeat a course they have failed during the same school year. These benefits may be helpful in coping with the state accountability measures.

The next 10 items concern programs designed to provide students with additional help related to the Standards of Learning and state tests. More than half (53.1%) of the respondents indicated that their school had initiated after-school tutoring. Other frequently mentioned interventions included special programs to help students prepare for state tests (31.5%), voluntary summer school for students who failed one or more state tests (26.2%), after-school homework assistance programs (23.1%), tutoring in English during the regular school day (16.9%), and use of teacher planning periods to help students prepare for state tests (15.4%).

The next 11 items involve changes in instruction in English courses that have come about in response to the state accountability plan. In this area, it appears that adjustments have been widespread. More than four out of five chairs reported SOL-type tests and test items have been incorporated into class-based testing in English and that review sessions are scheduled prior to state tests. Other frequently mentioned interventions included sharing English standards with students (72.3%); instruction in test-taking skills (70%); reduction in enrichment activities to accommodate greater focus on state standards (68.5%);

Table 6.2. Percentage of English Department Chairs Reporting Specific Responses to Virginia's Accountability Plan (*N* = 130)

School/Departmental Response	%	School/Departmental Response	%
Adoption of block schedule	23.1	SOL for English shared with students at beginning of year	72.3
Increase in class periods	10.8		
Increased time for English/reading/language arts	6.2	Focal SOL objective written on board each day	36.9
Abandonment of block schedule	3.1	Increases use of direct instruction by teachers	59.2
Schedule adjustment so all students take English at same time each day	1.5	Reduction in enrichment activities to accommodate SOL instruction	68.5
Pairing of English courses with another course	6.2	Teachers' lesson plans must reflect SOL and pacing guides	77.7
Change in certain English courses from one to two semesters	10.8	SOL test results must be used in course planning and student assistance	35.4
Change to year-round schedule	1.5	Teachers must prioritize course objectives	58.5
After-school tutoring program	53.1		
Special test preparation for state tests	31.5	Teachers set targets for improvement in pass rates on state tests	75.4
After-school homework assistance program	23.1	Focus on K–12 curriculum alignment	46.9
Tutoring program in English during regular school day	16.9	Acquisition of new textbooks to match SOL	45.4
Homework assistance program during regular school day	9.2	Teachers involved in analysis of SOL test results	78.5
Saturday tutoring/homework assistance program	5.4	Districtwide planning for English curriculum	60.0
Use of teacher planning periods to assist students in preparing for state tests	15.4	Development of curriculum pacing guides	45.4
Voluntary summer school for students who fail state tests	26.2	SOL target pass rates and related interventions incorporated into school improvement plan	63.8
Required summer school for students who fail state tests	10.8	School committee created to monitor SOL test results in all subjects	26.2
Expanded summer school offerings in English	3.8	Grade-level teams monitor SOL test results and plan together	18.5
Reduction in field trips, assemblies, and other interruptions to instruction	66.2	Creation of grade-level teams to handle instruction for particular groups of students	9.2
Use of pretests based on SOL items	63.8	Creation of common planning periods for teachers of the same subject	6.2
Use of SOL-type tests and test items for in-class tests	82.3	Standardization of grading practices in English	21.5
Regular use of classroom games linked to SOL	20.8	Standardization of tests in English courses	15.4
Instruction in test-taking	70.0	Committee created to coordinate SOL-related staff development	32.3
Review sessions prior to state tests	80.8		
Use of information management system for tracking student progress on SOL	36.9	English faculty share teaching tips related to SOL	69.2

reduction in field trips; assemblies, and other instructional interruptions (66.2%); use of pretests to assess student knowledge of SOL (63.8%); increased use of direct instruction by English teachers (59.2%); use of information-management systems to track student progress on standards (36.9%); and use of a focal Standard of Learning each day in class (36.9%).

The last 18 items pertain to teacher planning, departmental and district coordination, and staff development. Again, there is the strong suggestion that English departments and high schools have been active. In 77.7% of the 130 schools, teachers' lesson plans were expected to reflect Standards of Learning and curriculum pacing guides. In almost as many schools (75.4%), teachers were expected to set targets for improving their students' pass rates on state tests. Teachers were also expected to use state test results in planning their courses and identifying students in need of special help (35.4%). Objectives for English courses had to be prioritized, with those objectives related to state standards given highest priority (58.5%).

Districtwide curriculum alignment was a matter of great importance for nearly half (46.9%) of the respondents, and 60% indicated that the English curriculum was planned on a districtwide basis. Curriculum pacing guides were mentioned by 45.4%, and a similar percentage noted that new textbooks reflecting state standards had been purchased.

To help teachers understand the relationship between their instruction and student achievement, teachers were involved in analyzing and interpreting state test results in 78.5% of the 130 high schools. Data related to student performance and interventions to help struggling students served as a focus for state-required school improvement plans in 63.8% of the high schools. Department chairs reported that teachers met to share tips on ways to improve the teaching of state standards in 69.2% of the high schools.

State accountability initiatives were perceived to be standardizing English instruction in some of the responding high schools. Grading practices were reported to be standardized in 21.5% of the English departments, and 15.4% of the chairs indicated that English teachers had adopted common tests for the same courses. Grade-level teams (9.2%) and common planning periods for English teachers (6.2%) were relatively infrequent responses.

Overall, the responses of department chairs suggest that the operation of English departments and their host high schools has been affected in various ways by Virginia's accountability plan. Instructional planning and practice as well as approaches to assessment and remediation have changed in many high schools.

INFLUENCES ON DEPARTMENT CHAIRS' PERCEPTIONS

The responses of the English department chairs to the 31 Likert-scale items concerning the impact of statewide accountability measures revealed a number of variations across Virginia high schools. We wondered whether these variations might be associated with certain characteristics of the high schools. The funding level, as determined by per-pupil allocation, for example, conceivably could influence perceptions of impact. High schools with access to greater resources might be more able to control the impact of accountability measures than less fortunate high schools. Another independent variable was the pass rate on the first administration of the SOL tests in English. High schools with higher pass rates might be less likely to experience a great impact than those with relatively large numbers of failing students. We also wondered whether perceived impact was related to the high school's drop-out rate, based on statistics submitted by the high school to the state. The drop-out rate, after all, could be regarded as a possible consequence of state accountability measures. Finally, we wondered whether the size of the high school, in terms of student enrollment, might make a difference in terms of perceived impact. Much has been written lately about the benefits of smaller high schools. Were department chairs in smaller high schools in our sample less likely to perceive negative impacts resulting from the state accountability plan?

Table 6.3 contains correlations for the four independent variables (funding, pass rate on English SOL tests, drop-out rate, and school size) and the 31 Likert-scale items. Pearson correlations were run using SPSS. While none of the relationships is particularly strong, a few merit consideration. Per-pupil spending is positively related to greater time spent on British literature. Since more affluent schools tended to have higher pass rates on the SOL tests, it is possible that English teachers in these schools felt they could devote more attention to non-American literature, even though it received less emphasis on state tests. The pass rate on SOL tests in English was positively related to the chair's perception that English teachers had to move too quickly through the curriculum in order to cover all the Standards of Learning before the state tests were given. While speeding through course content might make teachers feel they were overlooking valuable supplementary material, their commitment to covering, however briefly, material on which students were to be tested could help to explain higher test scores.

School size was the only independent variable characterized by relatively high correlations with more than one of the Likert-scale items. The larger the high school the more likely English department chairs were to report that (1) teachers spent instructional time preparing students for state tests, (2) teachers moved too quickly through the curriculum in order to cover all the standards before state tests were given, and (3) most students understood the meaning of a standard of learning. To interpret the meaning of these relationships, it is helpful to point out that the size of the high school was correlated to the pass rate on state SOL tests in English (Pearson $r = .393$). Many of Virginia's largest high schools are located in relatively well-to-do suburban areas.

Table 6.3. Pearson Correlations of Perceived Impact of SOL and State Tests and Selected High School Characteristics

	School Funding			Pass Rate in Eng.			Dropout Rate			School Size		
	Pearson	Sig. 2 tailed	N	Pearson	Sig. 2 tailed	N	Pearson	Sig. 2 tailed	N	Pearson	Sig. 2 tailed	N
Teachers have retired early citing state reforms as their reason.	.171	.054	127	.100	.265	127	-.009	.922	127	-.017	.848	127
Teachers spend more time talking with each other about teaching.	.021	.814	130	.158	.072	130	-.046	.604	130	.120	.174	130
English teachers are engaged in more collaborative planning.	-.101	.254	130	.133	.130	130	-.098	.269	130	.032	.717	130
Teachers spend instructional time on preparing students for state tests.	.148	.094	129	.225*	.010	129	-.169	.055	129	.325**	.000	129
Teachers are afraid to try anything unrelated to SOLs in their classes.	.031	.723	130	.105	.233	130	-.139	.114	130	.188*	.032	130
Committee work for English Dept. faculty has increased.	.053	.551	129	.152	.086	120	-.133	.133	129	.130	.142	129
Teachers must teach more students as result of lowering class size in SOL courses.	-.107	.235	126	-.047	.601	126	.083	.358	126	-.096	.284	126

(continued on next page)

Table 6.3 (continued)

	School Funding			Pass Rate in Eng.			Dropout Rate			School Size		
	Pearson	Sig. 2 tailed	N	Pearson	Sig. 2 tailed	N	Pearson	Sig. 2 tailed	N	Pearson	Sig. 2 tailed	N
Most capable teachers have been assigned to teach courses in which students must take SOL.	.139	.115	129	.036	.687	129	−.031	.724	129	−.093	.293	129
Teachers requested to be transferred out of grades or courses where SOL testing is done.	.068	.444	130	.124	.160	130	−.160	.069	130	−.107	.226	130
English class sizes have been reduced.	.020	.817	130	.085	.334	130	.002	.982	130	−.031	.730	130
Teachers must move too quickly through curriculum to cover all SOLs before state tests.	.175*	.047	130	.340**	.000	130	−.185*	.035	130	.382**	.000	130
Course content covered after state tests are given is not taken seriously by teachers.	.035	.693	130	.050	.570	130	.051	.565	130	−.021	.811	130
Teachers are less likely to allow students to leave class for legitimate reasons.	.040	.652	130	.145	.100	130	.005	.956	130	.114	.195	130

(continued on next page)

Table 6.3 (continued)

	School Funding			Pass Rate in Eng.			Dropout Rate			School Size		
	Pearson	Sig. 2 tailed	N	Pearson	Sig. 2 tailed	N	Pearson	Sig. 2 tailed	N	Pearson	Sig. 2 tailed	N
Teachers spend more class time helping individual students.	-.952	.559	130	.167	.058	130	-.104	.240	130	-.092	.296	130
Teachers make more effort to differentiate instruction to reach all students.	-.180*	.041	130	.058	.514	130	-.128	.147	130	-.033	.708	130
Teachers stress conventional assessment rather than performance assessment to prepare students for SOL tests.	-.045	.612	130	.060	.497	130	.104	.238	130	.038	.669	130
Teachers spend more time teaching writing.	.173*	.050	129	.169	.055	129	-.058	.510	129	.034	.699	120
Teachers spend more time teaching American literature.	.031	.731	128	.190*	.032	128	-.201*	.023	128	-.037	.681	128
Teachers spend more time teaching British literature.	.248**	.004	130	.153	.081	130	-.006	.950	130	.052	.554	130
Teachers spend more time teaching reading comprehension.	-.020	.824	130	.027	.758	130	.104	.238	130	.074	.401	130

(continued on next page)

Table 6.3 (continued)

	School Funding			Pass Rate in Eng.			Dropout Rate			School Size		
	Pearson	Sig. 2 tailed	N	Pearson	Sig. 2 tailed	N	Pearson	Sig. 2 tailed	N	Pearson	Sig. 2 tailed	N
Teachers spend more time teaching oral language skills.	−.003	.969	128	−.027	.760	128	.072	.416	128	.003	.974	128
Teachers spend more time teaching research skills.	−.148	.095	128	.034	.703	128	−.095	.284	128	.021	.814	128
Teachers of some advanced courses are afraid overemphasis on SOLs will cause students to be inadequately prepared for advanced work.	−.098	.267	130	.094	.285	130	−.093	.293	130	.168	.057	130
Teachers feel they must spend too much time on factual knowledge and not enough time on reasoning, analysis, and higher-order skills.	−.043	.625	129	.117	.186	129	−.089	.317	129	.125	.157	129
Students further behind in English receive more assistance and attention.	−.054	.541	130	−.005	.958	130	−.126	.153	130	.058	.510	130

(continued on next page)

Table 6.3 (continued)

	School Funding			Pass Rate in Eng.			Dropout Rate			School Size		
	Pearson	Sig. 2 tailed	N	Pearson	Sig. 2 tailed	N	Pearson	Sig. 2 tailed	N	Pearson	Sig. 2 tailed	N
Students who take longer to learn are having more trouble keeping pace with classmates.	.038	.670	130	.132	.133	130	.002	.979	130	.186*	.034	130
Students close to passing English SOL tests receive more attention from teachers than students not close to passing SOL tests.	−.065	.460	130	.115	.193	130	.004	.966	130	−.002	.980	130
Most students understand what SOL means.	−.010	.907	130	.192*	.028	130	−.207*	.018	130	.336**	.000	130
Some students are encouraged to delay taking English SOL tests.	−.008	.931	127	.210*	.018	127	−.074	.406	127	.131	.143	127

Levels of significance: * = .05. ** = .01.

RESOURCES AND RESPONSES

One of the big policy questions that arises during the course of accountability initiatives is whether a school's capacity for responding to such measures
is tied to available resources. The correlational analysis of perceptions of impact
in the preceding section did not suggest that per-pupil expenditures were highly
related to perceived impact of Virginia's accountability plan. What about the
information on high school responses to the plan? We decided to divide our sample into two groups, high schools that spent less than $6,000 on each student
($N = 94$) and high schools that spent more than $6,000 on each student ($N = 36$).
Frequency counts and percentages were calculated for each of the 45 possible
responses listed on the survey.

Table 6.4 presents data concerning high school responses for the two
groups. Overall, lower-spending high schools averaged 16.5 responses (out of 45
possible responses), as compared to an average of 14.9 responses for higher-
spending high schools. When individual responses were examined, a number of
differences were identified.

If we look only at responses to the state accountability plan that were
reported for at least half of the high schools in either, or both, groups, we find that
lower-spending schools were more likely to have adopted the following responses:

9.   After-school tutoring program

19. Reduction in field trips, assembles, and other interruptions to
     instruction

20. Use of pretests based on SOL items

21. Use of SOL-type tests and test items throughout year

23. Instruction in test-taking skills

26. SOL shared with students at beginning of course

28. Increased direct instruction

29. Reduction in or elimination of enrichment activities

30. Require that lesson plans reflect SOL and pacing guides

32. Require that teachers prioritize course objectives

33. Require that teachers set goals for improvements in SOL test
     scores

34. K–12 curriculum alignment based on SOL

36. Faculty analyzes SOL test results

Table 6.4. Responses to State Accountability Plan and Per-Pupil Spending

Responses to Accountability Plan	High Schools Spending Less than $6,000 (N = 94)		High Schools Spending More than $6,000 (N = 36)	
	No.	%	No.	%
1. Adopted block schedule	25	27	5	14
2. Increased periods in day	13	14	1	3
3. Increased time for English	7	8	1	3
4. Abandoned 4-x-4 block schedule	2	2	2	6
5. All students take English at same time	1	1	1	3
6. Pairing of English with another course(s)	8	9	0	0
7. Change of certain English courses from 1 to 2 semesters	11	12	3	8
8. Adopted year-round schedule	1	1	1	3
9. After-school tutoring program	52	55	17	47
10. Special preparation sessions for SOL tests	31	33	10	28
11. After-school homework assistance program	18	19	12	33
12. English tutoring program during school hours	16	17	6	17
13. Homework assistance program during school hours	9	10	3	8
14. Saturday tutoring/homework assistance	4	4	3	8
15. Use of planning periods to provide SOL help	14	15	6	17
16. Voluntary summer school for students who fail SOL tests	22	23	12	33
17. Required summer school for students who fail SOL tests	11	12	3	8
18. Expanded summer school offerings in English	5	5	0	0
19. Reduction in field trips, assemblies, and other interruptions to instruction	67	71	19	53
20. Use of pretests based on SOL items	62	66	21	58
21. Use of SOL-type tests and test items throughout year	83	88	24	67
22. Use of games to review SOL items	20	21	7	19
23. Instruction in test-taking skills	67	71	24	67
24. Review sessions prior to SOL tests	75	80	30	83
25. Information management system for tracking student progress on SOL	31	33	17	47
26. Reduction in or elimination of enrichment activities	68	72	21	58

(continued on next page)

Table 6.4. *(continued)*

Responses to Accountability Plan	High Schools Spending Less than $6,000 ($N = 94$)		High Schools Spending More than $6,000 ($N = 36$)	
	No.	%	No.	%
27. Lesson plans must reflect SOL and pacing guides	79	84	22	61
28. SOL scores must be used in course planning	32	34	14	39
29. Teachers must prioritize course objectives	58	62	18	50
30. Teachers set goals for improvements in SOL test scores	72	77	26	72
31. K–12 curriculum alignment based on SOL	47	50	14	39
32. New textbooks based on SOL	44	47	15	42
33. Faculty analyzes SOL test results	75	80	27	75
34. Districtwide planning for English curriculum	55	59	23	64
35. Pacing guides developed	44	47	15	42
36. SOL targets and interventions incorporated into school improvement plan	60	64	23	64
37. School committee created to monitor SOL scores	22	23	12	33
38. Grade-level teams created to monitor SOL scores and plan together	17	18	7	19
39. Grade-level teaching teams created	7	8	5	14
40. Common planning periods for same-subject teachers	7	8	1	3
41. Standardization of grading practice in English	19	20	9	25
42. Standardization of teacher-made tests in English	15	16	5	14
TOTALS	1555		535	
Mean Responses per School	16.5		14.9	

Responses that were more likely to characterize higher-spending high schools, and that were mentioned for at least half of the 36 higher-spending schools, included the following:

24.   Review sessions prior to SOL tests

37.   Districtwide planning for English curriculum

Since lower-spending high schools were somewhat more likely to have lower pass rates on the SOL tests in English (Pearson $r = .22$), it is understandable that they would be characterized by a higher average number of responses. A review of the most frequently mentioned responses for lower-spending high schools further reveals that most of the items represent low-cost interventions and strategies. Responses that are likely to represent a substantial investment, such as summer school and Saturday programs, were mentioned infrequently by lower-spending high schools.

CONCLUSION

This chapter presents a study of the views of English department chairs regarding Virginia's accountability plan. Conducted during the second year of the plan, the study involved responses from 130 chairs, representing 45% of the high schools in the state. Department chairs, though rarely queried in policy implementation research, constitute an important link in the high school leadership chain.

What was learned from English department chairs that might help policy makers understand the process of implementing a statewide accountability initiative?

First, chairs provided a balanced assessment of the impact of curriculum standards and statewide testing. They noted both costs and benefits. Concerns included fears (1) that teachers felt compelled to move quickly through the curriculum, regardless of whether or not all students were understanding the material, and (2) that higher-order thinking was taking a backseat to the memorization of facts. Teachers of advanced subjects worried that overemphasis on "the basics" might harm brighter students when they enrolled in upper-level honors courses.

On the positive side, chairs recognized that teachers were spending more time discussing curriculum matters and coordinating content coverage. Teachers were reported to be taking the state tests seriously and devoting considerable time to preparing their students for the tests.

Second, the study revealed considerable variation across schools in terms of perceptions of the impact of state initiatives and school-based responses to the initiatives. While some chairs believed the impact of the accountability plan had been slight, others indicated that teachers and students had been greatly affected. Impacts ranged from changing the school schedule and creating special summer programs to standardizing lessons and assessment practices. While some responses were more popular than others, no responses characterized all of the schools in the study. It will be important in the future for researchers to investigate why particular responses to the accountability plan were chosen and how well they are working.

Third, the variations in responses to the accountability plan for the most part were unrelated to school funding, the pass rate on English SOL tests, school drop-out rate, and school enrollment. This finding came as a surprise. We had anticipated that high schools with fewer resources, fewer students passing state tests, more dropouts, and larger enrollments would implement different programs, practices, and policies than other high schools. Perhaps these differences will emerge over time. Data for the present study were collected in the second year of the accountability plan.

A concluding reflection concerns the role of department chair. While the purpose of the present study was not to investigate this role, we could not help but wonder whether the state's accountability plan would lead to changes in the responsibilities of chairs. Given the attention to curriculum prompted by the Standards of Learning, the advent of state tests tied to the SOL, and publication of test results on a school-by-school and subject-by-subject basis, we would imagine that department chairs, at least in subject matter areas where state tests are given, would become increasingly important members of the high school leadership team. Department chairs would seem to be in an ideal position to supervise curriculum alignment, review student performance on state tests, evaluate how teachers are covering the Standards of Learning, and implement improvement plans. They also might be expected to exercise leadership in arranging for remedial instruction, tutoring, and staff development related to the Standards of Learning. Access to state test results also might mean that department chairs, like principals, will increasingly be subject to outcomes-based evaluation of their performance.

REFERENCE

Siskin, L. S. (1991). "Departments as different worlds: Subject subcultures in secondary schools." *Educational Administration Quarterly, 27*(2), 134–160.

Chapter Seven

HOW SUPERINTENDENTS IN VIRGINIA DEAL WITH ISSUES SURROUNDING THE BLACK-WHITE TEST-SCORE GAP

MARGARET GROGAN

AND

WHITNEY H. SHERMAN

Demands for school improvement including the current emphasis on standards have redefined the role of educators nationwide. While reform must be dealt with by teachers, administrators, parents, and community members alike, the role of the superintendent is most critical. Although superintendents are constrained by board policy, they hold powerful positions in our educational systems. Current expectations for superintendents include advising the board, managing resources, and communicating to the public (Carter & Cunningham, 1997). However, as the pressure to measure accountability through standardized testing increases, superintendents are expected to demonstrate competency as instructional leaders as well (Ashbaugh, 2000). More than ever before, superintendents are expected to be aware of student achievement as measured by standardized tests. In line with the American Association of School Administrators' (AASA) standards, Virginia's recent superintendent evaluation criteria and performance indicators state that a superintendent "monitors and assesses the effect of the programs and/or curricula on student achievement" (*Guidelines for Uniform Performance Standards*, p. 41). Thus, the superintendent must be concerned with test scores as well as other indicators of student achievement. Over the past 3 years, reform efforts in Virginia have begun to include high-stakes tests, which have provided school districts with rich sources of data.

The purpose of this paper is to report on a qualitative study of Virginia superintendents that was conducted to find out what their perspectives were on the black-white test score gap[1] that has become evident in the wake of the recent Standards of Learning (SOL) testing. The study was prompted by a growing nationwide awareness that not all students were performing equally well on standardized tests. We targeted superintendents for this study because of the potential power superintendents have in their districts to make changes.

"Superintendents must be in a position to distribute power and influence in such a way that it supports the capacity to continuously improve schools" (Carter & Cunningham, 1997, p. 16). The quality of the superintendency, many times, is reflected in the quality of the schools in the district. Therefore, superintendents must be dedicated to the continuous improvement of all schools and diverse populations of students in their districts. Superintendents, as instructional leaders, must also be attuned to test-score data and discrepancies that may exist between various racial groups if they want to be sure that all students have a chance of reaching their potential.

According to a 1996 Horace Mann League report, superintendents believe one of the top 10 destructive factors in education is the lack of attention to social issues such as the imbalance of wealth and intolerance of difference (Carter & Cunningham, 1997). Issues of race and ethnicity coupled with increasing poverty today create the urgent need for systemic reform. Rizvi (1993) argues that education systems "not only reproduce inequality [they] also *generate* it" (p. 205) (italics in the original). Superintendents must understand the environments of their schools and respond to them with a critical awareness. Inconsistent quality for individual schools or for groups of students is unacceptable and contributes to test-score gaps. According to Wills & Peterson (1995), the interpretive schemata of superintendents affect their reform efforts. If superintendents fail to perceive and identify differences in the academic achievement between diverse populations of students as a problem in their school districts, their responses to calls for reform will not include strategies to meet the needs of students from various racial and cultural backgrounds. Superintendent-approved plans of action must reflect determination and creativity to achieve equitable outcomes for all populations of students. To date, there is little evidence that inequities across the country have been eliminated.

THE BLACK-WHITE TEST-SCORE GAP NATIONWIDE

According to results released by the Department of Education, the achievement gap between black and white students that had narrowed in the 1980s widened from 1990 to 1999 ("Racial gap," 2000). The same report indicated that the average black 17-year-old can read only as well as the average white 13-year-old. In fact, "African Americans currently score lower than European Americans on vocabulary, reading, and mathematics tests, as well as on tests that claim to measure scholastic aptitude and intelligence" (Jencks & Phillips, 1998, p. 1). The gap exists before kindergarten and continues into adulthood. While black students are struggling to catch up on basic skills, white students are soaring past them, thanks in part to higher expectations and more advanced work assignments. The gap continues to increase the longer students remain in school. White students are more likely to populate honors and gifted classes, while black students are found more often in special education classrooms and are more likely to be suspended from school (Lipman, 1998; Zernike, 2000).

Although low achievement among black children was once attributed to the effects of poverty and disadvantage and considered to be an urban problem, current data show that the low achievement of black students exists across socioeconomic groups, making it a suburban problem as well ("Racial gap," 2000; Zernike, 2000). Children from wealthy black families do not perform as well as children from wealthy white families. In many instances, wealthy black children perform only as well as children from poverty-stricken white families (Zernike, 2001).

The black-white test-score gap has been researched since World War I when the U.S. Army conducted the first mental testing program in 1917 (Jencks & Phillips, 1998). While many biological determinists have utilized the test-score gap data to support the notion that whites are genetically superior to blacks, many social scientists are convinced that this is not the case. These scientists define race as a social category rather than a biological category.

According to Jencks and Phillips (1998), the debate between genetic and social explanations of the black-white test-score gap remains unresolved. While genetic explanations for the test-score gap have been discounted by social scientists, the acceptance of a simple cultural explanation as the sole contributing factor to the gap has been discounted as well. Scientists are finding explanations of the black-white test-score gap to be more complicated than once believed. Studies have shown that the test-score gap exists between black and white children despite instances of the same schooling, income, and wealth. Teachers in schools with a majority of African-American students typically have lower test scores than teachers in schools with a majority of European American students. For this reason, some question the quality of teachers in minority schools. Studies have also shown that most teachers tend to have lower expectations for black students and that black students themselves resist peer pressure to raise their own expectations. Moreover, because demographic trends in the United States show increasing diversity (Ward, 1993), the gap is likely to widen if left unaddressed.

In her study of the restructuring of two schools, Lipman (1998) discovered that teachers explain the low achievement of African-American students in one of four ways. The most commonly held belief is the deficit model, which attributes low achievement to the social and economic conditions of families as well as parents' disregard for education. Second, the social relations model attributes the low achievement of African-American students to the absence of support from educators in the form of mentoring relationships. Third, the critique of racism emphasizes the role of racial inequality, racism, and powerlessness in the alienation of African-American students. Fourth, the educational critique of low achievement emphasizes curriculum, instruction, and school policies.

While a superintendent alone cannot restructure a school system to make it more equitable for all children, he or she can reinforce the importance of all students achieving success and set the tone for change. The literature reveals that it is a problem that touches all educators—teachers and administrators; however, superintendents must lead school districts in creating shared visions that nurture students of all races and socioeconomic levels. Do superintendents make it a priority to create plans of action that will eliminate the achievement gap?

METHODOLOGY

We designed an exploratory study of superintendents in Virginia to examine their perspectives on the black-white test-score gap. The two research questions were: If there is a black-white test-score gap in SOL test scores in the district, what does the superintendent think about it? What, if anything, is the superintendent doing about it? In this investigation, 15 current superintendents, 7 males and 8 females, were interviewed in individual sessions of 60 to 90 minutes. Participants were chosen purposively based on the desire to sample superintendents from rural, urban, and suburban districts representing a cross-section of the state. The majority of participants were selected from districts where at least 30 percent of the student body was African-American. While women superintendents represented mainly rural districts or districts they described as rural/suburban, men superintendents represented rural, urban, and suburban districts. All superintendents were informed of the purpose of the study. Participation was voluntary.

All interviews were conducted with the use of a standardized, open-ended interview guide (Patton 1980). The guide was developed to ensure that all respondents addressed the same issues. Open-ended questions were used to allow respondents the freedom to speak in their own voices and to elaborate on their perceptions of the black-white test-score gap in their districts. Notes were taken during each interview session and all interviews were audiotaped and transcribed. To cross-check the accuracy of superintendents' statements (LeCompte & Preissle 1993), triangulation was achieved by the analysis of district documents including reports of disaggregated test scores over a 3-year period, strategic plans, and other plans or policies pertaining to the reduction of the test-score gap.

THEORETICAL FRAMEWORK

Data analysis was informed by the new politics of race and gender (Marshall, 1993). This approach draws attention to the failure of the various liberal agendas for school reform put forward during much of the twentieth century. There is evidence that equity values were subordinated to excellence and quality values over this period. Marshall argues that conventional liberal solutions to various inequities, including school desegregation, affirmative action, federal entitlements for the poor, Title IX, bilingual and multicultural education have lost support and impetus (p. 2). There has been little critical inquiry into who is being best served by policies and practices. The new politics of race and gender considers that administrative work undertaken especially by superintendents with the positional power to make change to be socially and culturally formed (Rizvi, 1993, p. 214). That is to say, administrators devote energy to solving problems they consider worthy of their time and resources. But administrators define problems according to their own social and cultural perspectives. For too long policies and practices that reflect administrators' perspectives have been considered neutral with regard to race and gender. This new conceptualization has helped us to consider how administration is related to the structural conditions shaping schooling in each district.

FINDINGS

Though superintendents represented a broad range of districts, the majority placed great emphasis on the regional and historical influences permeating any discussion of schools and schooling. While most of the communities were poor and had low tax bases and relatively high unemployment rates, especially among the African-American population, one community was among the wealthiest in Virginia and four were described as representing a fair percentage of all income levels. Three of the superintendents spoke of low literacy rates among adults in the community, but 1 spoke of having a highly educated population of community members, and 5 spoke of having a large portion of well-educated members in the community. Three of the communities were undergoing a shift in population from majority black to majority white. Superintendents reported that the student populations of 7 of the 15 districts included 50% or more African-American students and the populations of an additional 3 districts consisted of at least 40% minority students. Representing central, south central, southwestern, and northern areas of the Commonwealth, district sizes ranged from small to medium to large. Student populations ranged from 970 to over 50,000. At the time of the interviews, superintendents' tenure in their current district ranged from one year to eight years. There were 11 Caucasian superintendents in the sample and 4 African-American superintendents. Eight superintendents were women and 7 were men.

Findings can be grouped under the following headings: (1) geographical and community context, (2) SOL testing context, (3) working with the board, (4) the risks of going public, and (5) action.

GEOGRAPHICAL AND COMMUNITY CONTEXT

Test-score data in all districts revealed a persistent gap over 3 years of recent SOL testing. The average gap on any SOL test was a 30% point difference between African-American students' scores and white students' scores. While the data from several districts showed decreases in the gap in single subject areas, in only two districts was there evidence of a decrease in the average gap of five points or greater during that time period (1998–2000) (see Figure 7.1).

Many of the superintendents in this study described their cities and towns as part of the old south. One of the localities was the site of school closings after *Brown v. Board of Education* (Brown II), 1955, for a 5-year period in the early 1960s. Several superintendents discussed racial tension in their communities. One superintendent mentioned, "long-standing divisions between blacks and whites in the community . . . and long-standing frustration and bitterness" (PW,[2] 21). The majority of the superintendents talked of relatively homogeneous communities within their districts where some schools consisted of over 80% of either Caucasian or African-American students, and one commented that while certain sections of the city are diverse, other sections are not diverse, "they are segregated in the sense of housing patterns" (NL, 2). In talking about community attitudes and perceptions, one of the superintendents remarked:

DH: This part of the state is very much the old south.

INTERVIEWER: Can you explain what you mean by that?

DH: I really believe there's a belief that the white population is superior and you really can't expect more from the African-American population. It still exists here and that's not just my perception . . . in the educated African-American population, our Rotary is integrated. To a great extent as much as you have businesses that are run by African-Americans some of those participate in Chamber, but our churches are not integrated. Most other things aren't. The schools are [integrated] on the surface. But there really is that old south kind of feeling that there's a place for the African-Americans and the whites are supposed to rule. (DH, 31)

And another superintendent put it this way:

White teachers accept their black children for where they come from, where they are, who they are, but do not expect them to accomplish the same thing that their own personal white children that they have at home accomplish. They have lower, lower, standards for our black children. (WF, 22)

Figure 7.1. Average Black-White SOL Test Score Gaps in 1998, 1999, and 2000

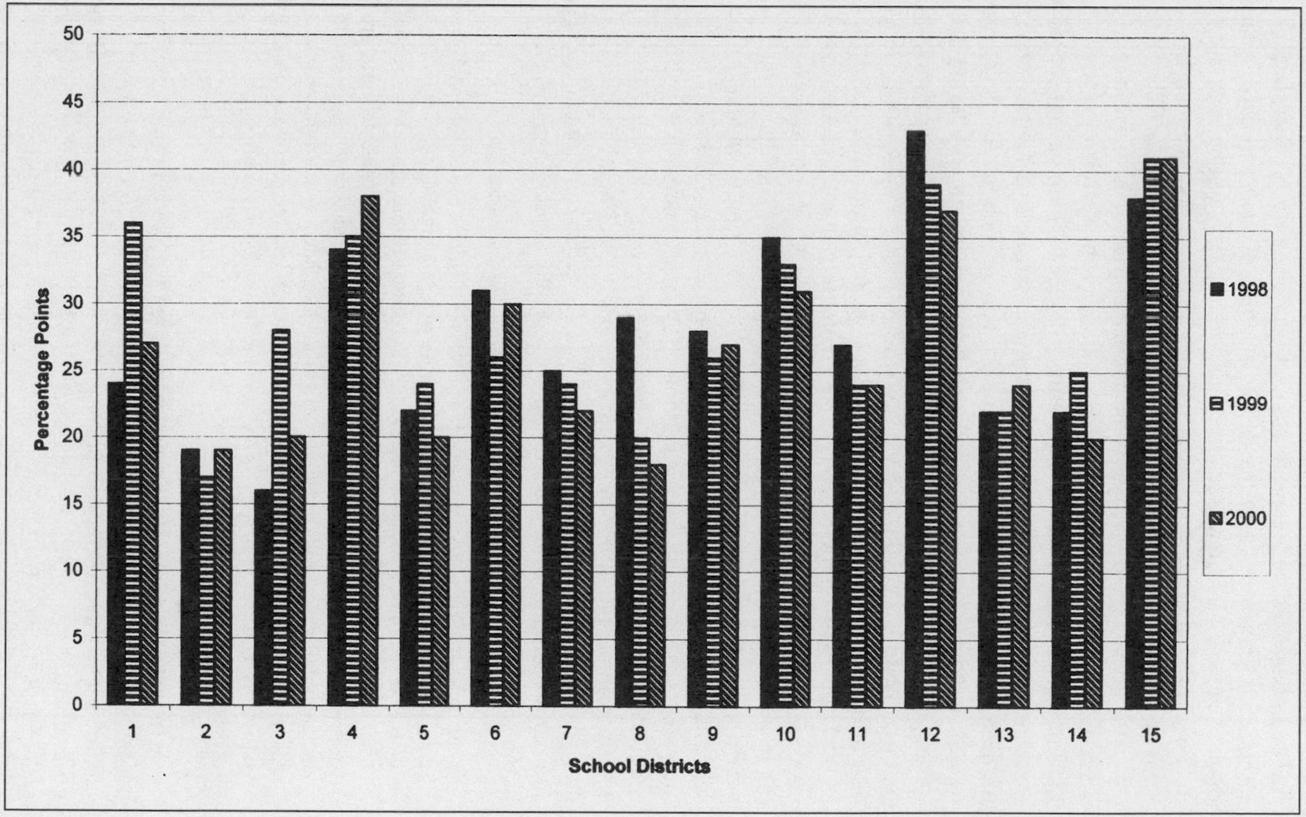

When talking of the district, superintendents commented often that teachers' expectations of student performance was a key issue. A superintendent spoke of her current drive to raise teachers' awareness of their practices in the classroom. She said, "I think it's really important to keep working with our teachers to help them understand their expectations, what their body language says about what they expect, sort of small comments they make . . ." (LC, 22).

In order to help us understand the context of their discussion about the black-white test-score gap, the superintendents painted vivid pictures of societal racism rooted deeply in their communities and largely unquestioned. Related to these attitudes were the depressed economic conditions that characterized many of these districts. Those that formerly relied on tobacco farming were searching to find an industry to take its place. And even those communities that had industry of some kind were uncertain about their economic future. However, while many of the superintendents in the economically depressed districts spoke of the difficulties in raising taxes to increase local school funding, the superintendents of the larger districts mentioned strong community support for increased school taxes. One superintendent commented that, although less than 20% of the people in his county have children of school age, over 80% of the population supported the last bond referendum. In fact, all of the superintendents in the larger school districts enjoyed community support for schools. According to the superintendent of one of the largest districts, "There is a pervasive feeling that the schools in [this] county are great places to have their kids educated. And that comes from people in the community [who] have children in school, and those that do not have children in school" (TV, 2). Another superintendent attributed community support to the fact that the white and wealthy had a vested interest in the school system:

> [This school system] has embraced the diversity that's in the community. The fact that [this system] continues to have a larger percentage of students who are white than who are black or of color signifies an anomaly because most urban school districts are predominantly students of color, and I think that speaks to why [this district] enjoys such a tremendous amount of support in the community because the influential, the wealthy, who are historically white, have a vested interest in having the best possible schools and so with that wealth and power goes decisions that will ultimately mean that the schools are going to be funded at the levels that will make them quality. (NL, 2)

In contrast, some of the smaller communities were attracting retirees from out of town who sought low taxes but who brought no children with them. In such districts, there seemed to be an uneasy truce between the school and local government. One superintendent characterized her community as complacent and fearful of change. She sought various ways to infuse some instructional expertise into the schools, fighting an uphill battle every time. "I have a split board. . . . [F]our of them have been very supportive and three of them don't want change of any kind" (DH, 24).

Though all of the superintendents were expected to do their best for every student, those in smaller districts were expected to do so with fewer material and human resources. Cautioned by the current shortage of teachers, several superintendents talked of faculties and administrators that had been on the job a long time. Superintendents also spoke of the need for better-informed instructional leaders in their schools. The superintendents were ready to move forward but the communities were not necessarily with them. As one explained:

> I will say that we have not changed our principals in years and years and years. I inherited all the principals that we have. Some of them have 20 some years experience each. . . . And I have been very vocal about not just putting a person in a building unless they have had instructional experience at that level. Somebody who knows elementary curriculum. We still sort of fight with the mindset of the fact that principals are building managers rather than instructional leaders. We are working on that. We've made lots of progress. But, the community has not yet bought into that. They don't have an understanding of that at this point. (AD, 15)

Therefore, community support in the form of resources, both human and material, varied across school districts in this study. The words of the superintendents reveal that history, location, and demographics of the region certainly shaped community perception of what was educationally important. In one respect, though, all communitities were alike: all were dealing with the new Virginia accountability plan.

SOL TESTING CONTEXT

This study was conducted during the initial stages of the implementation of the accountability plan in Virginia, 1999–2001. Participating superintendents had 2 or 3 years of data to guide them in their efforts to meet the newly tested state standards. Not surprisingly, most superintendents found themselves in the midst of much turmoil because few of their schools reached the mandated 70% passing rate for accreditation. Although some superintendents were dismayed by the test-score gap revealed in their data, few had given it long and serious consideration. Their primary focus was simply raising test scores. One superintendent spoke of focusing on the quality of the learning process in schools to improve instructional programs (LF). After seeing her district's SOL results for the second time, another superintendent expressed her resolve this way:

> Our Native Americans performed highest, but they are such a small percentage, a few extreme scores can throw things off. The black and white populations were congruent. Both were extremely low. . . . All of the scores have to be raised. (PS, 2).

Another superintendent, in a very large district, described his goals:

> The real issue for us, for me primarily, is how to . . . we're focusing on every child getting over the bar. So, in focusing on every child getting over the bar, you have to look at every child. I'm less concerned about our schools meeting state accreditation as I am about every youngster meeting SOL expectations. (TV, 3)

All of the superintendents discussed the strategies they had supported for raising test scores for all children. For the most part, these strategies included after-school sessions for several months leading up to the tests in the middle and elementary schools, remedial summer school for middle and elementary students who did not pass the tests, concentrated opportunities for teachers to increase their knowledge of content, and curriculum alignment with the standards and tests. Several of the superintendents remarked on teachers' lack of ability to help students pass the tests. Despite some slight gains in test scores in one of the districts, the superintendent felt that a much more concentrated effort was needed. She said:

> I'm going to go to the governor's best practice centers in regions around the state and see if they can help me teach the teachers how to teach the subject matter. I suspect that the high school teachers cannot answer the SOL questions themselves. (WF, 15)

Another superintendent talked of a district-wide emphasis on curriculum alignment as a result of disappointing test results.

> We did a total curriculum map. We spent a lot of time with Heidi Hayes-Jacob's materials. We talked with Appalachian Education Laboratory. We did some curriculum alignment and worked with them. We actually are working with a computer base, a data-base, on curriculum mapping and we got real specific and had the teachers, examine and map everything. (KP, 5)

Putting the whole movement toward testing into context, one of the superintendents admitted that, until the accountability plan became a reality, little attention had been paid to what was being taught in the classrooms. She knew changes had to be made, but it was not until after the first test results came back that a plan was developed.

> We began our first real curriculum development [94–95]. I would say prior to that, teachers just had a textbook and they taught the textbook. So, we really began more in-depth curriculum work mid-1990s. When the first SOL test came out, we were not ready curriculum-wise at all. We were not matched to the standards. We knew that we would not do well although our results were not as bad as they could have been. (AD, 3)

Speaking to the newly implemented accountability system, another superintendent commented:

> This was not the same kind of assessment change that we had experienced before. We truly had to have in place a system to change in order to deal with this latest challenge. And what we did [that year] was to adopt . . . [a] response to systemwide SOL readiness. (GM, 4)

Superintendents argued that they were mindful of raising the SOL test scores for all of the students. Only six of the superintendents, however, were truly tuned in to the notion of a gap in test scores. Since most of the test scores were disappointing in the first few years, any gains made were worthy of attention. In those communities where there was public notice given to the scores, superintendents had to make the most of any reasonable increase to demonstrate that the district was responding to the accountability plan. Most of the superintendents were pleased at the support that their efforts received from parents and other caretakers of the students who were struggling. Not all communities embraced the need for summer sessions, however. Superintendents in small, agricultural, and poor communities found themselves having to fight to implement summer school programs. Some families preferred their children to work in the summer, while other families did not want the inconvenience of sending their children to school.

> See part of the issue is these kids attend sporadically, you know. They don't have anyone to get them up, get them dressed, so the judge has started to actually fine truant children's parents. This past summer, for example, summer school and a lot of these, some are black, some are white, but a lot minority, said, "I'm not sending my kid to summer school. (GM, 27)

This superintendent, however, did not give up on the idea. She persevered and gradually had all of the middle school students who had failed the SOL tests attend summer session. She got powerful help as she explained:

> We used every air conditioned trailer that we had to run summer school but I wanted these children who failed all four [tests] and they were not just to learn, but they were all essentially fed in the morning. . . . We also do some fun things at the end of summer school because these kids don't have anything else to do in the summer. So we required them to attend summer school under compulsory attendance law and a lot of parents said, "I'm not sending them." So I sent all their names to the judge and the judge helped me round them all up and before the end of the first week we had them all in summer school. (GM, 28)

Another superintendent talked of parental resistance to summer school. "I had angry, angry, angry parents and they wanted their children to work. Their children needed jobs" (WF, 13). For most of the superintendents, though, summer sessions and after-school sessions have proven successful. They point to test-score gains for many grade levels and subject areas since they have implemented these strategies. One superintendent commented on the fact that he will try to restructure the summer school concept in his district for coming years to maximize its effectiveness.

> So, instead, this year, we're going to do it from the middle of July to the middle of August as a way to try to prepare kids for success in coming into the year as opposed to trying to repair weaknesses from the past year. And we're going to evaluate that effort. Not only during the summer, but throughout the year to see to what extent that intervention had some staying power and influenced teacher perception at the beginning of the year and student success at the beginning and middle of the year. (TV, 10)

There seems to have been no precedent for this single-minded focus on instructional issues in Virginia public schools. And a by-product of this focus has been an in-depth analysis of the data provided by the SOL tests. Although standardized test data long have been available to school administrators, it is not clear how much they were scrutinized or for what purpose. The existence of a racial gap in SAT or Stanford test scores, for instance, does not seem to have been cause for much concern. The black-white test-score gap has been documented for years, but apparently few paid attention to it in many school districts studied.

Most of the superintendents in this study, however, seemed to take the achievement gap to heart. As one superintendent remarked, "I'm concerned about gaps and how the gaps offer testimony or the lack thereof of how we're fulfilling our mission as public educators who haul students along towards the common goal we have of an educated citizenry" (GM, 7). Another stated, "I think that anytime that we see discrepancies we should be attentive to it" (WD, 19). None of the superintendents felt that they would be achieving their goal of raising test scores for all children, if the gap were to persist. One articulated a common belief among all the superintendents this way, "Oh, I think that we have to shoot for 100% and even contemplating being satisfied or okay with 70% would be a horrid statement about our commitment for all children" (WD, 15).

Many superintendents argued that their efforts at remediation helped to close the gap because the African-American students were the ones who were struggling the most. Few of these same superintendents, however, would have gone on record saying that these strategies were *aimed* at the minority students. Most argued that sensitivity to the wishes of the board precluded such statements.

WORKING WITH THE BOARD

After discussion with us, and a long look at the district data, the majority of the superintendents recognized that there is a black-white test-score gap in their districts. A few superintendents, for whom the data were not readily available during the interviews, could not speak to whether a gap existed, but suspected that one did. Of paramount importance was the board's perspective. Several of the school boards had not asked for SOL data to be broken down by race, gender, or socioeconomic status. In fact, some of the superintendents had not disaggregated their SOL data until we asked them to do so for this study. Others had broken down the test data, but their boards did not allow them to communicate the results to the community in a public forum. However, the reasons for lack of board interest in the disaggregated test data or the lack of communication to the public differed from locality to locality. One superintendent in a predominantly African-American district explained it this way:

INTERVIEWER: Has your board asked for a breakdown?

WF: No and I don't think they ever would. They soft-pedal racial differences in the county and the county is divided along racial lines but it's subtle, it is more covert than overt. Most of the time.

INTERVIEWER: Do you have any idea why they don't want to see a breakdown?

WF: Because they feel that it makes black people look bad, and this is a majority black county. (WF, 11).

A similar discussion about the board revealed the following:

INTERVIEWER: Did [the board] ask to see a breakdown?

DH: No.

INTERVIEWER: Do you have any ideas about why they may not have chosen to ask for a breakdown?

DH: They don't ever ask for that kind of breakdown. . . . Having never discussed it with them, I don't know. I would assume that that is true in the population in general [here] that there seems to be a feeling of, our scores can't go up in the general population because the emphasis seems to be we have a large minority population so that will always keep our scores down. It's the general thing I hear in the general public. (DH, 6)

Another superintendent defended her decision not to report the test-scores by race:

[The board] just didn't want me to stir it up, so to speak. That was the term. "Don't stir it up by putting those numbers out there. It'll cause more stink.". . . There's also a contingency of blacks who are very militant with a chip on their shoulder. So any time their kids get expelled or suspended, they file suit against a principal for discrimination. So there have been lots of those. The feeling was that, if you come out with [these numbers], we'll get another suit filed against us. (GM, 8)

According to this superintendent, one of the most surprising facts was that the press did not report the scores broken down "in any way shape or form" (GM, 8). Likewise, in another community, "The newspaper has not questioned [the figures]. In fact, here, the newspaper hasn't had a whole lot to say about the test scores one way or the other" (DH, 4).

While some superintendents expressed concern about the lack of communication to the community about the test-score gap, others supported their board's decision not to report disaggregated data. One superintendent, when asked why his board had not asked for the district's SOL test data broken down by race and gender responded:

What we've tried to focus on together is not giving ourselves permission to exclude some children and include others. So, our focus has been on every child. And in doing that, you get around some of those other issues that sometimes people think that by focusing on one group, you're not going to focus on another. We're going to focus on every child who is not meeting reasonable progress, to meeting these high expectations. (TV, 8)

Further, some school boards and superintendents have been unwilling to attribute the test-score gap to anything other than economics. Another superintendent, when asked if his board asked for a breakdown in SOL scores by race and gender, said, "They are aware and again the focus has been more along the line of what I would call economic stratification rather than racial stratification" (WD, 11). While this board has been uncomfortable expressing the achievement gap in terms of race, the superintendent described the board as

willing to differentiate resources and provide greater resources for schools that have determined need. . . . So, I think that is a courageous leadership staff in terms of their willingness to say we need to give more money to this school because students in that school do not have some of the amenities in life that our other children have. (WD, 10)

In this study, many superintendents did not have the board's encouragement to disaggregate their data, and while several superintendents *had* taken the initiative to disaggregate their SOL test data by race and gender, it is important to note that only four superintendents in the sample also had open conversations with their communities about the gap. According to one superintendent:

We began 4 years ago providing data broken down by grade, by course, by school, by gender, by ethnicity, and so people have the clear expectation that I'm going to ask questions and members of the superintendent's executive staff are going to ask questions about data—How many black students passed third grade science? For those students who didn't pass, what are you going to do about it? Why did this group of youngsters who happen to be male do better on the social studies portion of the exam than this other group? (NL, 4)

Similarly, another superintendent commented:

[F]or our public reporting it's by school and by district and then we've also reported ethnicity publicly because we have, essentially, two strategic goals in this district in our strategic plan. Two strategic goals, four instrumental goals, so six goals for the district here. The two goals have to do with raising student achievement on one hand and elimination of the achievement gap on the other hand. (PW, 5)

One other superintendent, though he did not disaggregate his SOL test data by race and gender, focused on the achievement gap in a somewhat different manner. In regards to his board, he commented:

Well, they have been focusing up until the last couple of years when we shifted to a test-driven accountability system, they were more interested in dropout rates and graduation completion rates and in those areas we had done a lot of work by race, so, for example, . . . in the last 5 years, we've cut our dropout rate in half. . . . [W]hat I saw was about 80% of our whites were graduating, but only 59% of our black students were finishing . . . so we had about a 23% increase in 5 years in the black graduation rate, and I think the best thing about that was when you measure the achievement gap by graduation. (CJ, 11)

Influenced by board reactions, superintendents had varying opportunities for a discussion of the SOL test-score gaps. When there was some public communication, the prevailing community response to a discrepancy between African-American students' scores and white students' scores on the SOL tests has been, in most cases, apathy at best and complete silence at worst. In addition, when we pointed out the gaps, which persisted over the 3 years of data, collected at grades 3–12, some superintendents indicated that their own knowledge of the gaps was somewhat sketchy. Most of the superintendents were primarily concerned with raising SOL test-scores across the board because the accreditation of their schools depended on it. The recent accountability plan in Virginia seems to be compelling superintendents to concentrate on getting every school to reach the benchmark of a 70% passing rate. Heightened public scrutiny in every district made many superintendents cautious about drawing attention to SOL test-score gaps.

THE RISKS OF GOING PUBLIC

Beyond board directives, superintendents had a wider community with which to contend. Keeping the historical and geographical contexts in mind, superintendents had to decide how to handle discussion of test scores both internally and externally. Mindful of their own tenure, superintendents talked of the effects of any action they might consider. Most took the line of encouraging internal discussion of racial or socioeconomic discrepancies in test scores but not public discussion. One superintendent said, "[Principals] have targeted lists of students . . . [data] have been seriously disaggregated in the buildings" (KP, 10). Another explained:

> I would have to say we do not talk about [the test-score gap] publicly in the sense of in the most public of settings such as the school board meeting or a public meeting to which a lot of parents or other groups have been invited. We do, however, talk about it in the public setting of a faculty meeting or administrative meeting which are not restricted in any way. Of course they're for the most part sort of work sessions as opposed to presentations about information and we try very hard to think about how we can address these issues. (LC, 5)

Another superintendent spoke of the political tensions involved with publicly announcing a test-score gap:

> [P]ublic education is the great equalizer and as a result, we as public educators have the responsibility to provide the greatest opportunity for each child and realize that in this current environment a lot of politicians don't like hearing that kind of thing. (GM, 9)

Interested in understanding the superintendents' thinking more clearly on this issue, we tried to get at the underlying risks superintendents' perceived in bringing the achievement gap to the attention of the public—especially for those superintendents whose boards had not specifically prohibited it. Some superintendents were unable to articulate their reasons beyond generalizing public concern. "[I]t's pretty emphatic [the school board] wants the best for everybody and, I think they're not sure in their minds if it's a race or a poverty issue" (KP, 7). "I think it's education level and economics and in some ways it may not stick out as much here because there's so much poverty here anyway" (CJ, 4). One superintendent acknowledged that there would likely be a shift in the approach her school board took in the future because of a recent addition to the school board.

> We do have an African American on the board [now] and I think this issue is going to become a lot more public than it has in the past. [This county] before SOLs came, ranked very well in the state on all testing. You know it was a blow when we

didn't have our schools fully accredited and I think there's probably some complacency because things have always been on the higher end not the lower end. So it
hasn't been talked about. It has not been talked about and that pattern has just been
carried through. (EB, 14)

This superintendent detected a change in public attitudes in that district
because minority voices, silent in the past, had recently been raised. She admitted that there had probably always been a gap in scores attained on the kinds of
standardized tests the district had traditionally given:

I think [the gap has] probably been there. This has not been looked at until this past
year, and when we started breaking down, gradually trying to take a look at where
are we falling down and that's when, actually probably the first time in a long time
that anything like this has been looked at. (EB, 14)

Another superintendent spoke of her sensitivity to the local context. Used to a
more open reporting system in her previous district, she realized that her new
community was too different for her to rely on past strategies.

In a community like this you have to be careful that what you do is balanced or
you're going to set one group off against the other. You have to do everything you
can but you have to do it subtly. (GM, 34)

And another superintendent made a similar point:

[Drawing attention to the gap] would cause trouble. I think I have to be aware of
it and I think everybody here, all administrators have to be aware of it, but I
think we have to solve the problem without making it a worse problem because
you don't. . . . If you attack sometimes things front on, you don't get anywhere.
(DH, 33)

Most superintendents argued that their knowledge of how the community
would react dictated their approaches to raising the issue of discrepancies in test
scores. Several expressed ambivalence as to whether these disparities were associated with race or socioeconomic status or both. A few superintendents
expressed the opinion that, drawing public attention to scores disaggregated by
any means, along race or gender lines, according to disability or giftedness,
would unsettle the community. Still, another expressed the opinion that, rather
than looking at data from groups of students, it was more important to concentrate on individual students.

In order to eliminate the gap, you first of all have to make sure you look at individual student performance. Even looking at groups of African American, Hispanic—

there will be a gap in there. So, if you look at average scores, you still are not going to be able to help to reduce the gap unless you look at individual youngsters. (TV, 11)

Yet, three superintendents felt passionately about eliminating the gap. One talked of her resolve to make a difference:

[O]n my watch [test-scores] can't go down. I must be up there with [neighboring communities]. I think we can do it. An effective school is having poor black children perform academically as well as rich, white children. That is my definition of an effective school. I didn't have to put in the ethnicity there, but I did. It's important. I'm not afraid to mention black/white. (WF, 16)

Another spoke of his belief in honest discussions about the test-score gap:

We don't hide it. We talk about it. We don't go out waving this around saying, "Oh, by the way, we have a gap!" . . . we've been up front. My school board about once a year has asked us about the gap and we're very pleased that we've been able to tell them we've made some inroads in the gap. . . . You see if you don't acknowledge you have a gap, you'll never do anything about it. You'll shortchange a lot of kids. We have no reason to hide from the fact that there's a gap. We want to keep getting better. (NL, 12)

ACTION

While all of the superintendents discussed the strategies they had encouraged to raise test scores for all students, only two superintendents spoke of specific strategies that they were using in their districts to eliminate the achievement gap. One additional superintendent spoke of strategies he was using to increase the graduation rate of African-American students, and although he has not specifically addressed the achievement gap in test scores, he is included in the following discussion of superintendents who have taken action to eliminate the gap.

District characteristics do not seem to account for whether or not superintendents have taken action to reduce the gap. When comparing the three active districts, district size, economic level, and district type were different. One school system was small, one was medium, and one was fairly large. While one of the communities had a large population of uneducated adults and was poverty-stricken, another had a large percentage of highly educated parents who were affluent, and the third district had a mix of both educated and uneducated adults as well as economic levels. One district was urban, one was rural, and one was suburban. Yet there were two similarities in districts where the gap has been addressed: (1) superintendents acknowledged publicly that there was a black-white test-score gap and believed not only that it was worth taking action to correct, but that schools can actually make a difference in eliminating the gap, and (2) school boards and communities were willing to publicly discuss the gap.

Superintendents in these three school systems have:

- implemented cultural sensitivity training for all employees;
- initiated mentoring programs that identify African-American students who have not taken rigorous classes and encourage them to take more challenging classes;
- established relationships with community centers and created tutoring sites in their neighborhoods;
- employed minority achievement coordinators in several schools to specifically target African-American males;
- coordinated college preparatory programs for African-American youths;
- rearranged high school schedules and provided transition programs for ninth-grade students;
- trained teachers and administrators in data analysis;
- implemented year-round schooling in target schools;
- and personalized education for high school students by breaking from the traditional high school pattern and adopting plans for alternative high schools with fewer students. (See Figure 7.2.)

Two of the three superintendents in these school systems cited specific goals and strategies written into their district plans as well as individual school improvement plans to eliminate the achievement gap while not allowing the scores of other students to fall. As one superintendent explained:

One of our goals in [the district] was to close the gap in achievement between African-American students and white students without holding those kids who are excelling down, so what you have to do is to push kids who are excelling to continue to excel at the pace at which they can, but to influence the kids who are at the low end to make up some ground they've lost. (NL, 6)

Another superintendent justified his actions this way:

Well, I think as far as the outcomes are concerned, we have the same expectations for all students irrespective of their population. How we get there I think

Figure 7.2. District Actions

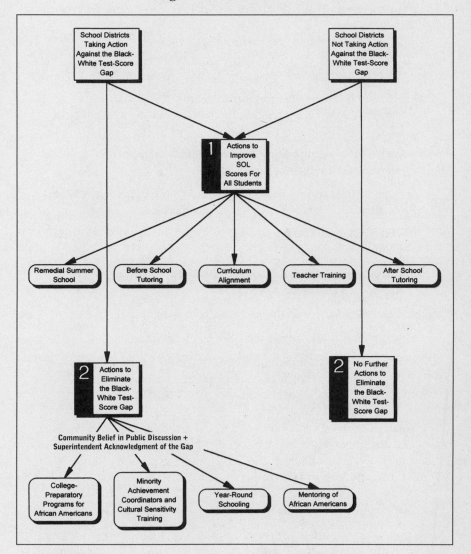

requires . . . quite a bit of differentiation and personalization of the whole educational process. [We] have been going through a transition from sort of cookie-cutter factory model type schooling to this system of lots of choice and part of the reason for the choice is to respond to the need for differentiation, so there's no point in . . . letting people choose if there aren't choices for them to choose from, so I think the differentiation is a recognition that one size does not fit all. (CJ, 9)

Interestingly, another superintendent spoke to the claim by some that the achievement gap is attributable to the socioeconomic status of the community.

> One of the issues that's often raised when this test-score gap is talked about is that some proportion of the variance is attributable to SES, and I'm sure that's true. One of the moves that we've made in terms of analysis is to look at the gap within the free lunch rates or free lunch conditions we should say. And we find the gap within the conditions as well. So, that essentially, when we're looking at the African-American/white achievement gap, just in that comparison, the highest scoring kids are white kids who are not on free lunch. The next high scoring kids are white kids who are on free lunch. The next high scoring are black kids who are not on free lunch. And then black kids who are on free lunch. (PW, 7)

In summary, three of the superintendents in this study not only publicly acknowledged the existence of an achievement gap in their school districts, but they also reported taking specific action to eliminate it. These superintendents held strong beliefs that they could make strides toward eliminating the achievement gap through their district leadership. And, most important, they transformed their beliefs into plans of action.

CONCLUSION

Superintendents of larger districts in this study tended to enjoy more financial support than superintendents of smaller districts. Another important fact to note is that while women represented over half of the participants in this study, in all cases, they were superintendents in rural districts that were experiencing some type of turmoil or were facing issues of community poverty. Superintendents of districts with greater financial support, most often male, tended to have the resources to hire better teachers. This generated support from the community for schools as well as trust that the school system was a good place to educate their children. A cyclical process characterized these districts. (See Figure 7.3.) Greater financial support leads to better teachers and materials. Better teachers and materials lead to greater student achievement. Greater student achievement leads to greater community support. Finally, the circle is completed as greater community support leads back to increased financial support for schools. In addition, more often superintendents of medium to large school districts, the majority of whom were male, revealed that they disaggregated their test-score data by ethnicity because of the greater numbers of diverse groups in their districts and because of community members that demanded a public discussion about the data.

Each of the 15 superintendents in this study made a good case for focusing on raising all test-scores in public. Only three, however, have taken specific actions to eliminate the achievement gap. Their sense of what was required stemmed from their perceptions of a district leader under the media spotlight of accountability. Of the 3 superintendents who have taken action to reduce the achievement gap in some way, one has seen a significant increase in the graduation rate of African-American students and one has seen evidence that the achievement gap is decreasing each year and will continue to do so in the future. While the third superintendent has not seen a significant decrease in the average gap in his district, he is confident that time will show that his programs have worked. Data in one additional district indicated that the gap may be decreasing. However, it was evident that disparities in test-results had long been ignored in the majority of these districts. Neither the African-American community nor the white community had asked for data to be disaggregated in many cases. The common practice in the school systems seems to have been to look at individual students rather than at certain populations of students. While that might have been acceptable in the past, the time is ripe for change.

Looking at the findings of the study through the lens of the new politics of race and gender, it becomes clear that superintendents express a lot of good

Figure 7.3. Cycle of Support

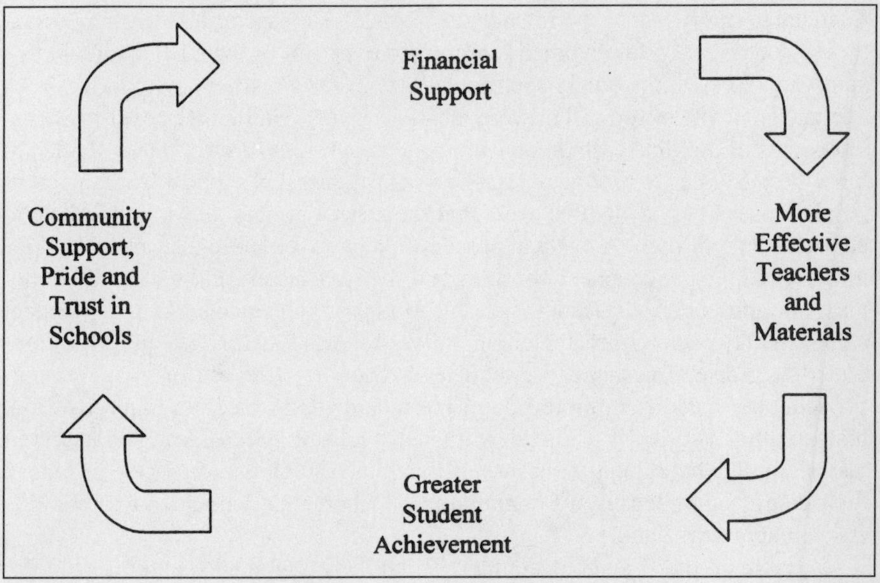

Financial
Support

Community
Support,
Pride and
Trust in
Schools

More
Effective
Teachers
and
Materials

Greater
Student
Achievement

will but not much commitment to action. Some of the participants argued that, if they were to expose the issue to public scrutiny and public discussion, they would be in danger of losing their positions. This is certainly a powerful disincentive to challenge the status quo. But, at the same time, if superintendents were to see their schools as *generating* the inequalities that exist between African-American and white students, instead of as addressing the existing discrepancies, there might be a greater moral imperative to "rock the boat." For too long, superintendents have hidden behind the claim that all students' needs must be met; no special attention should be given to those who are African-American or poor or who have another minority label. The notion of equity demands that we treat some groups differently so that they have a chance at performing as well as others.

Superintendents must include the interests of diverse populations of students in all aspects of school decision-making processes. In an effort to improve teaching and learning for all students, awareness of the black-white test-score gap must be increased. Knowledge of the gap and the data to illustrate what is happening over time have been two of the real benefits of the accountability reform. This study shows that superintendent leadership under circumstances of the reform is crucial to bringing needed resources to bear on the problem. As the literature suggests (see Bjork, 1993; Grogan, 2000; Kowalski, 1999), superintendents must not only be more involved in the instructional decisions made districtwide, but they must also be responsible for directing efforts to ensure that *all* children learn the most they can. This does not require a major departure from superintendents' past practices. However, it does require a shift in priorities. As awareness increases, so too must action to reduce the black-white test-score gap. Superintendents are measured by the quality of their schools and by what they do with their power. Core values of superintendents in an age of accountability must include the desire for equitable outcomes for all children. Superintendents have a moral imperative to serve the needs of all their students—representing all forms of diversity, racial, linguistic, gender, academic, religious, sexual, and so on. In this study, participating superintendents are aware of the achievement gap. However, awareness has not yet prompted the development of strategies to significantly reduce the gap. Community outcries, media frenzies, covert and overt racist attitudes, accountability pressures, and political agendas all serve as stumbling blocks. Nevertheless, for the sake of social justice, the black-white test-score gap must be recognized, reduced and, eventually, eliminated.

APPENDIX 7.1
INTERVIEW PROTOCOL

1. Please talk a little about the school district. How many students do you serve? What is the community like? How long have you been here as superintendent?

2. How have the SOL test scores in this district changed over the past 3 years?

3. Looking at specific scores on particular tests, is there a gap between the scores of students who are white and those of minority students?

4. What do you think causes this gap?

5. Is this something you can talk about in your community? Both inside the school system and in the public?

6. What is the attitude of the board toward discussing this information?

7. What are you doing as superintendent to eliminate the gap?

8. What problems do you encounter in trying to carry out your plans?

NOTES

1. There are many test-score gaps between white students' scores and the scores of students of other races or ethnic groups. This study focused on the gaps between black students and white students because (1) that was the minority population that all districts in the study had in common and (2) historically, in the districts studied, the interests of the African-American population were subordinated to those of the white population. In very few of the districts studied was there another minority population of any size.

2. Consistent with the reporting of qualitative studies, the identities of participants have been concealed. Page numbers and fictitious initials are used to refer to quotations from the transcripts of interviews.

REFERENCES

Achilles, C. M., Nye, B. A., Zaharias, J. B., & Fulton, B. D. (1996, March). *Education's equivalent of medicine's Framingheart Study*. Paper prepared for the Fifth Annual National Conference on creating the quality school, Oklahoma City: OK.

Ashbaugh, C. R. (2000). The superintendent's role as instructional leader. In P. M. Short & J. P. Scribner (Eds.), *Case studies of the superintendency* (pp. 9–21). Lanham, Maryland: Scarecrow Press.

Bjork, L. (1993). Effective schools-effective superintendents: The emerging instructional leadership role. *Journal of School Leadership. 3*(3), 246–259.

Carter, G. R., & Cunningham, W. G. (1997). *The American school superintendent: Leading in an age of pressure.* San Francisco, CA: Jossey-Bass Publishers.

Carter, S. C. (2000). *No excuses: Lessons from 21 high-performing, high-poverty schools.* Washington, D.C.: The Heritage Foundation.

Chaddock, G. R. (1999, November 30). Adverse impact? Tougher tests and zero-tolerance discipline are hitting minorities. *Christian Science Monitor*, 1–4. Retrieved June 6, 2000, from the World Wide Web: http://www.christiansciencemonitor.com.

Grogan, M. (2000). Laying the groundwork for a reconception of the superintendency from feminist postmodern perspectives. *Educational Administration Quarterly, 36* (1), 117–142.

Guidelines for uniform performance standards (2000). Division of Teacher Education and Licensure, Richmond VA: Virginia Department of Education.

How to close the achievement gap. (2000, February 2). *Baltimore Sun*, 1–5. Retrieved June 7, 2000, from the World Wide Web: http://www.baltimoresun.com.

Jencks, C., & Phillips, M. (Eds.). (1998). *The black-white test score gap.* Washington, D.C.: Brookings Institution Press.

Kowalski, T. (1999). *The school superintendent.* Columbus, OH: Merrill.

LeCompte, M., & Preissle, J. (1993). *Ethnography and qualitative design in educational research.* San Diego, CA: Academic Press.

Lipman, P. (1998). *Race, class, and power in school restructuring.* Albany, NY: SUNY.

Marshall, C. (1993). The new politics of race and gender. In Marshall, C. (Ed.), *The New Politics of Race and Gender: The 1992 yearbook of the politics of education association* (pp. 1–6). Washington, DC: Falmer.

Matthews, J. (1999, September 2). Gap in exam scores shrinks. Minority, white students improve passing rates. *Washington Post*, p. V1.

Patton, M. (1980). *Qualitative evaluation methods.* Newbury Park, CA: Sage Publications.

Racial gap in test scores grows. (2000, August 25). *Richmond Times-Dispatch*, pp. A1, A11.

Rizvi, F. (1993). Race, gender and the cultural assumptions of schooling. In Marshall, C. (Ed.), *The New Politics of Race and Gender: The 1992 yearbook of the politics of education association* (pp. 203–217). Washington, DC: Falmer.

Skrla, L., Scheurich, J. J., & Johnson, J. F. (2000, September). *Equity-driven achievement-focused school districts.* Report on systemic school success in four Texas school districts serving diverse student populations, The Charles A. Dana Center at The University of Texas at Austin.

Virginia Department of Education. (2000). *Guidelines for uniform performance standards and evaluation criteria for teachers, administrators, and superintendents.* Richmond, VA.

Ward, J. (1993). Demographic politics and American schools. In Marshall, C. (Ed.), *The New Politics of Race and Gender: The 1992 yearbook of the politics of education association* (pp. 8–18). Washington, DC: Falmer.

Wills, F., & Peterson, K. (1995). Superintendents' management of state-initiated reform: A matter of interpretation. In K. Leithwood (Ed.), *Effective school district leadership: Transforming politics into education* (pp. 85–116). New York: SUNY.

Zernike, K. (2000, August 4). Racial gap in student test scores polarizes town. *New York Times*, pp. A1, A25.

Chapter Eight

EDUCATORS' ETHICAL CONCERNS ARISING FROM THE VIRGINIA ACCOUNTABILITY PLAN

PAMELA D. TUCKER

AND

MARGARET GROGAN

During the course of collecting data for the various studies reported in this book, there were numerous references by principals and teachers to the quandaries posed by the current Standards of Learning (SOL) and Accreditation (SOA). Some of the participants labeled their concerns ethical or moral, while others described them in ways that led us to consider them moral or ethical.[1] We drew these conclusions from the context of the discussion or from the kinds of concerns identified by the participants in the studies. In this chapter, we chose to address the subtext directly with a cross-cutting analysis of the data to discern what bothered educators from an ethical perspective.

BACKGROUND

The SOL and SOA are so central to educational concerns in Virginia today that it is hard to remember any policy initiative that has so dominated the daily work of schools or the thoughts of those who work in them. Given that Virginia has had Standards of Learning for almost 30 years, however, it is interesting to consider what has changed so dramatically within the last 5 years. Was the curriculum articulated in the earlier standards followed by teachers and to what extent? How was learning assessed? How was the curriculum and student mastery of it used to make decisions about students' instructional needs? How was curriculum implementation coordinated or supported by building level principals and central office supervisors? These questions are important in light of what emerged from the data collected in the studies reported in this volume.

What were the practices, beliefs and values that existed before the adoption of the current SOL and SOA? By grounding the discussion of educators' current moral concerns in their attitudes and beliefs *prior* to the reform, we can understand better the sources of their current misgivings. Second, we can find ways to deal with them so that all students are served as well as possible. What follows is a discussion based on the responses of teachers and principals in several of the studies conducted for this book. The authors have reanalyzed the data with attention to ethical themes. For instance, phrases such as, "being fair to students," "loss of professional freedom," "harming students," and so on alerted us to the categories we have identified here.

We begin by tracing the ways teachers and principals reasoned prior to 1995 through a brief review of the literature. Most helpful to the discussion are issues of curriculum, testing and assessment, and standards. In addition, we look at how administrators and teachers worked together to deliver the curriculum. Then, we use a multidimensional ethical framework to examine the current practices and underlying assumptions of educators as they struggle with the implementation of Virginia's accountability plan. We intend to show that while some of the moral issues identified in the postreform climate are legitimate, others are based on an uncritical sense of educators' traditional rights and responsibilities. Using Starratt's (1994) three-part theoretical lens of the ethics of care, justice, and critique, we discuss both the possible ethical positions of educators prior to the reform and their current concerns. We conclude the chapter with our thoughts on potential ways to reconcile some of the moral dilemmas and their implications for leadership in an age of accountability.

IN RETROSPECT

For many teachers in Virginia, as in other parts of the country, the SOL traditionally served as a guide, a reference point for the general skills and knowledge that were to be taught. It was by no means the only point of reference for curriculum development. Each school division had the prerogative to create its own curriculum to reflect local priorities and preferences for both content and the scope and sequence of units or courses. In addition, the textbook adoption process at the local level also affected the "taught" curriculum. While school divisions tried to find books that met the local needs and the Standards of Learning that existed at time, alignment was only approximate. Ultimately, it was up to the individual teacher to make sense out of these conflicting influences and determine what was taught in the classroom (Johnson, 1990; Lortie, 1975).

Content across classrooms and courses shared some common threads but also varied depending on teachers' professional judgment of what was important to cover, their comfort with certain topics, their fascination with other topics, and perceived interest and mastery by their students (Johnson, 1990; Marzano, 2000). This relative autonomy allowed teachers to pursue their interests and passions for specific topics with creative units on butterflies, Native American tribes, leaf patterns of various trees, tangrams, origami, and others that supplemented the core curriculum as outlined in the Standards of Learning.

Pacing of lessons also varied because of the rate at which students learned new concepts or material. Without rigid curriculum timelines, most teachers preferred to slow down the pace of a unit if most students were having difficulty with the material. Teachers preferred the mastery of some content to mere exposure to the entire curriculum (Johnson, 1990). Students and teachers both felt more successful with this thorough approach to covering the content. The obvious result, however, was that some portions of the mandated curriculum were not taught by the end of the year (Strauss, 2001).

Measuring mastery of learning was another challenge typically left to individual teachers. While standardized, norm-referenced tests were administered, they were viewed as external measures of achievement that were minimally related to the "taught" curriculum. In addition, standardized test results were often of little use to the classroom teacher because (1) they arrived after students had departed for the summer; (2) they tended to be so global in their assessment categories, for example "math procedures," that they offered little diagnostic information to guide the instructional process; and (3) for secondary teachers, it was a Herculean task just to find the reports on over 100 students. When results were reviewed and shared with teachers, the message from principals and supervisors tended to be general: "The results are good and keep doing what you've been doing" or "The results were [disappointing] so we need to work harder" (workshop, Davenport, 2001). The feedback collapsed the efforts of *all* teachers across *all* subjects into a one-dimensional judgment that offered little guidance for improvement (Johnson, 1990).

At the local level, some school divisions used reading and math assessments in the early grades; but in most cases, teachers were expected to gauge student progress themselves and adjust instruction accordingly (Lortie, 1975). This individualized approach to assessment assumed that all teachers had expertise in test construction such that they could tap both surface and deep-level understanding of material and concepts in a valid and reliable manner, and that they could be objective in assessing the students for whom they had dedicated so much time and energy in teaching. Despite most teachers' efforts to do both, this method of measuring progress was idiosyncratic and made comparisons across classes, schools, and school divisions questionable, if not impossible (Marzano, 2000). For example, reading "on grade level" in one school division may not have been comparable to reading "on grade level" in another. It may not have even been comparable across classrooms in the same school. That determination varied based on the test that was used to judge it and the teachers' training and years of experience. Likewise, there may have been differences in the material covered in geometry in one school as compared to that in another, depending on the level of standardization required by supervisors from the central office.

Report card grades were the primary mechanism for quantifying cumulative progress and reflecting how well students were succeeding compared to the rest of the class. Grades, however, often combined judgments of actual mastery of material with other factors such as student effort, behavior, and attendance. In Virginia there was no objective measure of actual learning based on the "taught" curriculum that was not confounded by teacher perceptions, with the exception of the Literacy Passport Test of reading, writing, and math.

Success in this context was measured more by feelings of satisfaction on the part of principals, faculty members and parents than by objective assessments of learning. It was an intuitive process (Schmoker, 1999). Teachers judged whether they had done the best job they could, given the resources they had and their judgment of what students were capable of learning (Lortie, 1975). Teachers did not expect as much from some students as others (Chase, 2000; Haycock, 2001). Students were promoted so they would not feel bad about their poor work or so that teachers would not have to work with the same students again. Students who were having difficulties were put in less rigorous classes or even a different track of classes. While teachers worked hard to connect with and understand students, the lack of a common yardstick or benchmark made it difficult to determine what students were actually learning (Johnson, 1990).

At the school level, many principals believed that the best way to keep their teachers happy was to leave them alone to "do what they do best." Most teachers enjoyed the freedom from distraction and interference afforded by simply closing their classroom doors. The classroom was their world to create, organize, and maintain according to their vision of teaching and learning. This approach minimized the importance of common goals and the teamwork required to identify and achieve them. Many principals regarded teacher autonomy as a time-honored benefit of teaching (Johnson, 1990; Lortie, 1975).

The principalship constituted a role that involved managing a group of professionals who individually defined their work and success. As long as the principal and parents generally agreed on the success of the individual teacher, the teacher was allowed to exercise discretion in instructional matters. The principal supported the faculty by maintaining the school facility, providing the resources needed by teachers, managing student discipline, and organizing the daily schedule and annual calendar (Lortie, 1975). Principals tended to assume a more active role as instructional leaders only when they possessed substantial credibility as a teacher. As such, they would work directly on curriculum development, instructional strategies, and staff development. Principals did not tend to challenge the classroom autonomy of individual teachers unless there was some type of information that called into question the existing perception of satisfactory results, such as parent complaints or concerns from the central office.

Much as classrooms functioned as autonomous domains for teachers so did schools for principals. Assuming that faculty, staff, parents, and community members were generally happy, principals were encouraged to continue doing what they were doing. Schools reflected the communities in which they were located and were expected to maintain existing programs and community support. With only limited measures of effectiveness, such as attendance, promotion rates, and numbers of students enrolled in AP courses, few academic comparisons were made across schools or school divisions. Even results from standardized tests (such as the SAT or Stanford) were problematic because they were assumed to reflect the neighborhoods served by the schools (Johnson, 1990). With these limited data, it was difficult to question assumptions about what students were capable of learning and achieving. Schools were not expected to get the same results with different types of students (Falk, 2000). That was considered an unfair expectation for both educators and students.

FROM 1995 ON

In 1995, the educational landscape changed dramatically in Virginia with the introduction of the current Standards of Learning, followed by the Standards of Accreditation, school report cards, and Standards of Learning assessments (Timberg, 2000). In the near future, there would be high-stakes consequences for both schools and students based on the tests. To receive full accreditation, schools would need to have substantial percentages of their students pass each of the four Standards of Learning tests at the elementary and middle levels, and students would be required to pass six end-of-course tests to earn verified credits and graduate from high school. This accountability initiative challenged some of the aforementioned beliefs and teaching practices.

The curriculum followed by teachers became far more rigidly defined (Margheim, 2002). The Standards of Learning (Commonwealth of Virginia, 1995) no longer were viewed as guidelines but as the essential core of the curriculum for all school divisions. Many divisions undertook curriculum alignment efforts to integrate the SOL, instructional materials, and local curriculum guides. In some places, this work was done school by school, but in most cases, it was done as a divisionwide enterprise to ensure horizontal and vertical alignment. Typically, the SOL served as the organizing framework for the new curricula versus the dusty reference of the previous 20 years.

Today, many Virginia teachers feel that they exercise far less discretion over what they teach and how it is organized (Margheim, 2002). Given the rigorous pacing that the SOL require, teachers complain that there is little time for enrichment, in-depth projects, and field trips. In addition, teachers are concerned that students are being left behind when they push forward with new material based on the timelines delineated in pacing guides (Portner, 2000). Teachers feel unable to teach deeply or creatively because of the schedules that must be followed in order for all the topics to be covered before the tests. Only after the tests are administered in the spring do teachers feel at liberty to deviate from the SOL and teach special units.

Measuring mastery of material remains a challenging task even with the development of the SOL assessments. While they do provide an *objective* measure of learning that is valid and reliable ("Experts attest," 2000) in the early grades, they are only administered in grades three, five, and eight. Thus, in the elementary and middle grades, there is no annual assessment of student learning to determine student progress on a more frequent basis so that appropriate instructional adjustments can be made or to identify specific skills and knowledge that need reteaching. In response, many school divisions are developing their own assessment tools or buying commercial products to meet these needs during off-cycle test years. Some individual teachers also have aligned their tests with the SOL, the SOL assessments, and the locally developed benchmark tests. These test results typically are used for internal purposes of instructional improvement and are not shared publicly. For most divisions, student report cards continue to be the common vehicle for reporting academic progress.

One of the dramatic shifts that has taken place as a result of the current accountability initiative is the measurement of both school and classroom success. School report cards with their information on passing rates for SOL assessments are publicly shared and disseminated (see, e.g., Benning, 2000 or Swenson, 1999). They are mailed to parents, posted on the Virginia Department of Education web page, and published in the newspaper. The general public knows the success, or failure, of each school on the SOL assessments. In smaller school systems where there may be only one high school and one teacher for each subject area, end-of-course test results reflect directly on the success of individual teachers. Because there is consistency in content and format on the SOL assessments, it has become possible during the last 3 years for parents and community members to make comparisons among schools and school divisions based on specific curriculum objectives. As noted by a grandmother in Washington County, a small rural county in southern Virginia, "It's focused all our attention on education, and I don't think that's bad" (Seymour, 2000, p. B1).

Likewise, teacher success can now be judged, in part, by the SOL assessments. Other factors, such as parent satisfaction and proper coverage of the curriculum, continue to be important but they are only part of the equation that includes testing. This emphasis on assessment has changed how many teachers plan and teach their classes (Portner, 2000). There have been cascading implications of the changes in terms of decisions about content, pacing, extra assistance to students, and teacher-made tests (Benning, 2000; Mathews, 1999; Portner, 1999). Along with the SOL assessments comes a heavy sense of responsibility to help each and every student pass the tests. Teachers have responded in a variety of ways with most struggling to find strategies to help students succeed (Cawelti, 1999; Mathews, 1999; Portner, 2000).

According to Virginia statute (8 VAC 20–131–210A), principals ultimately are responsible for student progress. In addition, the very public nature of the information on student passing rates in the four core subject areas has put a great deal of pressure on principals to maintain and improve their testing results. They have responded to this expectation primarily by giving far more attention to instructional issues (Portner, 2000; Seymour, 2000). They now have information that allows them to make not only external comparisons with other schools like the rest of the public, but also internal comparisons across teachers. Analyzing and making sense of these data have become sensitive, yet critical parts of being a responsible administrator (Cawelti, 1999; Schmoker, 1999).

In sum, the reform initiative has had a remarkable impact on the educational process at both the classroom and school level. It has had an effect on curriculum, instructional pacing, assessment, measurement of success, and issues of professionalism. It has focused attention on the outcomes as well as the processes of education. It has, ultimately, disrupted the comfort teachers and principals had with schooling in Virginia. Many educators contrast their working conditions and educational priorities today with those of the past. They express serious concerns based on whether this movement is changing education for the better or worse.

AN ETHICAL FRAMEWORK

Good educators always consider their work in a moral sense (Purpel, 1999). To get a better understanding of the context of curriculum and assessment, the two areas at the heart of the accountability plan, we need to consider the possible moral and ethical dimensions of the issues described above concerning educators prior to 1995, and then now. Moral principles can certainly be detected in teachers' reasoning patterns. For instance, traditionally, teachers could argue that it was fair to make sure every child was keeping up with the curriculum. Rather than serving the needs of the quicker learners at the expense of those who needed more time, a middle ground was often reached. Not teaching the prescribed curriculum could be framed as the right thing to do because it was fairer to students. Teachers could also argue that they were meeting individual students' needs by grouping students and not exposing all to the same curriculum. For the past 50 years, parents and other individual rights' advocates have pressed for specialized programs based on these strategies for both the gifted and the learning disabled.

As for assessment practices in the classroom, teachers could make the case again that it is fairer to assess students only on what they have been taught in ways that are idiosyncratic to the particular classroom because that is how students have learned the material. In addition, assessment practices that are based in the classroom do not subject students to the kind of public scrutiny and pressure that standardized tests do. It could be argued that students were less traumatized by teachers' tests. Few people other than the teacher, the student, and parents or caretakers ever saw the results of particular assessments, and few questioned the progress of the student. It was the teacher's responsibility to ensure adequate learning in the classroom.

This reasoning uses elements of both an ethic of care and an ethic of justice. As Starratt (1994) points out, "the ethic of justice demands that the claims of the institution serve both the common good and the rights of individuals in the school" (p. 51). From a traditional perspective, educators have wrestled with this moral issue in the development and implementation of curriculum by tracking students, allowing teacher autonomy in the classroom, and using periodic assessment to identify students who have not mastered enough material to be promoted to the next grade. In some settings, serving the common good has meant lowering standards and providing instruction that could be described as minimal or basic. Individual rights were met for some by gifted classes and honors tracks, and for others by special education. For the vast majority of students, however, those in the average or standard levels, little attention was paid to rights.

The competing interests of individual rights and the common good are rarely satisfactorily reconciled. Communities struggle with policies aimed at reducing the tension on an ongoing basis. For most educators, this dilemma is the one they are most familiar with and the one about which they have the strongest opinions. Prior to the high-stakes testing accompanying the accountability plan, however, most educators were relatively satisfied that the policies and procedures being implemented in their own settings were addressing the issue as well as could be expected. Just as they had faith in the decisions they made at the classroom level, educators often approved of school-based and district-level opportunities for students to take specialized courses and programs. Fairness was understood in local terms and was expressed most often in terms of efficiency or cost-effectiveness.

The ethic of care could be used similarly to justify traditional instructional practice. Teachers "cared about" students who were experiencing personal hardships or struggling with the curriculum and thus did not expect them to perform as well as others who were succeeding in the system. This sense of care encouraged teachers to slow their pace and reduce the material to be taught or to extend their favorite units because students liked them best. Care could also be mistaken for pity, prompting teachers and principals to lower expectations in general for certain students. With the best intentions, educators labeled decisions usually designed to maintain the status quo as caring ones. Such decisions included student academic placement, opportunities for electives or remediation, options for participation in extracurricular events, and rewards or sanctions for certain behaviors. Elevated to a moral level, care has been cited to justify many of the approaches educators chose that are inconsistent with following externally set guidelines, covering all the material or challenging all students.

A more robust ethical framework such as the one Starratt (1994) suggests includes an ethic of critique. The traditional ideas of justice and care both benefit from the addition of critique. Critique "forces educators to confront the moral issues involved when schools disproportionately benefit some groups in society and fail others" (p. 47). "In order to promote a just social order in the school, the school community must carry out an ongoing critique of those structural features of the school that work against human beings" (p. 51). The moral dimension afforded by critique highlights disparities associated with race, gender, class, disability, sexual orientation, and other factors that render individuals outside what has been considered the norm. We are encouraged to question who benefits from social arrangements in the school. Who is least well served by existing structures, policies, or decisions? Critique raises the level of justice to the ideal of a social justice that recognizes inequities and prompts action. The conflict between individual rights and the common good is framed more clearly in terms of which individuals enjoy more rights and whose values have determined the "common" good.

Similarly, an ethic of care needs critique. A commitment of care requires more than an expression of pity or even sympathy. First and foremost, caring emerges from the experience of relationships with others (Noddings, 1984). "Care as a practice involves more than simply good intentions. It requires a deep and thoughtful knowledge of the situation, and of all the actors' situations, needs, and competencies" (Tronto, 1993, p. 136). Regarding ourselves as being in relation with others is the key concept. However, more often than not, expressions of pity arise from detachment. Educators feel sorry for those whose circumstances seem to limit their chances in the system. Whether for reasons of class, race, or other distinguishing feature, educators most often see themselves as apart from students whom they "care" about but with whom they do not wish to become involved. Thus, care can become an empty emotive acknowledgment unrelated to the needs of the individual student.

An ethic of critique again induces us to ask whether the best interests of the students are being met by responses often described as caring. It also means that we need to see the student from his or her own perspective rather than from the more generalized perspective of what educators think is best for him or her. "When I care, I really hear, see or feel what the other tries to convey" (Noddings, 1992, p. 16). Care combined with critique forces us to question whether each student is benefiting from practices that we would design for our own children, for instance. Above all, when fairness and care are sharpened by critique, they are elevated from what Burns (1978) calls modal values that can remain within the realm of reciprocity and good intentions to end values that are concerned with "the broadest and most comprehensive" (p. 430) of principles such as justice, equity, and human rights.

APPLYING JUSTICE, CARE, AND CRITIQUE
TO EDUCATORS' CONCERNS ABOUT SOL TESTING

With Starratt's multidimensional framework in mind, we next consider educators' ethical concerns arising from the accountability plan. Based on the research reported in other chapters in this book, we have identified the issues that seem to cause educators the greatest sense of unease. In order that we might offer some constructive ways to deal with these concerns, we have tried to understand the conflicts from the theoretical perspectives of justice, care and critique. The most frequently cited issues are those of: (1) the injustice of using standardized testing and the unfairness of failing students on the basis of these one-dimensional assessments; (2) the harm of limiting instruction for certain groups to drilling for the tests and remediation; (3) and the loss of teachers' individual rights, freedom, and autonomy in determining curriculum.

Standardized Tests

Using an ethic of critique, we see that standardized assessments have illuminated the discrepancies that exist in learning outcomes for different groups of students—especially those standardized tests, like the ones in Virginia, that are content based. A great deal of concern has been expressed regarding their high-stakes nature, but as one writer put it: "High stakes are imposed not so much by promotion and graduation policies, but by the educational neglect that allows children to fail in the first place" (Taylor, 2000, p. 41). If all students are being taught the same curriculum, it follows that all should have equal opportunities to score at a passing level on criterion-referenced tests such as those in Virginia. But until the advent of the tests, there were no publicly scrutinized data showing that some groups, mainly African-American and Hispanic, were scoring disproportionately low (see chapter 7 for a fuller discussion of this).

Although the pressure to produce better test scores has resulted in targeted assistance for some students who are not achieving at equitable levels (Glickman, 2000), schools are still striving to develop effective strategies for achieving equity. As highlighted by Kohn (2001), Robinson and Brandon (1994) found that socioeconomic factors (number of parents living at home, parents' educational background, type of community, and state poverty rate) account for 89% of the variance in state scores on the 1992 NAEP math scores. An opponent of the standards movement, Kohn argues that standardized tests offer a "remarkably precise method for gauging the size of the houses near the school where the test was administered" (p. 349) and for this reason, we should fight the current emphasis on standardized tests because they tell us nothing about classroom quality.

To accept this argument at face value smacks of academic fatalism based on poverty; that no matter how good the teachers and schools may be, standardized tests will always correlate with socioeconomic status. Some argue that the acceptance of this reality as an immutable fact is precisely why we cannot discard testing but we must use it to document and monitor student progress. The fundamental belief in the futility of education to change the "wealth-equals-achievement" equation has led to the acceptance of low-test scores for minority children despite research documenting research to the contrary (Scheurich, Skrla, & Johnson, 2000). We suggest that instead of killing the messenger (testing results) that provides feedback on an educational system of neglect, that we use testing as a means of measuring equity of results for all students. "Standards and accountability expose the sham that passes for education in many heavily minority schools and provide measurements and pressure to prod schools to target resources where they are needed most" (Taylor, 2000, p. 56).

Therefore, the standardized test that is not norm referenced, but content based, can shed some necessary light on who has been best served by the curriculum and instructional practices that have helped maintain the status quo. This is with the understanding that the test itself must be only one source of information to be gathered about a student's learning. The criticism that the multiple-choice test is limited in its capacity to describe a student's knowledge and skill level is a valid one. Again, from the perspective of an ethic of critique, standardized tests assume that one size fits all. They deny students the opportunities to express themselves in culturally diverse ways, through different learning modes and in authentic situations. Thus, while it can be seen that they serve the socially just purpose of exposing inequitable access to curriculum, standardized tests also contribute to perpetuating mainstream interests and expectations of the educational process. Other forms of assessment must supplement standardized tests.

Limiting Instruction for Certain Groups

Following from the above position, there is a concern that minority students, some special education students, and other marginalized groups will be denied a rich curriculum once the state enforces the 70% passing rate. Educators fear that the standards will be reduced to basic facts and that certain students will be drilled relentlessly to achieve a passing score. Many summer remediation efforts are similarly criticized. Having studied the TAAS tests in Texas, McNeil (2000) argues that the teaching associated with that reform "creates a new form of discrimination as teaching to the fragmented and narrow information of the test comes to substitute for a substantive curriculum in the schools of poor and minority youths" (p. 730).

An ethic of justice requires us to take this criticism seriously. It cannot be seen as contributing to the common good if, once more, structures are put in place to confirm the dominant discourse that is founded on "haves" and "have nots." Those who advocate for an accountability system that produces this unintended consequence find themselves, as Purpel (1999) laments, "engaged in maintaining and revitalizing a social structure in the form of a social triage in which some flourish, many struggle, and far too many perish" (p. 73). It is instructive to realize that reforms focused on ensuring broad access to a privileged curriculum can become assimilated into the bureaucratic practice of "business as usual." The forces at work generating inequality in our school systems can be more powerful than the mandates created to fight against them.

The most difficult aspect of this concern about the disparate treatment of students is that disparity is relatively hidden. Few of the educators interviewed for the studies in this book expressed unease about it and many would deny the discriminatory effects of emphasizing basic instruction for some groups. Focused primarily on raising student test scores across the board, principals and teachers in Virginia are putting their efforts into ensuring that the appropriate curriculum is covered and that extra help is available for those who need it. Reacting to situations where it became clear that teachers did not have the necessary materials, time, or expertise to guide students through the assessments, superintendents and principals mobilized available resources to meet the state benchmarks. That some of these efforts result in disparate treatment of certain student populations is not immediately apparent. Unless viewed through the lens of an ethic of critique, many of those strategies will be heralded for their responsiveness. In the eyes of some educators, the drilling and repetitive remediation will be associated with caring for students and wanting to do what is best for them under the circumstances of externally imposed assessments.

However, critique encourages us to probe more deeply both our actions and our intentions. If students' best interests were really at the heart of these practices, they would be modified or abandoned in their diminishing forms. Teachers need *more* creative approaches to material that is hard to grasp, not fewer. Remediation must not be interpreted to mean a duplication of the same instructional activities that were found to be inadequate in the first place or, even worse, more tedious ones such as mindless repetition of facts. Indeed, Tomlinson (2001) implores teachers to teach skillfully in a time of standards. They will accomplish this

> by having a sense of mission, by organizing what they want to teach in ways that make the best use of time, by teaching individuals rather than masses, by helping students make sense of and apply their learning, by actively engaging students in their lessons, by caring deeply about those who entrust their learning to them, and by acting on the belief that each student will leave the classroom markedly stronger than when he or she arrived. (p. 46)

Loss of Teacher Autonomy

There is no doubt that educational reforms inhibit teachers' creativity, freedom, and autonomy, in the broadest sense of these terms. Going back to the kind of general beliefs that were prevalent in states before such reforms as Virginia's accountability plan, teachers saw the exercise of these liberties as a measure of their professionalism. However, those freedoms were always meant to be curtailed by the curriculum guides or standards that were in place. District policies and state standards have traditionally provided the backdrop for teachers' classroom decisions on instructional strategies, methods of assessment, and content delivery. Thus, autonomy was always limited.

Moreover, respect for teacher autonomy taken to the extreme can result in a lack of cohesive goals and focus for a school. Without goals, how can schools improve and address existing inequities? Goals are a means of motivating and mobilizing a group to action, to achieve at a level higher than has been previously attained (Schmoker, 1998). Teacher autonomy shaped by the desire for an overall increase in the common good of education is a worthy aim. Yet, not all teachers who argue for a return to more freedom and autonomy in the classroom are thinking of the general good. Too often, these liberties are coupled with teachers' perceptions of what is best for the students in the classroom. Biases and prejudices color those beliefs of what students are capable of learning. So it becomes the freedom to limit students' opportunities rather than to expand them. And sometimes it is the freedom to remain mediocre and not to grow professionally that teachers are seeking.

Starratt (1994) argues that a school cannot fulfill its mission if administrators do not promote freedom, creativity, and autonomy among their teachers and other staff members (p. 48). But the ethic of critique forces educators to look at what that mission is. It "calls the school community to embrace a sense of social responsibility, not simply to the individuals in the school or school system, not simply to the education profession, but to the society of whom and for whom the school is an agent" (p. 48). Thus, the freedoms teachers are seeking are legitimate if they are embraced within the parameters that allow for all children to succeed. In Virginia, there are still many opportunities for teachers to design their own approaches to the material, to craft their own assessments, and to enrich students' experiences beyond what is required for the SOL assessments. Tomlinson (2001) makes the point that "if educators accept responsibility for the effective practice of education, it is within their professional reach to ensure that standards support rather than undermine excellent curriculum" (p. 39). Accepting standards is part of an educator's ethical commitment to students. Ensuring that every child has a very good chance to reach those standards is a moral imperative.

DEALING WITH ETHICAL CONCERNS SO THAT ALL STUDENTS BENEFIT

Clearly, educators must grapple with the ethical issues identified above. For educators in this book and others whom they represent, the issues are real and pervasive. The ability to recognize the ethical dimensions of these concerns is a first step in finding ways to reconcile them. We believe that Starratt's (1994) multidimensional framework sheds light on what is happening. Teachers and administrators in the midst of their struggle to implement accountability initiatives need some guidelines on how to reason through their task. They are torn between meeting the demands of various interest groups—some who clamor for the immediate abandonment of the high-stakes assessment and others who insist on its rigor—and providing the most positive environment for student success. This is not an easy climate in which to educate all children to reach their potential.

It is imperative, therefore, that all educators exhibit leadership and take a moral stand on these issues. Informed by the ethics of care, justice, and most important, critique, teachers and administrators should direct their energies toward two policy-making environments: the local and the state. First of all, educators should question the *local* policies and procedures that have been created in response to the accountability reform in Virginia. The very nature of reform should imply improved practices and the promise of better outcomes for students—especially students whom we have failed in the past. However, unless we adopt a penetrating approach to our evaluation of what the reform is achieving, we are likely to miss indications that it is not reform at all but reinforcement of the status quo. Purpel (1999) reminds us that "education . . . is a critically important mode of attaining an edge in achieving privilege in a society that embraces and legitimates an unequal distribution of wealth" (p. 68). Surely, we must work to make sure that all students have the opportunities that education offers. Teachers and administrators must see to it that in their own buildings and districts they do not exacerbate the effects of the state imposed reform in contributing to the traditional hierarchies associated with privileging the few.

Teachers' responses to this charge must include a vigilant monitoring of instruction in the classroom. The push for equal access to a rigorous curriculum is accompanied by curriculum mapping, pacing guides, and even lesson plan templates that threaten to remove all creativity from the classroom. Yet, as many have argued (see, e.g., Grogan, 2001; Moon & Callahan, 2001; Tomlinson, 2001), the SOL assessments do not *require* teachers to abandon quality teaching practices. Assessments of learning can continue to include those that are performance based as well as those designed to develop students' multiple-choice skills. Teachers can continue to tailor learning experiences to meet the needs of the individual student, allowing for cultural differences, learning preferences, strengths, and weaknesses.

Principals and superintendents, in their reinvented role of instructional leaders, must help to garner the necessary resources to support teachers' efforts in the classroom and provide professional development that is not confined to basic information about the standards and assessments. As authors of various chapters in this book and others (see Kaplan & Owings, 2001) have advocated, administrators must use their power to ensure that students are offered the most enriching opportunities to achieve passing scores on the tests. This is what leadership means in an age of accountability: to use the tools of assessment to spotlight high-powered teaching and learning. Management structures such as schedules, teacher-student ratios, allocation of faculty and staff, and before- and after-school opportunities including summers should be created to facilitate the best possible educational experiences for students. Above all, administrators must strive to ensure that their responses to the accountability reform are just and humane ones rooted in a strong sense of community both within the schools and outside. Starratt's framework is based on "assumptions about the social nature of human beings and on the human purposes to be served by social organizations" (p. 48). This reminds us that along with providing students an academically demanding environment, school leaders must also commit to preparing "the young to take their responsible place in and for the community" (p. 48). That is, despite the pressure for accountability, they should strive for balance in the purposes of schooling.

In addition, all educators should work toward refining and strengthening the reforms at the *state* level. The responsibility to work at creating better assessment tools, more meaningful resources, and more reasonable conceptions of student academic and social success rests with all of us in the field of education. This kind of leadership resides with the expertise that is distributed throughout systems (Elmore, 1999). At the state level, teachers and administrators can express their concerns to legislators and in public forums created to develop further the standards and assessments. In concert with efforts at the local level, teachers and administrators must use their professional knowledge and expertise on statewide task forces and committees to see that negative consequences of the accountability plan are eliminated.

In this chapter, we take the position that the reform effort is underway but that it is not yet what it could be. The worthy goals of equitable access to academic rigor and high-quality instruction must not preclude other educational goals that we should keep in sight. Although teachers and administrators have a duty to accept state mandated reforms, they do not have a duty to accept them uncritically. They must take the initiative to work for needed changes and the necessary resources to meet the challenges encountered. "As responsible professionals, [educators] are uniquely positioned to affirm the capacity of education to contribute to a consciousness of compassion and justice" (Purpel, 1999, p. 69). Thus, as educators ourselves, we encourage deep reflection on efforts to meet the demands of the accountability reform. How can our collective energies best serve all young Virginians? Using the framework of justice, care, and critique, we advocate a watchful stance and the courage to grasp opportunities. We cannot rest until the goals of accountability are consistent with the goals of equity and true social reform. Educational leadership in an age of accountability, then, is synonymous with proactive leadership for social justice.

NOTE

1. The terms *moral* and *ethical* are used interchangeably in this chapter.

REFERENCES

Benning, V. (2000, February 18). Fairfax to build up failing high schools. *Washington Post*, p. B7.

Benning, V. (2000, November 2). Number of schools to meet SOL goals rises. *Washington Post*, pp. VA 1, VA 10, VA 11.

Burns, J. M. (1978). *Leadership*. New York: Harper & Row.

Cawelti, G. (1999). *Portraits of six benchmark schools: Diverse approaches to improving student achievement*. Arlington, VA: Educational Research Service.

Chase, B. (2000). Making a difference. In D. Meir (Ed.), *Will standards save public education*? Boston: Beacon Press.

Commonwealth of Virginia. (1995). *Standards of learning for Virginia public schools*. Richmond, VA: Author.

Experts attest to merits of SOLs. (2000, November 22). *The Daily Progress*, pp. B1, B3.

Elmore, R. (1999, September). *Leadership of large-scale improvement in American education*. Paper prepared for the Albert Shanker Institute.

Glickman, C. (2000). Holding sacred ground: The impact of standardization. *Educational Leadership, 58*(4), 46–51.

Grogan, M. (2001). Positive and not-so-positive effects of preparing students to pass standards of learning tests in Virginia's high school classrooms. *NASSP Bulletin, 85*(622), 5–14.

Haycock, K. (2001). Closing the achievement gap. *Eductional Leadership, 58*(6), 6–11.

Johnson, S. M. (1990). *Teachers at work*. New York: Basic Books.

Kaplan, L., & Owings, W. (2001). How principals can help teachers with high-stakes testing: One survey's findings with national implications. *NASSP Bulletin, 85*(622), 15–23.

Kohn, A. (2001). Fighting the tests: A practical guide to rescuing our schools. *Phi Delta Kappan 82*, 349–357.

Lortie, D. C. (1975). *School-teacher: A sociological study*. Chicago: The University of Chicago Press.

Margheim, D. E. (2002). What do the teachers think? A survey of teacher attitudes about SOL testing. *Virginia Journal of Education, 95*(7), 11–14.

Marzano, R. J. (2000). *Transforming classroom grading*. Alexandria, VA: Association for Supervision and Curriculum Development.

Mathews, J. (1999, May 9). Va. schools tackle test preparation. *Washington Post*, pp. C1, C8.

McNeil, L. (2000). Creating new inequalities: Contradictions of reform. *Phi Delta Kappan, 81*(10), 729–734.

Moon, T., & Callahan, C. (2001). Classroom performance assessment: What it should look like in a standards-based classroom. *NASSP Bulletin, 85*(622), 48–58.

Noddings, N. (1984). *Caring*. Berkeley, CA.: University of California Press.

Noddings, N. (1992). *The challenge to care in schools: An alternative approach to education.* Berkeley, CA.: University of California Press.

Portner, J. (1999, May 19). Va centers help teachers gear up for exams. *Education Week,* pp. 14–15.

Portner, J. (2000, December 6). Pressure to pass tests permeates Virginia classrooms. *Education Week,* pp. 1, 20.

Purpel, D. (1999). *Moral outrage in education.* New York, NY: Peter Lang.

Robinson, G. E., & Brandon, D. P. (1994). *NAEP Test Scores: Should they be used to compare and rank state educational quality?* Arlington, VA: Educational Research Service.

Scheurich, J. J., Skrla, L., & Johnson, J. F. (2000). Thinking carefully about equity and accountability. *Phi Delta Kappan, 82,* 293–299.

Schmoker, M. (1999). *Results: The key to continuous school improvement.* Alexandria, VA: Association for Supervision and Curriculum Development.

Seymour, L. (2000, September 25). SOL exams a boon for rural districts. *The Washington Post,* pp. B1, B4.

Starratt, R. (1994). *Building an ethical school.* Bristol, PA: The Falmer Press.

Strauss, V. (2001, May 29). When clock beats curriculum. *The Washington Post,* p. A9.

Swenson, E. (1999, August 29). With SOL deadline in mind, area schools make strides. *The Daily Progress,* pp. A1, A8, A9.

Taylor, W. L. (2000, November 15). Standards, tests, and civil rights. *Education Week,* pp. 56, 40–41.

Tomlinson, C. (2001). Standards and the art of teaching: Crafting high-quality classrooms. *NASSP Bulletin, 85* (622), 38–47.

Tronto, J. (1993). *Moral boundaries: A political argument for an ethic of care.* New York, NY: Routledge.

Chapter Nine

EDUCATIONAL LEADERSHIP
IN AN AGE OF ACCOUNTABILITY

DANIEL L. DUKE
MARGARET GROGAN
AND
PAMELA D. TUCKER

If Americans entering the new millennium needed a reminder that they are living in an Age of Accountability, they need look no further than George W. Bush's initial set of education proposals. Among the key elements of Bush's legislative package were the following items (Broder, 2001):

- Annual state tests in reading and math for grades 3 to 8 to measure performance of pupils and schools.

- Schools that do not make enough progress in 1 year will receive aid to improve.

- If a school fails for 2 years, pupils may choose another public school as corrective action continues.

- If a school fails for 3 years, disadvantaged students may use federal funds to attend a private school or get tutoring.

To some observers, it might seem as if public demand for educational accountability has been around since Horace Mann's efforts to establish tax-supported common schools. The truth, however, is that educational accountability is a relatively recent phenomenon. When Lessinger (1971, pp. 62–63) traced the emergence of the idea, he gave credit to President Richard Nixon:

In his March 3rd (1970) Education Message, President Nixon stated, "From these considerations we derive another new concept: *Accountability*. School administrators and school teachers alike are responsible for their performance, and it is in their interest as well as in the interest of their pupils that they be held accountable."

Within a year of Nixon's remarks, states and school systems began to implement accountability initiatives ranging from performance contracting with private providers to new systems for evaluating teachers and schools. The Commission of the States announced that its central theme for the 1970s would be accountability. The *Washington Post* proclaimed that the school systems of America had entered "an Age of Accountability" (Lessinger, 1971, p. 64).

While the term "accountability" has been with us ever since the early seventies, its meaning has not necessarily stayed the same. Duke (2000, pp. 17–18) contends that the original notion of accountability—to give an accounting of— has shifted over time. Today many use the term as if it connoted a guarantee that students will learn what they are expected to learn. Others equate accountability with severe consequences for educators whose students fail to meet established standards.

The purpose of this concluding chapter is to make several key points regarding educational leadership in an Age of Accountability. These key points include the following:

- The sociopolitical context in which educational leaders must lead is changing.

- Educational leaders are realizing that "business-as-usual" is an unacceptable response to the challenges of educational accountability.

- Educational leaders are responding to accountability initiatives without a clear sense of the possible long-term impact of their actions.

- What it means to be an educational leader is changing as a result of pressure for greater accountability.

After sharing some reflections on the changing conditions under which educational leaders are working, we raise several questions regarding the possible costs of accountability. The next section presents some of the benefits that have come with Virginia's accountability plan. The chapter closes with a discussion of the implications of accountability measures for the preparation, recruitment, selection, and evaluation of educational leaders.

THE CHANGING CONTEXT OF EDUCATIONAL LEADERSHIP

The impetus for the contemporary wave of accountability initiatives, including Virginia's four-part accountability plan, was the publication in 1983 of *A Nation at Risk*. The blue ribbon federal commission that produced this seminal document linked the security and prosperity of the United States to the quality of public education. Declining student achievement was blamed for the decline in the U.S. economy.

In the almost two decades since *A Nation at Risk* first appeared, the Soviet Union has fallen, the U.S. economy has surged ahead, and the United States has laid claim to a position of preeminence in the world. Despite these developments, public education remains under attack. Schools and teachers apparently are guilty when the nation's prospects dim, but they receive no credit when circumstances change for the better.

In one sense, then, little has changed for educators since the rise of accountability as an influential public idea. Educational leaders continue to face criticism from parents, politicians, pundits, and policy makers. In other respects, however, the context in which educational leaders work has changed. The process of holding educators accountable has been systematized. Unlike the past, today's superintendents, principals, department chairs, and teachers are responsible for seeing that students learn material that they have had little voice in selecting. Standards have been set, but front-line educators have played little or no role in the process. To ensure that standards are met, statewide tests have been developed and aligned with the standards. Test results are published for all to see. The public can compare student achievement in different schools and school systems, thereby enabling dissatisfied parents with sufficient means to move their children to high-performing schools. States like Virginia also have established standards for schools. If these standards are not met, schools face various punitive actions, from loss of accreditation to state takeover.

Contemporary educational leaders consequently confront challenges that existed only as bad dreams for their predecessors. School performance problems have become front-page news. Principals are subject to dismissal or transfer if their schools' test scores are not sufficiently high. Bonuses and merit pay schemes for principals and faculties have been created by some school systems in an effort to promote greater achievement. Educational leaders are required to develop School Improvement Plans that specify exactly how performance deficits will be corrected. Principals are expected to hold teachers accountable for improving their instruction and, ultimately, the performance of their students.

The Age of Accountability, then, can be characterized by certain widely held assumptions about education and schooling.

First, publicly reported high-stakes tests are believed to be the best way to ensure that educators are held accountable for their performance. Teachers and administrators presumably must be pressured into working harder to improve student performance by publishing test scores and encouraging comparisons across schools. No serious consideration, at least in Virginia, seems to have been given to other accountability measures, such as warranty programs and expanded options for dissatisfied educational consumers. Furthermore, the high-stakes tests, with a few notable exceptions, tend to focus on multiple-choice questions and the recall of factual knowledge. Questions that test higher-order thinking are relatively rare. Only a handful of states, including Maine and Maryland, have experimented with performance-based tests that determine how well students can apply what they have learned and exhibit critical thinking skills.

A second assumption holds that explicit standards and high-stakes tests will motivate students who otherwise might care little for school-based learning. Although many students reportedly are taking the tests more seriously due to the possible consequences (Mathews, 2000), test proponents have not given equal consideration to the possibility that the tests could actually have the opposite effect—discouraging some students from continuing to exert effort in the face of possible, or repeated, failure on state tests.

Accountability advocates also assume that standards and tests will benefit poor and low-achieving students. Their argument suggests that the disparities in student achievement that currently characterize American education can be narrowed by insisting that all students meet higher content and graduation standards. The possibility that accountability measures might actually increase the gap between groups of young people has not been publicly acknowledged by policy makers.

Those bold enough to challenge these assumptions are often discounted as card-carrying members of the "education establishment," romantics who are out of touch with the realities of the global economy, and elitists. The most surprising characteristic of the present moment is not the popularity of the "standards and tests" prescription for educational progress, but the virtual absence of experiments with alternative systemic approaches to raising student achievement and increasing educational accountability. Is fear—in the form of threats to punish schools and withhold diplomas—the only spur to flagging achievement that we can come up with? It would appear that the first victim of the Age of Accountability has been imagination, or what some in previous times might have been called American ingenuity.

It is hard to believe that a decade ago, coalitions of politicians and business leaders were calling on American educators to "break the mold" and boldly explore new ways to promote learning. What happened to the impassioned calls for teaching critical thinking skills (Marshall & Tucker, 1992; Murnane & Levy, 1996)? What happened to the initiatives to reinvent and restructure schools (Stringfield, Ross, & Smith, 1996)? Where are the voices of reason to remind us that young people are more than just test scores (Duke, 1995; Duke, 1996)?

THE NEW MEANING OF EDUCATIONAL LEADERSHIP

If Virginia's experience with accountability reform is indicative of changes elsewhere, several hallmarks of public education are vanishing. With state standards of learning, accreditation standards, and testing programs, as well as state funding and sanctions for poorly performing schools, have come the erosion of local control of education and the reduction of ambiguity regarding what schools are supposed to accomplish. The mission of schools is now crystal clear—get students to achieve state-dictated passing scores on state-commissioned tests so that schools can meet state-mandated passing rates and attain state accreditation. It is our belief that the new context in which educators must practice their profession—a context characterized by centralization, a singular focus on test performance, and negative consequences for poor performance—has occasioned a new understanding of what it means to be an educational leader.

Traditionally, the antidote to ambiguity regarding public education's mission presumably was strong leadership. Superintendents and principals were called on to provide a sense of direction and purpose to enable teachers to focus their energies and provide high-quality instruction (Duke, 1986; Duke, 1994). Direction and purpose today are provided by the state. Few can claim any longer that ambiguity exists concerning the mission of public schools. If educational leaders no longer need to determine or clarify what school is about, is there less need for educational leadership? We think not. We do believe, however, that there is a need for a different focus for educational leadership.

Educational leadership entails more than providing direction. It also involves inspiring commitment to the school's mission (Duke, 1994). Our studies suggest that schools where teachers are highly committed to preparing students for state tests are schools where test performance is relatively high. To achieve such commitment requires more than cheerleading on the part of superintendents, principals, department chairs, and teacher leaders. It entails an understanding of how young people learn and how to improve instruction. It involves freeing people of less important duties so that they can focus on teaching and learning. It calls for buffering teachers and students from the punitive aspects of standards and designing infrastructures to provide assistance to students and training to teachers. It necessitates winning the support of parents, who in many cases harbor serious reservations about high-stakes tests.

Achieving and maintaining commitment to the new accountability requires more leadership than one individual can provide. We agree with Leithwood (2001) and Elmore (1999) when they argue that the key to educational accountability is *distributed leadership*—a network of relationships focused on the continuing improvement of performance. Distributed leadership increases the likelihood that schools can become true learning communities characterized by collective, rather than individual, accountability. It is simply inappropriate to continue holding individual teachers accountable for expectations that only can be realized through collaboration among various professionals. We agree with Hogan, Curphy, and Hogan (1994, p. 493) when they argue that contemporary leadership involves "persuading other people to set aside . . . their individual concerns and to pursue a common goal that is important for the responsibilities and welfare of a group." Leading schools and school systems in an Age of Accountability will depend, to a great extent, on the capacity of leaders at various levels to initiate and sustain cultures of collective accountability.

Considerable complexity characterizes educational leadership today. Eliminating ambiguity of purpose has not meant that the tasks of educational leaders have become simpler or easier. Leaders, to be credible, now must know far more about learning, curriculum, instruction, assessment, diagnosis, and remediation than ever before. Distributed leadership does not mean that superintendents and principals are freed of the obligation to function as instructional leaders. Given the heavy demands of accountability, school leadership may have to become bifurcated like hospital leadership did decades earlier. Hospitals typically have administrators who are chiefly responsible for the business side of operations and medical heads who are in charge of patient treatment and care. Such a division of responsibility may be the only way that school principals can function as true instructional leaders (see chapter 4).

One critical function of instructional leadership that receives relatively little attention is *troubleshooting* (Duke, 1987). It is difficult to imagine implementing a program of continuing instructional improvement without leaders who are able to anticipate problems before they mushroom out of control or undermine student achievement. It is to the function of troubleshooting that we now turn our attention.

GUARDING AGAINST NEGATIVE EFFECTS

Conventional wisdom maintains that many educators confront reform with a "this too shall pass" attitude. If Virginia's experience is any indication, educators are not opting for the role of passive bystander. While they may not always be leading the reform parade, they clearly are marching along on the road to accountability. The studies reported in this book indicate that superintendents, principals, department chairs, and teachers are responding to Virginia's accountability plan with new policies, programs, and practices.

In order to respond conscientiously to the challenges posed by new Standards of Learning, Standards of Accreditation, and state testing, Virginia's educational leaders must do more than promulgate new policies and launch new initiatives, however. Responsible leadership recognizes that reform may entail costs as well as benefits. Consequently, educational leaders must become adept at troubleshooting. They must ask tough and sometimes politically incorrect questions and remain ever vigilant for unintended negative consequences of reform.

In this section we raise some questions that we believe educational leaders in Virginia need to be asking.

Is it possible to raise scores on standardized tests without improving the quality of public schooling? To listen to some accountability advocates, raising scores and passing rates on standardized tests is the sine qua non of educational excellence. They seem to believe that test performance is an end in itself rather than a means to an end.

Under certain circumstances, though, the quality of public schooling may be adversely affected, even as test averages and passing rates climb. If tests stress a limited range of thinking skills and knowledge, for example, they may cause teachers to deemphasize other important learning opportunities. If students far below the established cut score receive little attention because teachers feel they must concentrate their limited time and energy on helping students who are within a few points of passing, the school experiences of our most needy young people will suffer. If students far above the established cut score are compelled to bide their time while classmates master the standards, the school experiences of our most talented students will be compromised. If students become frustrated and discouraged because they feel that teachers care less about them than their test scores, the results can hardly be viewed as constructive. And if high pass rates on state tests become a justification for complacency and resistance to change, both students and teachers could pay a high price.

While we do not mean to suggest that these "ifs" are occurring in all schools, we know they are occurring in some. We know that teachers in some schools focus their assistance on students who are close to passing state tests, leaving the lowest-achieving students to fend for themselves. We know that test scores are being viewed as ends, not means, in some schools. As a director of testing for a school division told one of the authors, "It used to be when we sat down to meet, we talked about students. Now we talk about test scores." We know that many teachers feel they must sacrifice higher-order thinking skills and lessons that engage and intrigue students in order to cover required curriculum content. We know that teachers and administrators in some schools where a large percentage of students pass all the state tests are using this fact to justify inertia. Seeing that such negative by-products of educational reform are kept to a minimum is one of the major tasks facing educational leaders in Virginia and elsewhere.

Is Virginia's accountability plan reducing disparities between groups of students? Advocates of standards and testing frequently justify these measures in terms of narrowing the performance gap between low-achieving and high-achieving students. Exactly how this process works, however, often is left to the imagination of educators. Prudence dictates that the consequences of greater accountability be anticipated with caution. Among the *possible* consequences of accountability for Virginia's students are the following:

- Performance on state tests will rise for all groups, but the gap between different groups of students will remain stable.

- Performance on state tests will rise for some groups, but not for others. Depending on which groups improve, the achievement gap could narrow or widen.

- Performance on state tests will not rise for any group, and existing achievement gaps will continue.

- Performance on state tests will rise for students who remain in school until graduation, but the dropout rate will also increase.

The only consequence of the accountability plan that might be regarded as generally acceptable is for performance on state tests to rise for all groups, but for the rate of improvement for current low-achieving groups to be greater than for current high-achieving groups. Under this circumstance, the achievement gap would narrow while all students improved performance. It is worth noting that totally eliminating the achievement gap between groups of students might seem commendable, but it doubtless would generate a negative reaction from parents who expected *their* children to outperform other children. Policymakers often forget that many parents do not send their children to school so they can be just like other students.

If the perceived impact of accountability measures is to "hold back" high-achieving students while helping low-achieving students to improve, the consequences for public schools could be devastating. Parents with the means likely would move their high-achieving children to schools where they could excel, leaving many public schools socioeconomically isolated and filled with relatively low-achieving students.

It is too early to know what impact Virginia's accountability plan will have, but educational leaders must carefully monitor performance trends within and across school systems if they are to be prepared for possible negative fallout from shifting patterns of achievement on state tests.

Is Virginia's accountability plan making it more difficult to manage schools? No one leads all the time. Even the most capable educational leader must spend considerable time managing the affairs of their school. It is therefore important to ask whether accountability measures are having an adverse effect on school administration.

In surveying the impact of California's Public Schools Accountability Act on San Francisco Bay Area schools, Hatch (2001) has noted that the biggest threat to reform may be "system overload." In other words, it is not necessarily the case that particular accountability measures are inappropriate or counterproductive. Instead, it is the sheer number of simultaneous measures that can pose a threat to those who must manage change. Hatch points out in this regard that Bay Area schools

> are struggling to respond to a dizzying set of state and district initiatives. In the areas of curriculum and assessment alone, these include recent state efforts to refine curriculum frameworks in language arts, mathematics, and several other subjects; to establish tutoring and reading academies; and to deal with California's Public

Schools Accountability Act, which provides rewards and sanctions to encourage schools to improve the performances of their students on the Stanford Achievement Test-9th Edition. (Hatch, 2001, p. 44)

Educational leaders in Virginia have had to manage a comparable collection of new initiatives. Local curricula have needed to be aligned with the revised Standards of Learning. New textbooks and instructional materials have been reviewed, ordered, and distributed. Arrangements have had to be made for preparing students for state tests, administering the tests, and analyzing the results. New policies and programs related to the accountability plan have been implemented. Meetings to orient parents and students to the SOL and SOA have had to be scheduled. Teachers and administrators have had to receive training concerning the SOL and how best to help students learn them. School Improvement Plans have had to be developed, monitored, and reported on. All this in addition to doing everything that already is required of administrators makes it understandable that some individuals have felt overwhelmed.

Another management problem that could result from the accountability plan concerns the increased stress on and public scrutiny of educators. These factors may deter capable individuals from becoming teachers and administrators and drive into retirement those already in the ranks. If this happens, and some believe it already is happening, the task of recruiting people to fill positions in schools will become even more challenging than it currently is. The schools that will face the greatest difficulty with recruitment predictably will be those with the lowest-performing students. What incentives and inducements can educational leaders offer to people to work in schools that face the prospect of public criticism, loss of accreditation, and state takeover?

A third administrative challenge involves maintaining a culture of cooperation in schools, especially secondary schools, where accountability measures have stalled efforts to promote interdisciplinary planning and teaching, and revived traditional departmental divisions. The public sharing of test results may lead to finger-pointing between departments, particularly when low scores in one or two departments threaten the entire school with loss of accreditation and community criticism. Principals must ensure that lines of communication between departments remain open and that faculty in various disciplines remain committed to schoolwide goals. Needless to say, the selection of department chairs has become one of the most important decisions for secondary principals.

An area of school administration that consumes considerable time and generates a great deal of anxiety is the supervision and evaluation of teachers. In order to increase the likelihood that teachers regard these functions as constructive, many principals have preferred to use their supervisory interactions and evaluations as mechanisms for promoting professional growth. Whether this orientation will be possible in light of accountability measures is unclear. In some

Virginia school divisions, board members and superintendents have let it be known that they expect student performance on state tests to serve as a basis for teacher evaluations. Supervision in many schools now focuses on the extent to which teachers cover the SOL. Under such circumstances, some teachers may grow to resent supervision and evaluation, thereby making the already difficult job of school administration even more so.

Do Virginia's Standards of Learning and state tests reflect what students should know and what good evaluation practice should be? The development of the SOL and tests to measure them has been marked by considerable controversy. Mention already has been made of the tendency for test items to focus on factual recall and overlook higher-order thinking. Problems concerning the SOL in social studies still have not been resolved as of the writing of this chapter. Complaints continue to be heard regarding particular test items, how they are scored, and the length of time it takes to return scores to schools. While the state has established advisory boards to oversee the SOL and the state testing program, local educational leaders also have an obligation to monitor the standards and especially the tests to make certain that students are protected from curriculum content that is narrow and politically motivated as well as inappropriate testing practices.

Given the serious consequences that can result from poor performance on state tests, cheating has become a source of concern. Several Virginia school divisions have reported cases of teachers coaching students in inappropriate ways and test answers being changed. Educational leaders at all levels must take whatever precautions are necessary to prevent such practices from giving certain teachers and schools an unfair advantage.

APPRECIATING THE BENEFITS OF ACCOUNTABILITY

While Virginia's educational leaders must remain vigilant regarding the potential costs of accountability measures, they also have noted various consequences of the state's accountability plan that represent promising developments. Leaders at all levels have nurtured these developments.

One encouraging sign has been the willingness of teachers and department chairs across the commonwealth to work together to make certain that the SOL are incorporated into their lessons. Teachers in many school divisions report that they cannot remember a time when they worked more closely with colleagues or devoted as much professional effort to discussing issues of curriculum, instruction, and assessment. In this regard, the accountability measures seem to have served as a powerful impetus to staff development, professional growth, and communication among teachers.

In the past, it frequently has been difficult for educators to tell whether or not staff development and professional growth actually made a difference. The state tests, however limited, now provide an annual measure of student learning and teacher effort. In schools where passing rates have risen from one year to the next, teachers express considerable pride and sense of accomplishment. Seeing that training, cooperation, and curriculum focus can pay dividends serves as a substantial boost to teachers' sense of individual and collective efficacy. In the absence of any benchmarks, educators can only guess about the impact of their efforts.

The SOL have been around for 3 decades, but until state tests were developed and accreditation standards were linked to student performance on the tests, the SOL were not of much value in guiding efforts to help low-achieving students. The SOL now drive the assistance and remediation process. Students no longer have a vague idea of what they must learn in order to succeed in school. Teachers, too, have a clearer idea of what to focus on. In many school divisions, the result has been the development of various programs—before- and after-school tutorials, special test preparation sessions before state tests are given, increased instructional time in difficult subjects like Algebra and summer schools—to provide students with the assistance necessary to pass the tests. It goes without saying that remediation efforts are much more likely to succeed when students and teachers have a clear sense of what to accomplish in order to avoid the consequences of low achievement.

The advent of the state accountability plan has provided enterprising educational leaders with opportunities to press for long-needed improvements. Because students who fail state tests may require intensive remediation during the summer, for example, principals have lobbied for air conditioning for their schools. Class sizes have been reduced for some SOL courses, and additional specialists in reading, mathematics, and learning disorders have been hired. Reluctant at first to give additional funds to school divisions, the state has begun to provide money to offset the impact of the accountability plan.

The benefits derived from Virginia's accountability plan are not limited to improvements in teaching and schools. Realizing that the only way they can guide the accountability process and minimize negative consequences is through cooperation, education groups across the commonwealth have created an unprecedented alliance. Organizations representing teachers, principals, superintendents, and parents have begun to share information, monitor the impact of accountability measures, and lobby legislators to make certain all students are well-served. The implication for educational leaders at all levels is clear: leadership in an Age of Accountability necessitates political action as well as educational competence.

LEARNING TO LEAD AND LEADING TO LEARN

In this book we have looked at the changing context of educational leadership. We have examined both the promising and the problematic consequences of Virginia's accountability plan. We have indicated the implications of account-ability measures for policy makers, superintendents, principals, department chairs, and teachers. In closing, one other set of issues needs to be considered. What are the implications of accountability for the preparation, recruitment, selection, and evaluation of educational leaders?

Is it necessary to rethink how educational leaders are prepared? Does lead-ership in an Age of Accountability require knowledge, skills, and dispositions that traditionally have received inadequate attention in graduate programs for school and district administrators and teacher leaders?

When the first calls for instructional leadership were made in the early 1980s, educational administration programs were slow to respond. Educational leaders were not losing their jobs because of poor student performance. Schools and school districts were not faced with loss of accreditation and state takeover. Today, of course, the situation has changed. With the advent of serious conse-quences for poor student performance, educational leaders must possess the knowledge, skills, and dispositions to function as instructional leaders. In Vir-ginia, the Standards of Accreditation actually mandate principals to exercise instructional leadership.

If educational administration and teacher leadership programs are to rise to the challenge of accountability, they will need to provide training in three areas: (1) monitoring student achievement, (2) coordination of student assistance, and (3) supervision of instructional improvement.

How well students perform on state tests is now front-page news. Taxpay-ers in Virginia, as elsewhere, can readily compare how different schools are doing. Under such circumstances, educational leaders must monitor student achievement, explain to the public how well students are performing, and point out where they need help. They must be able to explain to parents how tests are designed and scored. They must be able to help parents and students understand what test scores mean. They must know the difference between randomly dis-tributed errors and patterns of errors on tests. Teachers must realize that depart-ment chairs, principals, and central office administrators are aware of student performance, that they compare student grades with their scores on state tests, and that they are prepared to raise questions when large numbers of students in particular classes receive good grades, but do poorly on tests.

It is of little value to track student achievement if no effort is made to help students who are performing poorly. Educational leaders must be prepared to coordinate the delivery of assistance to students in need. Teachers cannot always be expected to take the initiative because student assistance often depends on factors beyond their control, such as scheduling changes (extended school day, before-school tutorials, modified class schedules, double or blocked periods), reallocation of staff (intervention teams, paired teaching arrangements), and special programs (Saturday school, summer school). In order to be effective coordinators of student assistance, it is essential for educational leaders to understand what kinds of interventions work and under what conditions. They need a basic understanding of reading problems and learning disorders. They also should know what remediation materials and software have proven helpful to struggling students.

Educational leaders do not personally teach all of the students who have difficulty learning the required standards. Consequently, they must be able to support the continuous improvement of instruction by teachers. To do so requires an understanding of how learning occurs as well as instructional theory. Department chairs and principals must be capable of describing what goes on in classrooms, working with teachers to analyze these data, and making recommendations concerning how to improve the classroom learning environment. When teachers lack the knowledge to implement the recommendations, educational leaders need to make arrangements for inservice training. Successful inservice training, in turn, depends on leaders' understanding of how adults learn and grow professionally.

Becoming adept at monitoring student achievement, coordinating student assistance, and supervising instructional improvement entails the acquisition and application of certain technical skills, such as classroom observation and data analysis. Other critical knowledge for educational leaders includes the principles of good assessment and a thorough understanding of the standards teachers are expected to teach and students are expected to learn. Knowledge and skills are necessary for leadership in an Age of Accountability, but they are insufficient without certain dispositions. Leaders must believe that all students can learn, and they must possess the will and ethical commitment to use their knowledge and skills toward this end.

If for whatever reason educational administration programs fail to prepare leaders in these ways, it is likely that primary responsibility for the preparation of educational leaders will shift to school systems, professional organizations, and state departments of education. To some extent, depending on the state, this process already has begun. It remains to be seen whether graduate programs can reinvent themselves in order to prepare educational leaders who are equipped to meet the challenges of accountability.

It is one thing to prepare capable educational leaders and another to see that they are placed in positions where they can make a difference. School systems must insist on hiring administrators with demonstrated competence in instructional leadership. This may require superintendents and principals to encourage the strongest teachers to consider educational administration as a career option. These individuals are in a far better position than members of graduate program admissions committees to recognize instructional leadership potential. Once hired, principals will need far greater support and latitude to achieve state-mandated academic objectives.

If policy makers believe that educational leadership is a key to raising student performance, they will need to do two things. First, they must take a hard look at what educational leaders are expected to do. Unreasonable expectations must be changed. One recommendation is to restructure the principalship and create two positions—a school manager and an instructional leader (Richard, 2000). Hospitals have operated on the basis of a differentiated leadership model for years. Second, educational leaders must receive remuneration commensurate with the proclaimed importance of the job. Districts that lack the fiscal resources to offer competitive salaries will need state assistance. Failure to revise job descriptions for leaders and offer proper incentives will render moot any efforts to improve recruitment and selection.

Educational leadership in an Age of Accountability calls not only for changes in the preparation, recruitment, and selection of leaders, but also changes in how leaders are evaluated. The most obvious change so far has been the inclusion of student passing rates on state tests as one basis for evaluating the performance of educational leaders, particularly principals. At the time this chapter was written, the director of one state administrators' organization indicated that six Virginia principals were in litigation over dismissals linked to low test scores. While the details of these cases are unknown, it is disheartening to think that test scores alone might be used as the basis for firing principals.

Principals also are being evaluated on the extent to which the objectives of School Improvement Plans have been met. In Virginia, these plans are used as the basis for addressing problems associated with low student performance on state tests. Low-performing schools receive help in identifying where problems exist and how to address them from Academic Review Teams dispatched by the Virginia Department of Education. Teams consist of staff from the state's eight regional Best Practice Centers and the Department of Education as well as practitioners with particular subject-matter expertise. Each team spends up to 3 days at a school working with the principal and faculty to identify issues affecting student performance. Classroom instruction is observed and discussed with teachers. Between November 2000 and March 2001, 205 schools in Virginia were assisted in developing 3-year School Improvement Plans so that they could meet state accreditation standards.

If principals are evaluated on student achievement and how well faculty implement School Improvement Plans, an argument can be made that they need broader authority than they currently possess. While such a step has not yet been taken in Virginia, it is worth noting that Arizona is entertaining a proposal to reshape the principalship. The Local Education Accountability Plan (LEAP) would allow a principal, with the approval of the local board of education, to control everything from the hiring and firing of teachers to bus schedules and school supplies (Stricherz, 2001). Not surprisingly, the proposal has drawn strong criticism from Arizona teachers' organizations. Still, it is unreasonable to hold principals solely accountable for that over which they exert little control. Principals should be evaluated on the broad range of responsibilities they fulfill and not a narrowly defined set of outcomes.

A FINAL THOUGHT

Whether we are witnessing a tectonic shift in the educational landscape, or simply another tremor, is impossible at present to determine. The prevailing view is that leadership during this Age of Accountability has become more stressful, more political, more complex, and more time-consuming. There is another view, rarely voiced, that bears consideration, however. Accountability programs such as Virginia's just possibly could make the job of educational leadership easier.

How can such a case be made? For years, educational leaders have complained that the goals of public education are ambiguous. No longer can that claim be made, at least not in Virginia, where the goal is clear—achieve state accreditation. To achieve accreditation, the objectives are clear—achieve passing rates of 70% on state tests. To achieve passing rates of 70% on state tests, the strategy is clear—insist that teachers teach the Standards of Learning. Such clarity of mission has not existed in the past. Nor have educational leaders enjoyed the leverage to bring teachers into line that they now enjoy.

The question, of course, that remains is whether educational leaders will embrace this clarity, or instead long for a return to ambiguity.

REFERENCES

Broder, D. S. (2001, February 15). Panel starts clock on education bill. *Washington Post*, p. A15.

Duke, D. L. (1986). The aesthetics of leadership. *Educational Administration Quarterly, 21*(2), 7–27.

Duke, D. L. (2000). *A design for Alana: Creating the next generation of American schools*. Bloomington, IN: Phi Delta Kappan Educational Foundation.

Duke, D. L. (1994). Drift, Detachment, and the Need for Teacher Leadership. In D. R. Walling (Ed.), *Teachers as leaders* (pp. 255–274). Bloomington, IN: Phi Delta Kappa Educational Foundation.

Duke, D. L. (1987). *School leadership and instructional improvement*. NY: Random House.

Duke, D. L. (1995). *The school that refused to die*. Albany, NY: State University of New York Press.

Duke, D. L. (1996). Seeking a centrist position to counter the politics of polarization. *Phi Delta Kappan, 78*(2), 120–123.

Elmore, R. (1999). Leadership of large-scale improvement in American education. Paper prepared for the Albert Shanker Institute.

Hatch, T. (2001, February 14). It takes capacity to build capacity. *Education Week*, pp. 44, 47.

Hogan, R., Curphy, G. J., & Hogan, J. (1994). What we know about leadership. *American Psychologist*, 49(6), 493–504.

Leithwood, K. (2001). School leadership and educational accountability: Toward a distributed perspective. In T. J. Kowalski (Ed.), *Twenty-first century challenges for school administrators* (pp. 11–25). Lanham, MD: Scarecrow Press.

Lessinger, L. M. (1971). The powerful notion of accountability in education. In L. H. Browder, Jr. (Ed.), *Emerging patterns of administrative accountability* (pp. 62–73). Berkeley, CA: McCutchan.

Marshall, R., & Tucker, M. (1992). *Thinking for a living*. New York: Basic Books.

Mathews, J. (2000, October 22). First class faces SOLs in Virginia. *Washington Post*, pp. C-1, C-9.

Murnane, R. J., & Levy, F. (1996). *Teaching the new basic skills*. New York: Free Press.

Richard, A. (2000, November 1). Panel calls for fresh look at duties facing principals. *Education Week*, p. 5.

Stricherz, M. (2001, January 17). Law giving principals new powers under fire in Arizona, *Education Week*, p. 22.

Stringfield, S., Ross, S., & Smith, L. (Eds.). (1996). *Bold plans for school restructuring*. Mahwah, NJ: Erlbaum.

CONTRIBUTORS

Dan W. Butin an assistant professor of education at Gettysburg College in Gettysburg, Pennsylvania. He specializes in the social and cultural contexts of education, with an emphasis on issues of multicultural education, social exclusion, and alternative assessment. His most recent work investigates the potential for community service learning in teacher education programs. He received his Ph.D. from the University of Virginia in social foundations.

Daniel E. Curry-Corcoran is currently a doctoral student at the University of Virginia in the Foundations, Leadership, and Policy Department where he is studying educational evaluation and policy. Before completing an M.Ed. in educational evaluation at the University of Virginia in 1999, Mr. Curry-Corcoran taught English at the secondary level for 2 years first at an inner-city school in Norfolk, Virginia, and then at an alternative school in Charlottesville, Virginia. Along with his current studies, he is working with Brunswick County Public Schools and Old Dominion University as an external evaluator for the PT3 (Preparing Tomorrow's Teachers to Use Technology) grant initiative.

A one-time high school history teacher and administrator, **Daniel L. Duke** has been a professor of educational leadership for over a quarter century. After serving on the faculties of Lewis and Clark College and Stanford University, Duke joined the University of Virginia as chair of the Department of Educational Leadership and Policy. In 1996 he obtained funding for the Thomas Jefferson Center for Educational Design, an interdisciplinary organization devoted to the design of new learning environments. As. director of the Jefferson Center, Duke coordinates a wide range of research, evaluation, design, training, and consulting activities.

An established researcher and author, Duke has written or edited 22 books and nearly 150 articles on a variety of subjects, including the reform of secondary education, innovative learning environments, educational leadership, school safety, and organizational change. He has consulted with more than 200 school systems, government agencies, and institutions of higher education in the United States and abroad. Duke has served as president of the University Council for

Educational Administration and Editor of the Series on Contemporary Educational Leadership for the State University of New York Press. Recently he was selected as the Outstanding Professor in the Curry School of Education at the University of Virginia.

Duke received his bachelor's degree from Yale University and his doctorate from the State University of New York at Albany. He lives atop Pantops Mountain in Charlottesville with his wife, dog, and cat and awaits Thomas Jefferson's return.

Margaret Grogan is professor and chair of Educational Leadership and Policy Analysis at the University of Missouri. She teaches educational leadership and codirects the UCEA Center for the Study of Leadership and Ethics. She edits a series on Women in Leadership for SUNY Press. Her current research focuses on the superintendency, the moral and ethical dimensions of leadership and women in leadership. Among her publications are: *Voices of Women Aspiring to the Superintendency* (1996), "A Feminist Poststructuralist Account of Collaboration" (1999), and "Equity/Equality Issues of Gender, Race and Class" (1999). Additionally, she has coauthored with Cryss Brunner and Lars Björk (2002), "Shifts in the Discourse Defining the Superintendency: Historical and Current Foundations of the Position." Together with Mary Gardiner and Ernestine Enomoto, she wrote, *Coloring Outside the Lines: Mentoring Women into Educational Leadership* (2000). She received her bachelor's degree from the University of Queensland, her master's from Michigan State University, and her Ph.D. in educational administration from Washington State University.

Walt Heinecke is assistant professor of Educational Evaluation and Policy Studies at the University of Virginia's Curry School of Education. He teaches courses in research and evaluation methods and the sociology of educational policy. His research interests include the relationship between policy and educational practice, educational accountability, standards and testing, and the evaluation of educational technology. He is currently conducting evaluations of projects in the U.S. Department of Education's Preparing Tomorrow's Teachers for Technology (PT3) Program. He is coeditor of *Political Spectacle and the Fate of American Schools* (forthcoming). He is editor of the series *Research Methods in Educational Technology* for Information Age Press and has coedited Volume 1 of that series: Evaluating Educational Technology. He serves on the editorial board of the *Journal of Technology and Teacher Education* and the *Journal of Technology, Learning and Assessment*. He received his Ph.D. from Arizona State University in educational policy studies.

Tonya R. Moon, Ph.D., is an assistant professor in the Curry School of Education at the University of Virginia and a principal investigator for the National

Research Center on the Gifted and Talented. Her specialization is in the areas of educational measurement, research, and evaluation and she works with state departments across the country on technical issues associated with educational assessments designed for accountability purposes. She also works as a consultant with school districts and schools on using better assessment techniques for improving instruction and student learning. She has published numerous articles, book chapters, and research monographs dealing with the areas of student achievement, generalizability of performance scores, technical issues associated with performance assessments, and gifted education. She is past president of the Virginia Educational Research Association. Her e-mail address is *trm2k@virginia.edu*. She received her Ph.D. from the University of Virginia in educational measurement, research, and evaluation.

Brianne L. Reck is currently a middle school administrator in a school division in the Greater Richmond Metropolitan Area. She has served as an adjunct professor in the leadership department of the University of Virginia. She received her Ph.D. in educational administration from the University of Virginia. Her research interests are in school reform and leadership.

Pamela B. Roland is assistant, professor, Center for K–12 Education, School of Continuing and Professional Studies at the University of Virginia. She has education degrees from Radford College and the College of William and Mary, and a doctorate from the University of Virginia in educational administration. She has been adjunct faculty for Mary Baldwin College and the Curry School of Education at the University of Virginia and a visiting professor at University of Wisconsin at Platteville; Center for the Education and Young Adolescent (CEYA); SUNY/Fredonia, NY; and Midwestern State University, Wichita Falls, TX. In her current position, she is the primary instructor for the University of Virginia Career Switcher Program and for a distributed learning course on the Internet, *Teaching for Standards Based Mastery*. She is often a key presenter at State and National Program conferences for the School of Continuing and Professional Studies. She can be reached at *pre3c@virginia.edu*.

Whitney H. Sherman has a Ph.D. in administration and supervision from the University of Virginia. Her dissertation was entitled "Women's Experiences with a Formal Leadership Program for Aspiring Administrators." She received her M.Ed. in administration and supervision at Virginia Commonwealth University and her B.S. in Psychology and Early Childhood Education at James Madison University. She served as the conference director for the UCEA Charlottesville Conference on Ethics and Leadership in October, 2001. Ms. Sherman was an invited participant at the 2001 David L. Clark Graduate Seminar in Educational Research sponsored by the University Council for Educational Administration in

Seattle, Washington, in April, 2001. She is also the recipient of the Administration and Supervision Women's Fellowship as well as a dissertation grant award offered by the University of Virginia. Dr. Sherman is currently an assistant professor at Georgia State University.

Amy Sofka earned her master's of education degree, focusing on the social foundations of education, in 1996 from the Curry School of Education at the University of Virginia (UVa); she is now working on a doctorate from the same institution. Research interests include the impact of the Virginia Standards of Learning on K–12 schools, the relationship between local communities and their school divisions, and the role of higher education institutions in supporting and training schoolteachers, as well as administrators. Recently hired by UVa's School of Continuing and Professional Studies, Ms. Sofka is engaged in content course programming for school divisions throughout Virginia, and is in charge of the School's alternative teacher licensure programming.

Pamela D. Tucker is an assistant professor of education in the Curry School of Education at the University of Virginia and serves as the director of the Principal Internship Program. Her research focuses on various aspects of teacher evaluation and the nature of school leadership. Books coauthored with others include, *Evaluation Handbook for Professional Support Personnel* (Center for Research on Educational Accountability and Teacher Evaluation), *Teacher Evaluation and Student Achievement* (National Education Association), and *Handbook on Teacher Portfolios for Evaluation and Professional Development* (Eye on Education). Articles address topics such as the "Legal Context for Teacher Evaluation," "Helping Struggling Teachers," and "Guidelines for Linking Student Achievement to Teacher Evaluation." As a special education teacher and former administrator in a school for learning disabled students, she has worked with a variety of student populations and has a particular concern for students who are most at risk for school failure. She earned her Ed.D. in educational administration from the College of William and Mary.

INDEX

Accountability, 7, 30, 106, 109, 111, 112, 194, 207; advisory committee, 55; age of, 2, 3, 5, 106, 112, 114, 131, 177, 182, 195, 201, 202, 210, 212; collective, 202; educational, 4, 11, 14, 36, 46, 53, 56, 60–62, 135, 201; high stakes, 24, 28, 99, 185; initiative, 1, 2, 3, 4, 14, 19, 56, 63, 90, 105, 136, 141, 143, 150, 185, 186; measures, 3, 69, 84, 136, 137, 141, 144, 206; plan, 1, 4, 37, 48–63, 70–73, 76–83, 85, 86, 88, 89, 92, 135–37, 140, 141, 144, 153, 154, 164, 165, 170, 187, 188, 190, 193, 195, 204, 206, 207; reform, 3, 7, 8, 10, 26, 131, 177, 194, 195, 201, 205, 207; student, 20; systems, 8, 16–19, 21–22, 153, 191; and testing, 18, 63

Accreditation, 25, 163, 212; full, 114, 185; school, 2. *See* Standards of Accreditation

Achievement: expectations of, 103, 107, 111, 118, 127, 156, 162, 174, 188; student, 90–91, 99, 111

Achievement gap: Black-White, 155–58, 165, 166, 172, 173, 176, 177. *See* testing

After-school: homework assistance programs, 141; tutoring, 89, 141, 150

African American, 190; community, 176; students, 157, 159, 166, 169, 172–74, 176; racism, 157, 162; superintendents, 159

American Association of School Administrators: standards for, 155

A Nation at Risk, 14, 15, 17, 38, 199

Assessment, 17, 104, 109, 111; classroom, 87; -driven reform, 9, 10; performance, 140; standardized, 122; student, 106; system, 17, 20, 130. *See* testing

Authority: centralization of, 86, 88–89

Autonomy, 88, 182, 190, 193

Best Practice Center, 4, 114, 130, 211

Capacity: local, 129–31

Change, 128, 162, 176, 186, 195

Common Core of Learning. *See* curriculum

Curriculum, 100, 103, 105, 107, 110, 118, 130, 135, 139, 157, 184; Advanced Placement, 56, 86, 185; alignment, 122, 129, 143, 154, 164; blueprint, 118; character education, 108–9; Common Core of Learning, 42, 61–62; horizontal articulation, 72; mapping, 164, 194; pacing, 85, 87, 103, 143, 185, 194; prescribed, 100, 102, 187; SOL courses, 86–88; "taught," 182–84; vocational, 86

Diploma: alternative, 121; certified, 13; modified standard, 56

Dropout rates, 22, 121, 144, 153–54, 205

Duke, Daniel L., 3–5, 99, 101, 131

Education Commission of the States, 18, 19, 25, 26

Education Summit, 41, 43